'[This book] illuminates not only our social and economic history but also the moral economy of underdeveloped capitalism . . . reminds one of Adam Smith and Marx on early capitalism.'

Sabyasachi Bhattacharya, *former Professor of History at Jawaharlal Nehru University, former Chairman of the Indian Council of Historical Research, and former Vice-Chancellor, Visva-Bharati University, India*

T0382899

THE SOCIOLOGY OF GREED

The Sociology of Greed examines crises in financial institutions such as banks from the vantage point of the greed of the people at their helm. It offers an intensive analysis of the banking crises under the conditions of colonial capitalism in early twentieth-century Bengal that led to institutional and social collapse.

Breaking new ground, the book looks at the moral economy of capitalism and money culture by focusing on the victims of banking crises, hitherto unexplored in Western empirical research. Through sociological analyses of political economy, it seamlessly combines archival records, survey and statistical data with literary narratives, realist fiction and performing arts to recount how the greed of bank owners and managers ruined their institutions as well as common people. It argues that greed turns perilous when the state and the market facilitate its agency, and it examines the contexts and histories, the indifference of the fledging colonial state, feeble political response, and the consequences for those who were impacted and the losses, especially the refugees, the lower-middle class and women. The volume also re-composes relevant elements of Western sociological scholarship from classical theories to early twenty-first-century financial sociology.

An insightful account of the social history of banking in India, this book will greatly interest researchers and scholars in sociology, economics, history and cultural studies.

Prasanta Ray is Professor Emeritus in Sociology, Presidency University, Kolkata, and Honorary Visiting Professor, Institute of Development Studies, Kolkata, India. He was Professor and Head, Department of Political Science, Presidency College; Professor-in-Charge, Department of Sociology, Presidency College; Guest Faculty member, Department of Sociology, Calcutta University; Member, Calcutta Research Group; and Member, Working Group on Under-Graduate Colleges in India, National Knowledge Commission, 2006. His books include *Conflict and the State: An Exploration in the Behaviour of the Post-Colonial State in India* (1991) and *Pratyaha: Everyday Lifeworlds: Dilemmas, Contestations and Negotiations* (co-edited with Nandini Ghosh, 2016).

THE SOCIOLOGY OF GREED

Runs and Ruins in Banking Crises

Prasanta Ray

Routledge
Taylor & Francis Group

LONDON AND NEW YORK

First published 2018
by Routledge
2 Park Square, Milton Park, Abingdon, Oxon, OX14 4RN

and by Routledge
605 Third Avenue, New York, NY 10017

First issued in paperback 2020

Routledge is an imprint of the Taylor & Francis Group, an informa business

© 2018 Prasanta Ray

The right of Prasanta Ray to be identified as author of this work has been asserted by him in accordance with sections 77 and 78 of the Copyright, Designs and Patents Act 1988.

All rights reserved. No part of this book may be reprinted or reproduced or utilised in any form or by any electronic, mechanical, or other means, now known or hereafter invented, including photocopying and recording, or in any information storage or retrieval system, without permission in writing from the publishers.

Trademark notice: Product or corporate names may be trademarks or registered trademarks, and are used only for identification and explanation without intent to infringe.

British Library Cataloguing-in-Publication Data
A catalogue record for this book is available from the British Library

Library of Congress Cataloging-in-Publication Data
A catalog record for this book has been requested

ISBN 13: 978-0-367-73494-7 (pbk)
ISBN 13: 978-0-8153-8672-8 (hbk)

Typeset in Sabon
by Apex CoVantage, LLC

To Susama Gupta, my maternal aunt, the first collateral victim of the Bengal banking crisis, whom I knew.

CONTENTS

TABLES

ACKNOWLEDGEMENTS

I am indebted to the Institute of Development Studies Kolkata (IDSK) for offering me an Honorary Visiting Professorship, which has enabled me to conduct this research. I am grateful for the help and guidance warmly rendered to me by Ashok Kapoor, P. Ravi Kiran, and Dr. Rajib Lochan Sahoo of the RBI Archive in Pune. Similarly, Dr. Hoom gave me access to all the papers available in the SBI Archive, Kolkata. I have benefitted enormously from the library at IDSK, the Secretariat Library, Writers' Buildings, Kolkata and the Presidency College library. Dr. Santanu Ghosh of the West Bengal Education Service helped me locate appropriate data in the RBI Archive. My friend Professor Abhijit Mitra introduced me to the two novellas written by his father, the late Narendranath Mitra, and acquainted me with latter's literary works. Professor Sabyasachi Bhattacharya kindly commented on the manuscript and encouraged me to publish it. I have gained immensely from observations on the draft by Professor Amiya Kumar Bagchi. Dr. Rukmini Sen and Professor Pradeep Bandyopadhyay gave their valuable comments on the draft. I acknowledge Taboban Bhattacharyya's assistance in my archival research. Madhusri Ghosh and Asok Patra of the IDSK library were enormously helpful in procuring books and journals. The production of the manuscript has been enriched by professional expertise of Mandira Sen and Madhuparna Banerjee. Needless to say, the responsibility for misreading the history of the banking crisis lies with me.

A CONVOLUTE

But the frequent bankruptcies to which such beggarly bankers must be liable, may occasion very considerable inconveniency, and sometimes even a very great calamity, to many poor people who had received their notes in payment.
                                                          – Adam Smith (1776)[1]

From now on the bankers will rule.

                                                          – Jacques Laffitte (1830)[2]

Society prepares the crime and the guilty is only the instrument by which it is accomplished.

                                                          – Adolphe Quetelet (1835)[3]

I have never seen a class so deeply demoralised, so incurably debased by self-ishness, so corroded within, so incapable of progress, as the English bourgeoisie; and I mean by this, especially the bourgeoisie proper, particularly the Liberal, Corn Law repealing bourgeoisie. For it nothing exists in this world, except for the sake of money, itself not excluded.

                                                          – Friedrich Engels (1845)[4]

Money is therefore not only the object but also the fountainhead of greed.
                                                          – Karl Marx (1857–1858)[5]

How it happens that some societies have more, and some, fewer thieves.
                                                          – Emile Durkheim (1890–1900)[6]

But victorious capitalism, since it rests on mechanical foundations, needs its (ascetic rationalism) support no longer. . . . In the field of its highest development, in the United States, the pursuit of wealth, stripped of its religious and ethical meaning, tends to become associated with mundane passions, which often actually give it the character of sport.

                                                          – Max Weber (1904–1905)[7]

xiii

In reality, money in its psychological form, as the absolute means and thus as the unifying point of innumerable sequences of purposes, possesses a significant relationship to the notion of God. . . . The essence of the notion of God is that all diversities and contradictions in the world achieve unity in him.

– Georg Simmel (1907)[8]

What is a picklock compared to a bank share? What is the burgling of a bank to the founding of a bank?

– Bertolt Brecht (1928)[9]

Greed, provided it is sufficiently regulated, is tolerable.

– *The Economist* (18 October 2008)[10]

Notes

1 Adam Smith, *The Wealth of Nations*, Introduction by Alan B. Krueger (New York: Bantam Books, 2003): 412.
2 Laffitte was 'the liberal banker' who was active in the triumph of Louis Philippe, Duke of Orleans, who became the king of France following the July Revolution of 1830. Karl Marx, *The Class Struggles in France, 1848–1850* (Moscow: Progress Publishers, [1850] 1975): 27–28. Marx wrote: 'It was not the French bourgeoisie that ruled under Louis Philippe, but *one faction* of it: bankers, stock-exchange kings, railway kings, owners of coal and iron mines and forests, a part of the landed proprietors associated with them – the so-called *financial aristocracy*': 28.
3 Adolphe Quetelet, *Recherches Statistiques sur le Royaume des Pays-Bas*, [1835], quoted in Frank H. Hanking, 'Moral Statistics', in *Society: Critical Concepts in Sociology, Volume 1: The Origins of Society*, edited by Reiner Gundmann and Nico Stehr (London: Routledge, 2009): 200–213.
4 Friedrich Engels, *The Conditions of English Working Class* (1845), www.marxists.org/archive/marx/works/1845/condition-working-class/index.htm, accessed on 30 May 2017.
5 Karl Marx, *Grundrisse: Foundations of the Critique of Political Economy* (Rough Draft), translated with a Foreword by Martin Nicolaus (London: Penguin Books in association with *New Left Review*, 1973): 222.
6 Emile Durkheim, *Professional Ethics and Civic Morals*, translated by Cornelia Brookfield with a new preface by Bryan S. Turner (London: Routledge, 2003). Originally, these were notes for lectures delivered between 1890 and 1900, which were repeated in 1904, 1912 and before his death in 1917.
7 Max Weber, *The Protestant Ethic and the Spirit of Capitalism*, translated by Talcott Parsons (New York: Scribner's, 1958): 181–182.
8 Georg Simmel, *The Philosophy of Money*, edited by David Frisby, translated by Tom Bottomore and David Frisby, 2nd enlarged ed. (London: Routledge, 1990): 236.
9 Bertolt Brecht, *The Threepenny Opera* (New York: Grove Press, [1928] 1964): 92.

10 Quoted in Nancy Folbre, *Greed, Lust and Gender: A History of Economic Ideas* (Oxford: Oxford University Press, 2009): xx, xxxii. This was by way of suggesting that we need to re-write Gordon Gekko's famous observation in the 1987 film, *Wall Street*, 'The point is, ladies and gentlemen, that greed – for lack of a better word – is good. Greed is right. Greed works'.

INTRODUCTION

This analysis of the sociology of greed is a many-faceted exploration subject to the limits of data and the limits of conjecture. It is in a way reconstructing institutional history with the victims of greedy bankers and the insensitivity of the state at the centre. In its folds is a special attention to personal loss and of women's sufferance of the calamities. That way, it proposes a different kind of social history of banking.[1] Taking data from late colonial Bengal as a case study, it argues that the misery of the small depositors, the victims, in which this book is interested, was due to greed on the part of the owners and the managers of the banks which eventually went into liquidation. Their moral failure was compounded by poor managerial skills and crisis in the economy in the war years. A number of colonial reports are used in this historical reconstruction of moral failure of individual owners and managers of banks, the institutional crisis such failure brought about, the public response through print media and discussions in legislature, the interventions by the state and the merchant community to calm the stakeholders and to retrieve public trust in the viability of the banking institutions, and of two contrary processes of negotiation with the crisis, one by the rich, powerful and well-placed stakeholders to deny the banks repayment of borrowings, and the other by the ordinary depositors. This is a thick narrative of cunning dispossession of meager money assets of the lower middle class. Thereby it brings out the moral economy of capitalism in the late-colonial setting in Bengal. In fact, it moves beyond monetary loss by trusting clients. It unravels how this precipitated moral confusion in intimate relationships.

In foregrounding greed on the part of the founder/owner of such banks in league with the power elite, the book discusses the victims of bank failure in Bengal.[2] It attempts at historical retrieval and looks for tragedies in course of institution formation – more

1

specifically the crisis in the 1940s and the 1950s and the 'runs' on banks.[3] It is common knowledge that tragic traces are easily effaced by the designs on the part of those who stand to lose their social esteem, maybe their wealth too, in case the details of a tragedy survive the proverbial brevity of public memory and fabrications of enquiry committees.[4] When such tragedies take place within the framework of an institution – in most cases they do – the traces become debris underneath the foundation of institutional renewal.

Almost all of the losers are now nameless and un-nameable. What is reconstructed here is the story of their loss and feeble resentment. Adam Smith had argued: 'It [the emotion of resentment] prompts us to beat off the mischief which is attempted to be done to us and to retaliate that which is already done'.[5] But the victims of fraud in Bengal could not 'return evil for evil', an intervention which would follow popular resentment towards the perpetrators of sufferance imposed on the victims as Smith anticipated. The victims belonged to Adam Smith's category of 'middling and inferior stations of life'. Their moralities sharply contrast with those of men of higher ranks who have an 'easy empire over the affections of mankind' and those who indulge in 'proud ambition and ostentatious avidity'.[6] The men in charge of the state organization were unconcerned about the misery of the victims of bank failures because they thought that they were not required to be concerned with notions of good and evil. They were 'naturally' adiaphoric.[7] This weakened their possible 'individual spontaneous outbursts of sympathy to take increased moral responsibility' towards the unfortunate losers.[8] But Adam Smith becomes more relevant in our understanding of the attitude of both the colonial administration and the post-colonial state in India. Neil Rabitoy has recounted a remarkable reversal in British policy of humanitarian intervention in Gujarat in the Bombay Presidency during a major famine in 1802–1803 towards management of another famine in 1812–1813. In the latter case, the administration 'regarded justice and humanity as outside its proper sphere of activity'.[9] In fact, it quoted 'extensively from Adam Smith for several pages to the effect that Government interference does not alleviate scarcity but causes it'.

Beneath and beyond the adiaphoric state and the greedy managers of other people's money, there is the mechanics of the unequal society which explains the recurrence of crime. Adolphe Quetelet's observation is worthwhile to recall. He wrote: 'Society prepares the crime and the guilty is only the instrument by which it is accomplished. . . . There is a budget which we pay with frightful regularity; it is that of prisons, chains and scaffold'.[10] But well-networked criminals often evade the penal laws and punitive institutions. The costs – much of which is inestimable – suffered by the ordinary victims are quite enormous: loss of painstaking small deposits, emotional cost of anxiety and monetary recuperation and spoilt intimacies. The ordinary victims were the low earning, small and possibly inconsistently saving, without reckonable collective fronts and without dramatic multi-media representations. They were largely invisible and inaudible.

One is struck by the silence of the colonial documents on who the ordinary victims were and the magnitude of their loss, money-wise and otherwise, except in terms of categories like 'refugees' from East Bengal or loss of 'life's savings'. Although the total quantum of documents on bank failures is not at all meagre in the archives in India, these offer hardly any clue.[11] The Reserve Bank of India or any other appropriate government department did have the task of collecting the details of the victims of the banking crisis. The RBI did appoint inspection teams. But the focus was on fraudulent banking staff rather than the ordinary depositors who lost their savings:

> The inspecting officers have been instructed to report on acts of fraud and misfeasance they may come across during the scrutiny of the books of the banks. The liability of the management and the directorate may arise in respect of fraud or breach of trust, the former punishable under the Penal Code and the latter incurring a civil liability.[12]

But the men in charge of inspection very often ran into many hurdles even when their inquiry was restricted to the top banking staff whose indulgence in financial impropriety can be traced through examination of official papers.[13]

One is intrigued by the fact that the 'silence' is still maintained even now. The higher officials, in both the RBI Kolkata liquidation wing and the Office of Court Liquidator (Department of Economic Affairs [Banking], Ministry of Finance, Government of India, Kolkata) refused to answer oral questions as elementary as what were the names of 32 banks, still in the process of trying to realize the amount from their debtors to be in a position to pay their creditors, particularly the ordinary savings bank account holders. No estimate was given by men I could manage to talk to, but who wanted to remain anonymous, about the number of savings bank holders who were still waiting to be paid and some of whom did call up the authorities from time to time. The reasons for refusal to talk as given by the officials are the following: (1) the fear of a reprimand by the court, and (2) instruction by the Government of India not to disclose anything to an 'outsider'. One informal idea was given by one official that the Nath Bank had about 21,000 savings bank account holders. He suggested that for the smaller banks, the number could be approximately 6,000. None gave me an idea of the amount of money still due to the savings bank account holders of those banks. I doubt whether the relevant offices had ever assessed that. But they did drop hints that many legal heirs of the original savings bank account holder would still ring up the liquidator's office to try to know when they might be compensated for the loss their forefathers had suffered. The officers also disclosed the tactics of evasion on the part of those on whom the banks had a rightful claim to gain back from them what they took from the banks in the form of loans: changing the residential address to remain incommunicable, or making an appeal to the Office of Court Liquidator that they might be exempted because they did not have the sound financial position to comply with the banks. In the first case, nobody from the Office would seek to trace them out. In the second case, the Office usually conceded their request for reprieve, although some officials suspected faking of financial misery by the legal heirs of the original debtors. While the cunning defaulters could stonewall the state's efforts to realize the amount due to the afflicted banks from them, the savings bank holders or their heirs were helpless in securing what would be theirs. Considering the fact that the real worth today of the amount of money they are entitled to get back must be paltry, and that the maze of illegalities and immoralities would normally turn them cynical, those who systematically get in touch with the Office of Court Liquidator must be in desperate need for the compensation. This is not to take for granted that the second or third-generation descendants have been unable to recover from the financial damage suffered by some of their elders due to run on the banks.

Since records, particularly quantitative estimates, are not available, a search for the victims and for a measure of their loss has to be organized at different sites. One would obviously be memory. I requested a few persons I met by chance whose grandfather, father or male breadwinner lost their small bank deposits, to try to remember what the reaction at home was. Almost all of them mentioned that they were too young then to comprehend the gravity of the sudden destitution. They could all remember a sad numbness in the elders, men and women, seated in a huddle with their hands on their heads.

One compared it with the eerie silence of the burning *ghat* (crematorium). There was sudden death in the family, the death of hope for a relatively secure future. The second option was study of contemporary literature, which this book has drawn upon.

The attempt is to bring back the grieving men and women to the centre of an analysis of a crisis which originated in banking but was aggravated by many other social institutions. The search is not merely for the names and the numbers of the victims and for the quantum of money lost by them. In fact, personal loss is given a much wider meaning here, beyond the conventional numerical estimates used in studies on collapse of financial institutions. There is no rigorous estimate as yet of the financial loss suffered by lower-middle-class refugees from East Bengal, who by all accounts suffered most because of 'run' on many banks. Bank pass books of individual depositors or ledger books could have been the ideal source of information. Faint outlines of miseries might have been drawn up based on information on average annual income, cost of living, dependency burden of the earning family members and kinship obligations that involved expenses. But firm indicators and dependable clues are not easy to come by. Financial miseries make deep inroads into the entirety of individual existence. The loss of vital savings plunged people at the margins to immeasurable psychological crises involving his or her own self and intimate relationships; more so for people, the lower-middle-class refugees, who were already marginalized by history. The expressions of their agony are profound in literature, visuals, biographies and autobiographies, diaries and letters. All reveal the interior of a suffering person and his or her relations as nothing else does.

The principal interest here is in the ordinary depositors, particularly their helplessness in the face of a crisis in the public sphere that intruded into their private spaces. The story of their agonizing impoverishment, of collapse of relationship within the framework of family, conjugality and friendship, and of the moral confusion of the individuals under stress, has been constructed from every available fragment of texts of all forms: a petition by a solitary woman, letters to the editor of news dailies, representations of depositors, pleas of the employees' unions, biographical notes, two novellas by a famous author who himself was a victim of the crisis. A reliance on literature is obviously dictated by an interest beyond numbers, either of individuals adversely affected by bank failure or the amount of lost deposit. What was ruined was not merely their economic security, but also their morals and relationships. The victims were reduced to pathetic human beings. This was truer about the women, particularly the wives and the daughters of owners, managers and employees of the affected banks. There was something patriarchal about the unscrupulous search for money. This is not to suggest even faintly that greed is an exclusively male vice. But exclusively male ownership and management of the banks definitely facilitated the male ego at work in money business. Hence is the need to examine male greed through womanly eyes. A common-sense caution is that no behavioural predisposition with the mentality in which it is embedded has a solitary existence, and it is both difficult and unnecessary to take out one from the whole constellation of predispositions, which do not always stand harmoniously to each other. It is as much difficult and unnecessary to locate it without an adequate reference to specific historical contingencies which evoke them.

The caution is necessary when one has to move from the tangible effects of the banking crisis to its impact on emotional bonds, that is, towards an intimate history; and hence epistemologically from positivism to hermeneutics, from 'hard' to 'soft' data, from measurement to meaning, from significance level of a statistical estimate to *verstehen*, from *etic* to *emic* positions.[14] After all, Sociology's locus as a 'third culture' between the natural sciences and the humanities nurtures a tension between the scientific mode and the artistic mode of cognition. Wolf Lepenies has summed up the predicament in his *Between Literature and Science: The Rise of Sociology*. He writes:

> On the one hand, when sociology desired to be sociography, it came into conflict above all with the realistic novel over the claim to offer an adequate representation of the 'prose of everyday circumstances'; when, on the other hand, it claimed to be social theory it incurred the suspicion of degenerating into a 'closet science', that is of belonging to that group of disciplines which . . . are unable to . . . express the 'poetry of heart'.[15]

Despite the dilemma, this book draws on literature. Rabindranath Tagore's *Sampatti-Samarpan* and *Bhaiphonta*, and Buddhadeva Bose's *Bhabishyater Baksho*, an autobiography, figure in Prathama Banerjee's paper, 'Social History of Banking in Bengal in the Late Nineteenth and Early Twentieth Centuries'. Unlike the two stories, the two novellas by Narendranath Mitra (1916–1975), drawn up on here, have the banking crisis as the critical episode. Narendranath Mitra himself was working in a bank which failed.[16] The bank, the Calcutta National

Bank, which he joined after the Second World War, went into liquidation in December 1952. In fact, he became a victim of the closure of the bank. The bank brought a lawsuit against him for approving a forged cheque. The case went up to the session's court where the British judge exonerated him from the charges.[17]

Sahridaya (Magnanimous Woman) (1956) and *Mahanagar* (The Great City) (1962) are his two writings on which this work draws. The later was based on his earlier short story *Abataranika* (Descent) (1948). It is the date of the publication that makes it so relevant for understanding the common human predicament due to liquidation of banks. Re-reading it after scanning the archival file, I was astounded by the completeness of the brief but literary representation of the facts regarding the crisis. Tagore's *Ghare Baire* (The Home and the World) (1916) also finds a place in this reconstruction.[18] In fact, these two novellas by Narendranath Mitra are trauma narratives with an autobiographical core, narratives read and re-read in Bengali homes, and with transcultural circulation through the agency of cinema (*Mahanagar* directed by Satyajit Ray) and Bengal Studies beyond Bengal.[19] This is how the specificities of locality and temporality of an episode dissolve, and the episode takes its place in a universe of similar experiences. Then, the brevity of a crisis and 'smallness' of the number of its victims, as in the case of the banking crisis in Bengal in the 1940s and the 1950s – both in comparison with the more catastrophic (as in the 'stormy decades' in Bengal), cannot be grounds for inattention. Invisibility and inaudibility of the ordinary depositors grieving over their loss must not be taken to suggest that they were unable to figure out the reasons of their misery. Their inaudibility and invisibility is due partly to banking crisis enquiry commissions' practice of leaving them out of the purview and partly because newspaper reports then did not focus on ordinary individual's reactions to injustice inflicted on them and to administrative silence. That explains the extraordinary significance of Narendranath Mitra and Satyajit Ray in giving them voice and visibility, and thereby an intelligible place in a people's history of the banking crisis in Bengal. The position taken here is that we better be like a 'chronicler who recites events without distinguishing between major and minor ones [and thus] acts in accordance with the following truth: nothing that has ever happened should be regarded as lost for history'.[20] We better acknowledge that 'everyone thinks, everyone speaks'.[21]

The reliance on aesthetic representations is an imperative for writing a history of human misery because nothing else offers a thick description better. Stefan Jonsson in his *A Brief History of the Masses (Three Revolutions)*[22] observes that the 'aesthetic representations should be taken seriously by social thought and political theory, for they serve as correctives of the political imagination and as testimonials of its shortcomings'.[23] Stefan Jonsson reflects on three astounding paintings: Jacques-Louis David's *The Tennis Court Oath* (1791), James Ensor's *Christ's Entry into Brussels in 1889,* (1888) and Alfredo Jaar's *They Loved It So Much, The Revolution* (1989), to show 'the ways in which human beings are partitioned, separated, and divided, [and] the visible and invisible lines drawn through the social terrain that prohibit the majority from approaching the centre of the picture'. To comprehend the plight of these people, we need 'trained sensibility: the sharp eye for cultural patterns, the novelistic feel for the shape of a story, the patience for synthesizing masses of abstruse data into meaningful wholes'.[24] Further, a turn to literature helps us partly compensate the silence of the archives.[25]

Victims of the banking crisis remained relatively unsighted because the tumultuous 1940s were crowded with victims of many kinds. But the current spate of Ponzi scandals in West Bengal and elsewhere in India points to continuous reproduction of victims of 'money-hunters' or 'money-grubbers'. In fact, this has been a global phenomenon. Researchers have established that there were 117 'systemic banking crises (defined as much or all of bank capitals being exhausted)' in 93 countries between 1970 and 2003.[26] Expectedly, there is great scholarly literature, theoretical as well as empirical, on the contemporary banking crisis. The economists bring out the enormous financial cost of the crisis at the level of the economy but are not interested about the social and personal cost inflicted on ordinary people by the greed and folly of some owners and managers of private banks. At most they make a cursory statement on human cost. Carmen Reinhart and Kenneth S. Rogoff provide a comparative analysis of banking crises all over the world and over a long period.[27] They point out the 'great social cost' of banking failures, in which this study is interested, but they do not detail the cost; nor do they elaborate on 'the Wreckage'.[28] There is only a semblance of interest in greed in their analysis of the recent banking crisis in Western economies.[29] This is unlike the analysis of money, banking and greed-induced fraud between 1840 and 1920 by western sociologists. One reason could be that 'economists have never argued that greed and lust are good: but they have not tried hard enough to figure out how to discourage both'.[30] The necessity of discouraging does not occur because, according to many economists, 'what drives free markets is not necessarily greed at all, it is the purposefulness of potential entrepreneurs whose purposes, in the disposition of their pure profits, may be altruistic, selfish, or whatever'.[31] Further, they are not bothered that 'these moral concerns are based on an inadequate understanding of the pure economic theory of pure entrepreneurial profit' (profit made out of 'other people's ignorance' or without 'effort or sweat').[32] Some research has shown 'that people's perceptions of greed, and their willingness to engage in – and justify – greedy behavior, are malleable'.[33]

This work has its point of departure in a moral concern about the victims of greed, which hopefully has not deflected it from pursuit of facts which disclose the avaricious schemes of individuals in strategic positions in the banking process and the helplessness of the victims both being located in the same spatiotemporal order. The search for the quantitative and the qualitative facts is towards grasping greed, which appears to elude exact definition, and locating its decivilizing outcomes.

Definitely, this is not the first examination of the banking crisis in Bengal. A reference to this crisis is a part of a comprehensive institutional history as in case of the three-volume history of *The Reserve Bank of India*;[34] or, a part of the history of the formation of the United Bank of India.[35] This research foregrounds the critical role of the moral lapse in the unrestrained avarice of the men who were at the helm of fledging banks in early twentieth-century Bengal. It offers a detailed description of indulgence in malfeasance and appropriation of public money, which is absent in a cursory reference to corruption as in various inquiry committee reports and in some academic researches. As it brings back humans in the analysis of corruption of institutions, it does not ignore the institutional frames, politics and history. In fact, it implicates banking institutions and law as, at least, unwitting facilitators of infectious greed. The late colonial state's indifference to the plight of the defrauded depositors is duly taken into account. The urgency of *udyog* in *swadeshi* concerns had unintended consequences in that it spawned financial misadventures motivated in many cases by the desire for improper pecuniary gains. Conceding the significance of these impersonal factors, we must reckon with the fact that some bankers and their accomplices/associates succumbed to and/or exploited the 'opportunities' created by a conjunction of the impersonal factors; some did not. Those who did also bracketed off the moral imperative of financial propriety and risks in the form of legal stricture, social stigma or troubled conscience as well.

In tracing the identity of those who created the preconditions of run on banks, those bankers who seized up on the chances, and those who became its victims – financial or otherwise, reference is made to class rather than to caste. Inset in the larger analysis is a specific exposition on the lower-middle-class refugees. Patriarchy finds an important place in the narrative on women's victimhood in the private familial space due to financial immorality of intimate men in their lives. By moving outside of the public domain, the inquiry is built on the need for a more comprehensive understanding of (financial) institutional crisis.

The book opens with a Convolute. The idea of a Convolute – 'grouped in sheafs' – is taken from Walter Benjamin.[36] The Introduction positions the empirical details in Chapters 1, 2, and 3 and 4 in a larger canvas of colonial capitalism and Bengali ethno-nationalism. Chapter 5 addresses to grasping greed theoretically. It brings out how classical economic sociology and classical political economy offered insights into greed, insights stimulated by some contemporary financial crisis involving banks. It goes on to argue that the 'classical' preoccupations have resurged in early twenty-first-century Western new financial sociology.

Chapters 1 and 2 bring out the magnitude of the institutional crisis. As their context, they offer a narrative on people being enticed into saving morality playing upon *swadesh* (patriotism) and *swartha* (self-interest). Persistent advertisements in the vernacular press, and books in Bengali on both money and banking written for school-going boys and girls as well as for adults to impart in them everyday financial education were towards the creation of a new money culture. This can be looked at as 'vernacularizing thrust of capitalism' in times of colonial nationalism.[37] These combined with valorisation of entrepreneurs in contemporary banking in Bengal. Chapters 3 and 4 are on the victims of both individual and institutional greed. These conjecture about the extent of loss by individuals framed conceptually by the official categories, namely, 'ordinary depositors', 'middle class', 'the poor' and the 'refugees'. These then re-construct the response by the victims, concluding with narratives on women's victimhood. Chapter 5 reconstructs history of theorizing financial crisis in the 'north', particularly in West European capitalist economies – a history which brings out the role of individual and institutional greed. Thereby it situates the banking crisis in Bengal in the 1940s and the 1950s in a global history of financial cunning and immorality. The Epilogue consolidates the discussion and points to unresolved issues.

10

Notes

1 The focus here is different from early scholarship on the crisis. See Prathama Banerjee, 'A Social History of Banking in Bengal in the Late Nineteenth and the Early Twentieth Centuries', referred in *Financial Intermediation in a Less Developed Economy: The History of the United Bank of India*, edited by Sugata Marjit and Indrajit Mallick (New Delhi: SAGE, 2008)
2 The state eventually formulated the Deposit Insurance and Credit Guarantee Corporation Act in 1961 and set up a larger institutional mechanism in the form of the Deposit Insurance and Credit Guarantee Corporation in 1978. The apparent re-invigoration of the financial institutions and practices was on the wreckages of ruined lives.
3 The crisis has already received scholarly attention by economists. See G. Balachandran, *The Reserve Bank of India, Volume 2: 1951–1967* (New Delhi: Oxford University Press, 1998): Chapter 12.
4 Kathie Weigel has created 'A *Virtual Cemetery of* Victims of the Great Depression in the USA'. This was inspired by Russian historian Boris Borisov's question about what became of over seven million American citizens who disappeared from US population records in the 1930s. Despite her best efforts, aided by the internet, she has so far managed to locate only five biographies – only one of them being a banker, three rubber workers and one poor person.
5 Adam Smith, 'Theory of Moral Sentiments', III.6 (I.440), quoted in T. D. Campbell, *Adam Smith's Science of Morals*, Routledge Library Editions: Adam Smith, vol. 3 (London: Routledge, 2010): 190.
6 Campbell, *Adam Smith's Science of Morals*, vol. 3: 175.
7 From Stoic philosophy – having neither merit or demerit.
8 Tommy Jensen, 'Beyond Good and Evil: The Adiaphoric Company', *Journal of Business Ethics* 96 (2010): 425–434. doi:10.1007/s10551-010-0475-4
9 Neil Rabitoy, 'The Control of Fate and Fortune: The Origins of the Market Mentality in British Administrative Thought in South Asia', *Modern Asian Studies* 25, 4 (1991): 737–764, www.jstor.org/stable/312751 About 100,000 people died in Ahmedabad city, but the administration did not do anything because that would interfere with 'the free operation of Mercantile Speculations in respect to grain'. It, however, made exceptions for supplies of grains to the troops.
10 Adam Quetelet, *Recherches Statistiques sur le Royaume des Pays-Bas* (1835) (Edinburgh: Robert and William Chambers, 1842).
11 Archives consulted: Reserve Bank of India Archive, Pune; State Bank of India Archive, Kolkata; State Archives, Kolkata Secretariat Library, Writers' Buildings, Kolkata (see Appendix 3).
12 Inspection of the four Bengali scheduled banks (Calcutta Commercial Bank Ltd., Mahaluxmi Bank Ltd., Noakhali Union Bank Ltd., Pioneer Bank Ltd.) under moratorium (inspection by the RBI, commenced on December 16, 1948, under section 3 of the Banking Companies [Inspection] Ordinance, 1946); the report, dated 16 Feb 1949, was submitted by Mr. L. K. Desai, Deputy Chief Officer, Department of Banking Operations, Bombay, who was deputed to Calcutta, to study the progress of the inspections.

13 The report from 'the staff still employed at the banks proved wholly inadequate and unsatisfactory. The salaries in these banks were low; the treasurer of the Calcutta Commercial Bank Ltd., drew about Rs. 200 per month, and every competent employee left the banks. Only a few remained in the services and they were irregular in attendance. . . . In the Calcutta Commercial Bank Ltd. With most of the senior officers under arrest or suspicion, none is left to sign any statement. In the Mahaluxmi Bank Ltd., where the Manager is still in service I did not succeed in looking into the Share Registrar as the book was in a cupboard, the key of which remained with an officer who was reported to have gone to his village and expected to return every other day. . . . Mr. Sen of the Mahaluxmi Bank prefers to attend late in the afternoons and the other two attend irregularly. . . . In none of these banks were books and vouchers stacked in proper order. The secretaries' registers, contracts for sale and purchase on investment accounts, documents relating to advances were difficult to access'.

14 *Verstehen* or understanding the *meaning* of action from the actor's point of view; field research done and viewpoints obtained: *emic* and *etic* refer to two forms of accounts of some aspect of the social world. The first is from the perspective of somebody (the subject) internal to a social situation; the second, from that of somebody (the observer) from the outside.

15 Wolf Lepenies, *Between Literature and Science: The Rise of Sociology* (New York: Cambridge University Press, 1988): 12–13.

16 His son, Professor Abhijit Mitra, has told me about entries in the author's unpublished diary on his personal predicament as a fall-out of the crisis. His two novellas border on autobiography. For, the financial fragility of the Calcutta National Bank in which Narendranath Mitra was employed, see Table 2.1 'Advances to Bengali banks', and for the significant service the bank rendered to trade and commerce, see the observation in Ditcher's Diary mentioned on p. 51.

17 Dhirendranath Mitra, 'Aamader Katha (Our Story)', in *Padakshep*, edited by Jyotirmoye Das and Asim Kumar Basu (Kolkata: Padakshep Sahitya Sansad, 2015): 25. Dhirendranath was Narendranath Mitra's brother. According to him, Narendranath joined the bank again only to resign.

18 Rabindranath Tagore, *The Home and the World*, translated by Sreejata Guha, Introduction and Notes by Swagato Ganguly (New Delhi: Penguin, 2005).

19 Astrid Erll, 'Traumatic Pasts, Literary Afterlives and Transcultural Memory: New Directions of Literary and Media Memory Studies', *Journal of Aesthetics & Culture* 3 (2011). doi:10.3402/jac.v3i0.7186

20 Walter Benjamin, *Illuminations* [1973], with Introduction by Hannah Arendt, translated by Harry Zohn (London: Fontana Press, 1992): 246.

21 Peter Hallward, 'Jacques Rancière and the Subversion of Mastery', *Paragraph* 28, 1 (March 2005): 26–45.

22 Stefan Jonsson, *A Brief History of the Masses [Three Revolutions]* (New York: Columbia University Press, 2008): 6.

23 Ibid.: 193.

24 The expression 'trained sensibility' is taken from Patrick Wilcken's biography, *Claude Lévi-Strauss: The Poet in the Laboratory* (New York: Penguin Books, 2010).

25 Prasanta Ray, '*Namer Sandhane* (In Search of Names)', Susobhan Chandra Sarkar Memorial Lecture 2015, organized by Ithihas Sansad and the Department of History, Presidency University, Kolkata.

26 Gurbachan Singh, *Banking Crises, Liquidity, and Credit Lines: A Macroeconomic Perspective* (London: Routledge, 2012): 227, note 2.

27 The Banca Monte dei Paschi di Siena (1472) is the oldest bank in the world which is still in operation today. For a brief history of banking in West Europe, see Thomas Crump, *The Phenomenon of Money* (London: Routledge & Kegan Paul, 1981): Chapters 10, 11; see also Carmen Reinhart and Kenneth S. Rogoff, *This Time Is Different: Eight Centuries of Financial Folly* (Princeton, NJ: Princeton University Press, 2009): 171, chapter 10.

28 Martin H. Wolfson and Gerald A. Epstein, eds., *The Handbook of the Political Economy of Financial Crisis* (New York: Oxford University Press, 2013).

29 Alexis Brassey and Stephen Barber, *Greed*, Foreword by Nicola Horlick (New York: Palgrave Macmillan, 2009); Reinhart and Rogoff, *This Time Is Different*.

30 Nancy Folbre, *Greed, Lust and Gender: A History of Economic Ideas* (Oxford: Oxford University Press, 2009): xxxii.

31 Israel M. Kirzner, 'The Economics of Greed or the Economics of Purpose', The 2010 June and Edgar Memorial Lecture, The Annual Proceedings of the Wealth and Well-Being of Nations, vol. 3 (2010–2011): 29, www.beloit.edu/upton/assets/Kirzner_Chapter.pdf

32 Ibid.: 28.

33 Long Wang, Deepak Malhotra, and J. Keith Murnighan, *Economics Education and Greed*, www.kellogg.northwestern.edu/~/media/Files/ . . . /Number399.ashx
It is interesting that use of films in economics teaching has received some attention in recent years. See David T. Flynn, 'Teaching Bank Runs Through Films', *American Journal of Business Education* 2, 67 (2009); Milica Z. Bookman and Aleksandra S. Bookman, *Economics in Film and Fiction* (Lanham, MD: R & L Education, 2009).

34 The volume relevant for this work is G. Balachandran: *The Reserve Bank of India, Volume 2: 1951–1967* (New Delhi: Oxford University Press, 1998).

35 Marjit and Mallick, *Financial Intermediation in a Less Developed Economy*.

36 Walter Benjamin, *The Arcade Project*, translators' Foreword, translated by Howard Eiland and Kevin McLaughlin (Cambridge, MA: Harvard University Press, 2002): xiv. The German word is *Konvolut*, derives from Adorno. 'In Germany, the term *Konvolut* has a common philological application: it to a larger or smaller assemblage – literally, a bundle – of manuscripts or printed material that belong together. . . . It remains the most evocative term for designating the elaborately intertwined collections of "notes and materials" that make up the central division of this most various and colorful of Benjaminian texts'.

37 Benedict Anderson, *Imagined Communities: Reflections on the Origin and Spread of Nationalism* (London: Verso, 2006): 39.

1

THE INSTITUTIONAL CRISIS

The 1940s in Bengal was a tragic decade. 'These years brought to Bengal the warning signals of an all-encompassing crisis that would engulf Bengal and cast a shadow over many decades in the future beyond 1947'.[1] Possibly, the famines, the riots and the partition diminished the visibility of the crisis caused by the 'run' on the banks in Bengal in the 1940s (Table 1.1). In no way could the collapse of banks in Bengal within a brief span of time be dismissed as a local aberration. The following generalization holds true for the Bengal episodes also:

> Financial crisis would generally begin innocently enough with a surge of healthy optimism among investors. Over time, reinforced by cavalier attitudes to risk among the bankers, this optimism would transform itself into overconfidence, occasionally even into a mania. The accompanying boom would go on for much longer than anyone expected. Then, would come a sudden shock – a bankruptcy, a surprising large loss, a financial scandal involving fraud. Whatever the event, it would provoke a sudden and dramatic shift in the sentiment. Panic would ensue. As investors were forced to liquidate in a falling market, losses would mount, banks would cut back their loans, and frightened depositors would start pulling their money out of banks.[2]

The years 1947–1949 were most critical. The crisis is considered to be 'the most widespread' compared to the 1829–1832, 1857 and 1863–1866 incidents because 'many of the depositors were ruined'.[3] Compared to the other major Indian cities, Calcutta was the worst affected (Table 1.2). The banks in Bengal apparently were not a part of a widespread bank failure and liquidation in 1913.[4] But between 1947 and 1950, of

14

Table 1.1 Calcutta area: 81 cases of liquidation

Year	Number of Cases
1940	01
1941	01
1942	01
1943	01
1944	01
1946	01
1947	09
1948	13
1949	21
1950	07
1951	05
1952	04
1953	05
1954	03
1956	02
1958	02
1959	04

Source: Annexure No. 99 (vide Answer to Unstarred Question No. 588 Dated 28.2.61 Col. 2112), Lok Sabha Debates (Second Series) Appendix 1, Thirteenth Session, 1961, Lok Sabha Secretariat, New Delhi: 301–309. Archive, State Bank of India, Kolkata.

Table 1.2 Bank liquidation in major Indian cities (1930–1959)

City	Number of Cases
Bangalore	22
Bombay	22
Calcutta	81
Delhi	20
Kanpur	15
Madras	56
Nagpur	01
Trivandrum	74
All areas	291

Source: Annexure No. 99 (vide Answer to Unstarred Question No. 588 Dated 28.2.61 Col. 2112), Lok Sabha Debates (Second Series) Appendix 1, Thirteenth Session, 1961, Lok Sabha Secretariat, New Delhi: 301–309. Archive, State Bank of India, Kolkata.

all the states in India, West Bengal unfortunately suffered most in the respect of the liquidation of banking concerns (Tables 1.1, 1.2 and Appendix 1). The failure of the Nath Bank (1950) triggering a run on The Bengal Central Bank, the Comilla Union Bank, the Comilla Banking Corporation and the Hooghly, is well known.[5] The middle-class people of this state lost a major portion of their savings as a result of bank failures.[6] A large segment of this class was the refugees from erstwhile East Pakistan, previously known as East Bengal.

Bengal had a significant network of a variety of banks.[7] In the category, 'Banks other than Scheduled and Provincial Co-operative Banks', there were 80 with their branches, sub-offices and pay offices in Calcutta in 1947. This was minus the non-scheduled banks with capital and reserve below Rs. 50,000 and those which did not submit the required statistics for 1946 and 1947. Calcutta understandably had a concentration with 27 head offices, 2 central offices, 36 branch offices and 15 registered offices (Appendix 1). There were also 51 scheduled banks in Calcutta in 1947.[8] The proliferation in banking in Bengal was not exceptional. It was happening all over India. There indeed were political-economic imperatives for the phenomenal growth. But a certain lack of ethics was noted.

> The motives behind several of the new banking ventures were not altogether legitimate or worthy. There was evidently a desire to get control over public funds for speculative investments and trading activities and also for pecuniary gains in many ways through excessive salaries, bonus, commissions, and so on. There was, again, in some cases, a desire to control sizeable banking and insurance establishments; this interlocking of interests between banks, insurance companies and industrial concerns was detrimental to the interests of bank depositors.[9]

Surendranath Banerjee observed that profit appeared 'much easier to make and capital [was] correspondingly less shy'.[10]

According to official sources,

> two hundred and five of the 634 banks that went out of business during 1940–1951 did so after 1947. Of these, no fewer than eighty-three banks, having outside liabilities of Rs 26 crores (260 million), were from West Bengal alone. Some of these were listed in the second schedule of the Bank Act at one

time or the other and included such well-known names as the Nath Bank. But the large majority of the banks failing in this eastern state were little more than loan companies that had over-reached themselves by opening more branches than they could sustain on the strength of their resources and by making large loans against property or inadequate security.[11]

Interestingly, the offices of the non-scheduled banks were concentrated in West Bengal and in four other states.[12]

Disenchantment of the middle-class depositors with the bank management and the state followed their experience of infectious collapse of banks. The following report is only one instance of many. Mr. T. V. Datar of RBI Central Office, Department of Banking Operations, Bombay, wrote in 1950 'that as a result of the suspension of payment of the Nath Bank Ltd., there was a run on the Calcutta National Bank Ltd., and the Hooghly Bank Ltd'. But the failure of the Nath Bank was just a trigger, because the 'Calcutta National Bank had already exhausted its government securities amounting to about Rs. 7 lakhs'.[13] A declaration of 'an emergency under section 18 of the Reserve Bank of India Act' was proposed by Mr. Bhargava, RBI Manager, Calcutta. The onus of the banking crisis was placed on the depositors' panic. The banks were to be saved from this public panic by generous loans from the government. Letters, telegrams and flights to Calcutta by very senior office bearers were part of the crisis management drive. Nobody in officialdom thought about saving the depositors from the loot conducted by the bank directors and higher officials. Or of asking and answering a question as to why and how at all the depositors and the other stakeholders became victims vulnerable to panic in the first place. Mahesh Chandra Bhattacharyya (1858–1942), famous for his chain of allopathy and homeopathy medicine shops in Kolkata had observed: 'Banks prosper on the basis of depositors' money but they consider their shareholders to be intimate to them while treating the depositors as distant clients. Banks are always apprehensive that the majority of depositors would withdraw their deposits'. His tract titled *Byabosai* (The Businessman) was written for the fledging businessmen in Bengal.[14]

A more relevant measure of the crisis could be the number of the victims – the lower- and middle-class savings bank depositors and the middle-class shareholders. However, there is no official estimate of the number nor of the amount of money they lost. This is not denying that there were other stakeholders who suffered also due to liquidation of banks at least initially. The proviso 'initially' is urgent because some affluent stakeholders with useful social networks could retrieve what they had initially lost. Let us take this example:

> In conference between the executive committee of the bank (the Union Bank) and the trustees of Carr, Tagore and Company, the 18-lakh (1.8 million) debt was compromised to 6 1/2 lakhs (0.65 million).[15] Although Carr, Tagore and Company was not insolvent and its trustees had announced that they would pay their debts in full, the debt was sold at auction and purchased by Muddun Mohun Chatterjee, probably a client of the Tagore family, for a mere Rs. 40,500.

'It was a common practice for the debtors of the bank to purchase their own debts at a discount'. Or, some 'culprits' would just make them untraceable. Their lack of scruples did not expose them to any legal sanction because the 'government itself made no attempt to see that justice was done either to the creditors or to the shareholders, who were victims of fraud'.[16] In fact, the debtors' disappearing act was facilitated by a RBI practice.

> It also appears that in many cases the Reserve Bank informs the non-scheduled banks people to give up banking and go to something else. The result is that in many cases the party goes to the High Court, gets an order for altering the Articles and Memorandum of Association and start a new line, all the time cheating the depositors.[17]

There is no consensus on the number of helpless victims. According to Pramatha Nath Mukherjee, president, Nath Bank Employees' Association, 'forty thousand creditors' suffered from the collapse of the banks.[18] This could be more reliable because the estimate came from the highest office bearer of the employees' association of a prominent bank. The only other numerical estimate came from the report of a newspaper. The *Amrita Bazar Patrika* wrote in its editorial about 'thousands of families' in its edition 11 March 1950.[19] Even scholarly researchers could not manage anything more exact. The lack of aggregate data on the number of depositors in banks in Bengal then stands in the way of estimating the size of the victims of bank runs. The chairman of the Canara Industrial and Banking

Syndicate Ltd., claimed 30,000 small depositors in course of his speech at the company's Silver Jubilee celebrations: 'a porter was now able to buy a house from his pigmy savings deposited in the bank. It is said that the bank offers to collect even a fraction of a rupee to encourage thrift and savings'. All knowledgeable individuals were not in agreement with this observation. *Capital* commented: 'There is not a great body of precise up-to-date information to indicate how far efforts to collect rural savings have justified this [the chairman's] assertion'.[20]

Evidently, we have no clue to the number of persons who lost their monetary viability. Some of them could have been relatively well-off shareholders, the big depositors who had wealth or other sources of income. But there were low-income lower-middle-class depositors holding savings accounts also. And they were more numerous than the other categories of stakeholders. There is no way one could estimate the low-income low-middle-class clients suffering loss due to liquidation of some banks. They obviously differed among themselves in terms of current or savings bank account with such banks, and how much they lost due to bank failure. One Nihar Bala Sett from Sukhchar, West Bengal, observed that 'many persons of middle class people had suffered in this Bank crisis, where more than Rs. 150000000 had been lost'.[21] According to Arun Chandra Guha, a Member of the Indian Parliament, the Nath Bank Ltd., closed its transactions with about rupees two crores (20 million) as deposit.[22]

Even the trading class in Bengal drew attention of the authorities to the grievous loss by the middle class.

> A big section of the middle-class people of Bengal, who had put in their mites . . . the results of their life-long sufferance and services . . . were badly shaken. The action or, for that matter, inaction of the Reserve Bank was thus ethically wrong and economically ruinous in their case.[23]

There are brief biographical notes like the following. This relates to a Bengali singer Kamal Das Gupta (1912–1974) whose song '*Bhaalobaasaa More Bhikhari Korechhe*' (Love Has Turned Me Into a Destitute) made him very popular to the Bengali middle class. He earned a great deal as indicated by the fact that he paid Rs. 37000.00 income tax. He became a total pauper due to the financial collapse of a bank where he had his savings. 'In the meantime in the post-war period many banks failed. His life's savings suddenly became nil. Sick Kamal babu became a destitute and a broke'.[24] Evidently he was not in the category of lower middle class. But nobody except the novelists and the short story writers wrote their biography.[25]

The other form of estimate of suffering was in terms of class identity of the sufferers. The reference to middle-class victims recurred in the press and on the floor of the legislative bodies. The *Amrita Bazar Patrika* observed: 'The bulk of the creditors of these banks come from the middle class which has been the hardest hit by the present economic distress'.[26] In a letter to the Editor, *The Nation* on 20 March 1950, Nalini Ranjan Mitra, Sudhanshu Bhusan Sur, Phani Bhusan Biswas wrote:

> The common depositors of the Bengalee Scheduled Banks should be saved from an unprecedented economic crash. The common depositors are the middle class people of the Bengalee society. They are victims of political division of the country and just at present they are on the march to unknown destination for safely leaving their hearth, home and whatever little wealth they possessed. These Bengalee Banks mostly thrived on the support and savings of the middle class people who are generally the investors of these banks.[27]

Their saving was motivated by their need for security for the future; for the salaried people, security after retirement. But saving in a bank also carried a status mark in the middle-class' reckoning.

> For the larger number of middle- and lower- middle-class persons the possession of a bank account is itself an index of well-being. . . . But it must be realized that the middle classes do not look forward to acquiring wealth. They are at least seeking security against old age and the consequent loss of employment.[28]

Unfailingly, everybody representing the cause of the helpless victims focused on the refugees. But it was the middle-class individuals among them who suffered most because of the banking crisis.[29] Refugee depositors lost their savings, resulting in their destitution, which became deeper in view of the fact that organizations helping them to resettle here in West Bengal also suffered due to the failure of banks. Dr. John Mathai, Minister of Finance, Government of India, wrote to Dr. Rajendra Prasad, President of India, on 12 June 1949.

I mentioned to you the other day that some money of the *Gandhi Smarak Nidhi* which had been deposited with some scheduled banks in Calcutta is in danger on account of the banks having stopped payments. You were good enough to ask me to send you the details which I am giving below. I understand that apart from the loss that the *Gandhi Smarak Nidhi* may suffer, one of the banks had a large deposit from the refugees from East Pakistan to West Bengal. The position of these people is that of a person jumping from the frying pan in to fire. I wonder if anything can be done to rehabilitate these banks. They were, I understand, scheduled banks.

Our claims are as follows:

Calcutta Commercial Bank   Rs. 33720.00
The Pioneer Bank   Rs. 682.00[30]

A deeper resonance of the great tragedy was in a letter signed by 34 (unnamed) signatories from Chittagong, dated 14 April 1949 to His Excellency the High Commissioner of India in Pakistan:

That a few months ago six scheduled banks owing to various complicated cases stopped payments and that its effect has not only become disastrous for the commerce and industry of this place, but it has also reduced thousands of poor men of very small means to street beggars and that among them are East Bengal Refugees, students, helpless widows, orphans, etc. and the thousands of unfortunate employees of banks and business firms.

That the institutions which lent invaluable support to such people were rendered unviable was re-told herein:

Accounts of Gandhi Memorial Funds, Congress Organisations, Relief Organisations, Constructive Workers' Organisations, School, Semi-Government Institutions, Provident Fund money and a number of such other organisations doing good to society and the general public in different parts of the country were opened in scheduled banks and by the collapse of the above-mentioned scheduled banks the works of many public and charitable institutions have to be closed down thus doing great harm to the general in both the dominions.[31]

There is no way to have a measure of the amount of money the depositors, particularly the lower-middle-class refugees, lost. It is rather definite that they could not have saved a great amount. But the little they saved must have a great significance for them. As everywhere, in Bengal too, those suffering from income insecurity persisted with the practice of saving money in minute fractions, which they could do only by denying themselves satisfaction even at the level of necessities. They were socialized by their life's experience in what Bourdieu calls 'savings morality'.[32] That they thought would secure their future a bit. However, their modest hope became elusive due to the banking crisis. They lost their savings but ironically earned a low esteem for their alleged vulnerability to rumour and a proneness to panic. But as the chairman of the Canara Industrial and Banking Syndicate Ltd. claimed, 'the bank offers to collect even a fraction of a rupee to encourage thrift and savings'.[33] Projecting banks as institutions to help those with a surplus of 'a fraction of rupee' was a part of building trust with lower-middle-class clients. That was definitely not to help them secure their future. Inculcating in them the wisdom of thrift was a design of the players in the capital market. In fact, they were cajoled into saving by enterprising individuals.

> They (B. K. Dutta and his office staff) would then set up shop on the balcony of the bar-library at the district court, servicing the financial transactions of the numerous lawyers, clients, peasants, jotedars or substantial farmers and talukdar, landholders, who would regularly visit the court from all over the district (Comilla).[34]

This was by way of building personal trust rather than trustworthy institutions.[35]

Enticing the people

The offer of 'higher rates of interest to seduce depositors' became noticeable from the early twentieth century.[36] Nikhilesh in Tagore's *Ghare Baire* (The Home and the World) (1916) thought the same way.

> He felt that the reason no large-scale industries can be sustained in our country was because there were no banks . . . he felt it was imperative to inculcate the habit and the desire to

save money in banks among our people. So he started a small bank. The urge to save money in the bank was strong among the villagers because the rate of interest was very high.[37]

When one goes through the pages of both vernacular and English language dailies in the 1930s and 1940s, one is struck by the flurry of advertisements by Bengalee-owned banks. Each announced its capital and the rate of interest offered. When some banks were in crisis, other banks promised security of investment. Some banks even tried to convince the prospective clients about their gains in the form of interest. They took upon the task of imparting everyday financial education.[38] Consider the following examples from *Bangadut*, a vernacular daily (26 June 1819):

> The bank in Sreerampur: An article regarding opening of a Savings Bank in Sreerampur has been published last week in which it is stated on the basis of a calculation that there should not be any high expectation when money of a certain amount is deposited every month on the total of which an interest accrues, which together with the total already deposited fetches further interest in the first five to six years. But if the money is kept with the bank for ten to twenty years, a satisfying sense of gain is possible. If one rupee is deposited every month, then in ten years it becomes one hundred and seventy-four rupees, rupees five hundred thirty-one in twenty years, and rupees one hundred and sixty-six in thirty years. In these thirty years, the principal sum is rupees three hundred and sixty, and rupees nine hundred and six is the interest on the principal sum of rupees three hundred and sixty. And if rupees ten is deposited every month for ten years in a bank, then more than ten times is gained. This article has been published in English; in the coming week it will be published in Bengali for informing the Bengalis.[39]

As the dateline of the *Bangadut* excerpt shows, the drive by a variety of financial institutions towards vernacular communication began from early nineteenth century in the hope of reaching out to the large potential clientele. The focus in the advertisements was on the rules of transaction: the dos and the don'ts. The seductive power of promise of cumulative interest was well known to the men who managed banks and other deposit schemes.[40] Apparently, it was about creating a new saving culture, but fundamentally, it was raising the money from the multitude needed for infrastructural projects on roadways and canals, probably more accessed by the powerful and the privileged than the common people.

This culminated in creation of Savings Bank attached to the Post Office in 1887. The enterprise of the government was lauded because this would invigorate the saving habit of the people.

> The people, who spend excessively on entertainment only because there is no institution to save their money earned through their hard work, will have the benefit of saving money. There is no doubt that the savings bank will benefit the poor and the needy men and women.[41]

Tapping the poor people's small 'excess' income in personal holding has long been a part of the design of the bankers (as well as money-grabbers of all kinds). The gains for the multitude, apart from and along with the interest earned – it was argued – were many and durable: like, an enhancement of common people's attachment to the governance of their country because the money collected from them would be utilized for a number of beneficial projects, for example, creation of roadways, canal excavation, rescuing poor peasants from the clutches of usurious moneylenders, and progress in industry and trade. But above all – the argument continued – the strength of the imperial order would be invigorated. Amrita Lal De (1846–1911) is a good illustration of the propounders of this policy on savings by the common people. The man who was concerned with the well-being of the poor and the common people was ironically the editor (1846–1911) of the *Royal Chronicle*, which carried on the cover of each issue the announcement: 'The only Representative paper specially devoted to the Interest and Welfare of the Ruling Chiefs, Princes, Maharajas, Rajas, Nawabs, Zaminders and the Gentry of India and which contains Records of their Doings etc'.[42] He also founded and edited an English language journal, *News of the World* (1881). His preoccupation with wealth-making is evident in his two treatises, *How to Be Wealthy* (1879) and *The Path to Wealth* (1883), and in the story *How a Rupee became a Hundred Thousand* (1884). The 109-page treatise, *How to Be Wealthy* purported to be a complete tactical guide to becoming wealthy which included a work ethic of hard work and discipline. On the cover was a quintessential message.[43]

How to be Wealthy
Being
A guide to fortune for everybody, containing the most essential rules
and practical hints and suggestions for success in life,
And
Directing the ways
And means – How to earn, save, invest
And increase money
And
Be wealthy, and thereby live comfortably
Upon a substantial Income.

A book for persons of all ages and circumstances.

'Each day new wealth without their care provides,
They lie asleep with prizes in their nets'.
John Dryden

How to be wealthy or at least how to be financially secure was the contemporary refrain among the *bhadralok* middle class. The Hooghly Bank Ltd., projected itself as the 'middle class's own bank'.[44] The logical outcome was insistent advertising in the vernacular dailies to project an image of viability of a bank, and the promise of a high dividend was a way to motivate men to deposit their surplus earning in a bank. That most of the banks which failed, failed because they went out to seduce men and money, has been located as a major reason of failure of banks. S. K. Muranjan observed:

> Among many wiles employed to beguile the public into placing their funds with banks, none was more crude or more frequent than the advertisement of imposing figures of authorized or subscribed capitals as against very fractional amounts of paid up capital.[45]

The advertisement by Mahaluxmi is a good example of presentation of institutional self in everyday life in the financial field. Headquartered in Calcutta, it profiled itself as a scheduled bank, thus justifying its custodial claim to be 'the most secure and dependable institution' for deposits. That it had been serving the country for 36 years, as the advertisement informed its potential clients, was a proof enough of its dependability. Its financial viability was indicated in the amount of accumulated capital and reserve to the tune of Rs. 15 lakhs and more, and its effective fund/working capital of more than 2 crores of rupees. Its reach was indicated by the fact that it had branches and agencies in all the reputed centres of business in India – all efficiently directed by experienced and established businessmen. The whole enterprise was grounded on the motto that economic independence was the fount of national independence (*Ananda Bazar Patrika*, 22 May, 1948). What is interesting is that, central to the intertwining of the prospects of the nation with those of financial investment, the amount of capital was stated using bigger fonts. *Lakh* and *Koti* (crore) are not merely numbers in conventional quantitative mathematical sense. It is in the nature of what Lévi-Strauss signified as qualitative mathematics, which allows us to explore cultural meanings associated with numbers.[46] The terms, 'lakh' and 'koti', used to refer to cherished levels of financial status. Another advertisement, by Bengal Central Bank Limited, unfolded a prosaic mathematical reasoning to establish its claim of financial viability. It offered an intelligible proof why it would be in a position to pay back on demand the larger part of the deposit by an investor. It relied on numbers rather than emotional exhortations as in the earlier case: no appeal to 'freedom' and 'nation' (*Ananda Bazar Patrika*, 11, 13 and 15 May, 1948).

Equally interesting is the use of cultural icons like Tagore.[47] His poem *Sanchoy* (Savings) is used in an advertisement, published in the Bengali journal *Shonibarer Chithi* (c1941). It was probably composed for the particular advertisement. Originally in Bengali, the advertisement had an evident literary flavour.[48]

Savings

The rainy days of grief have come with threatening gloom,
O dear ploughman, come out of your home.
The dry wilderness has been softened by the rains,
Now is the time when you must sow.

Only a little amount of your daily expenses can eventually create a large fund of wealth through savings. The best way is the savings bank account. Start today. Any amount can be withdrawn through a cheque, and a three per cent interest is paid

Bank of Commerce Ltd.
12 Clive Street, Calcutta.
Branch: College Street, Calcutta, Kidderpore,
Ballygaunge, Bardhaman, Khulna,
Bagerhat and Jessore.

Bankers' interest in 'a fraction of a rupee' and in publicity of a multiplier effect converged easily with Tagore's 'only a little amount of your daily expenses' as every financial institution was after the small salary/wage earners in Bengal. Deployment of mathematics and metaphors was intended to excite elementary skills in calculation and capacity for reasoning; maybe, towards reversing inertia of non-institutional saving on the part of financial illiterates. Tagore's metaphors – 'rainy days of grief' and 'softened by the rains' – were intended to play on both fear and deliverance. One wonders why 'ploughman' was being sensitized about new opportunities for well-being. Could it be to mobilize holdings of small amounts of money left after expenses on the essentials among marginal and middle peasantry? We have already noted B. K. Dutt's interest in peasants, jotedars and talukdars in his informal search for clients.

Lest the imageries of nature would not be sufficient to motivate people to come out of the inertia of non-institutional saving, in another exhortation, which used lines composed by Tagore, religious symbols were set in what was otherwise secular reasoning. This advertisement in Bengali was by Calcutta-based Hindusthan Co-operative Insurance Society Limited. Captioned 'Well-being and Collection' read: 'The inner message of Lakshmi is well-being. It bestows wealth with prosperity. Kuvera's message is collection [of money] through which wealth increases'. The advertisement built on the cue in Tagore's couplet to announce that life insurance (organizations) represented the messages of Lakshmi and Kuvera.[49] The Life Insurance Co. collected small savings by individuals, the sum to be utilized for the welfare of the nation.[50]

At another level, easily intelligible books were written in the vernacular explaining the nature of banks in various countries and here in India. A good example is *Desh-Bidesher Bank* (Indigenous and Foreign Banks) by Narendranath Laha and Jitendranath Sen Gupta (1930).[51] Another is *Banglar Banking* (Banking in Bengal) by Harishchandra Sinha (1939).[52] The publisher of the first book categorically expressed the intention of educating lay persons about the intricacies of the banking industry. It used dialogue as the pedagogic method of explaining the specificities of the banking industry across countries and economies, keeping reference to theory to a minimum. The question–answer conversations were between Narendranath Laha, PhD, and Jitendranath Sen Gupta, MA, B. L. The former, a rich businessman, was the secretary of the Bengal National Chambers of Commerce and a member, Committee of Bengal Provincial National Chambers of Commerce, and also a member, Committee of Bengal Provincial Banking Inquiry Committee. The latter was the researcher in the Bengal Economic Association.

The book, the publisher hoped, would fill a void in 'scientific analyses of banking in Bengal'. Harishchandra Sinha's book also offered basic knowledge of banking. But it concluded on a moral tone in the face of what he thought an impending crisis of banking in Bengal. He believed that to be a leader, one must be free from desire for money and honour, and that banking in Bengal was lacking in such leadership. His premonition turned out to be correct.[53] Atul Sur's brief outline on constituents of money market in *Takaar Bazar* (1948) belonged to the same genre of writings towards financial education of lay persons.[54] But it did not take any sentimental position on Bengal economy.

Before analysing what such texts meant for grown-up men and women, we need to recall books in vernacular written for school-going students. One is *Arthaneeti O Artha Byabohaar (Economics and Uses of Money)* by Nrisingha Chandra Mukhopadhaya (1875).[55] It was written, as the announcement in the title page mentioned, for Normal and Bengali-medium schools, primary schools and for the use by common people. In fact, the announcement recommended the book as a must read for adolescent and tender boys and girls. Along with informative discussion on the themes represented in the title, it imparted the economic 'wisdom' that only an increase in the number of the rich individuals would probably relieve the misery of the poor people.[56] The author was also categorical that, depending on the measure of labour and intelligence used, some would be rich and some poor. The advertisement for the book argued that earning money was the principal objective of human life. 'Without money, we cannot carry on daily life. So for every family man, a king or a subject, a landlord or a tenant, a servant or a businessman, it is essential to know the basic principles of this [economics] discipline'.[57] Another title, *Arthaneeti: Elements of Political Economy* by Jogindra Nath Samaddar (1912),[58] the first writer of a book on economics in Bengali, was meant for general reading but underscored by the same urgency of learning the fundamentals of economics. Its exhortation of learning economics by everybody altered the rationale from its utility in conducting the everyday familial life to its contribution to the knowledge of the national economy. The author wrote in his Preface:

> The general public needs to know the rules which govern making of money and its distribution, internal and external trade, and revenue as these relate to social tranquillity and prosperity. From out of deliberations on these rules, the economy in society becomes well-ordered and justice is established.

Desh-Bidesher Bank was a higher-level treatise compared to the last two titles just mentioned. It is worthwhile to note how the book, *Desh-Bidesher Bank*, projected itself, including a reference to the academic attainments and positions of authority held by the two eminent writers. The popular treatise on the critical significance of banks for the individuals, industries and the country matched contemporary scholarly economists' reasoning. The economists were convinced about the prospect of Bengal's economic renewal. Leading them was Benoy Kumar Sarkar (1887–1949), an economic sociologist and a prolific author. Many of his books were in the vernacular. He used to write in colloquial Bengali with a good amount of metaphors to make his arguments comprehensible and attractive. Sometimes he would even sound rustic. He too chose the conversation-style in what later became known as 'In the *Majlis* of Benoy Sarkar' (In Benoy Sarkar's Gatherings). His writings in Bengali include *Ekaler Dhondaulat O Arthashastra* (Wealth of the Present Times and Economics, in two volumes) (1930–1935), *Naya Banglar Gorapattan* (The Foundation of New Bengal, in two volumes) (1932) and *Bartir Pathe Bangali* (The Bengalis on the Way to Growth) (1934). The last-mentioned work argued with considerable statistical data that the Bengali people were unmistakably on a path of economic development since early 1930s. The book runs in to close to 600 pages. His zeal to enthuse educated Bengali youth to work towards Bengal's development found another medium in the journal *Arthik Unnati* (Economic Development) he edited between 1926 and 1949. He was emphatic that the hope of Bengal's renewal lay in Bengalis turning to trade and commerce and manufacturing. He had great faith in both individual initiative and institutional capacity building. He held in adoration Alamohan Das, a 'self-made' industrialist in Howrah in West Bengal. In fact, he was transformed into a measure of development. Sarkar wrote that there were about 500 Alamohan's in Bengal (at the time of his writing), 'some in banks, some in factories, some in insurance, some in trade with other nations'; it marks an increase over around 200 such men in 1925, about a hundred in 1905.[59]

In 1944, in one of his famous question–answer sessions in his *majlis*, Sarkar observed that the number of hard-working Bengali entrepreneurs had increased between 1905, when it was not more than a hundred, and 1944 to not less than 500. Bengali youth were showing great resilience in every kind of work in production and in the service sector like bank and insurance. The Bengali presence in even the Marwari-dominated Burrabazar, the famous business hub in Kolkata was not negligible. For him, these were definite signs of Bengal's economic renewal.[60] In his earlier work, *Bartir Pathe Bangali*, he suggested another positive sign in the enhanced propensity to save either in the post office or in the bank on the part of the Bengali middle class. However, this surmise was based on an inference from all-India data on middle-class saving.[61]

Reading the above-mentioned text, one is stuck by certain euphoria about Bengal's impending and inevitable prosperity. The pieces of writing are very brief without deep probing and are overtly committed to celebrate the positive signs of growth. Only the compatible statistics – sometimes from the Census, sometimes from undisclosed sources – are cited. Here too, the intention is to make the analyses intelligible by simple designs of argument. The author uses a single indicator of growth for each block of argument.

Sarkar's understanding of the state of the Bengali-run banks is embedded in his optimism of Bengal's progress. In fact, he wrote a 97-page tract called *Bangalir Bank-Daulat* (The Wealth of Bengali Banks) drawing on data collected by the researchers of the Bengal Economic Association (*Bangyo Dhana Parishad*) set up by Sarkar. The data were used in the first volume of his *Applied Economics* (1932). The piece in Bengali is a part of his *Bartir Pathe Bangali*. It is evident in these writings that he was aware that the capital in Bengali-owned banking industry had just reached only the 50 lakh (5 million) mark in 1944 and 1945. But according to his estimate, the Bengal Central Bank, the Comilla Union Bank and others had added to their capital in 1943. He expected that a Bengali-owned bank with a capital of 1 crore of rupees (10 million rupees) was about to appear on the scene. Although he was apprehensive that many banks could fail in the post-war period, he was definite that some would remain viable. The future was bright in his estimate.[62] He was ecstatic that, when due to global crisis thousands of banks collapsed in the United States, the misfortune did not fall on many Bengali-owned banks.[63]

According to Sarkar, much of the Bengali success in banking and insurance was 'undoubtedly' due to their 'business skill, unity, honesty and banking practices'.[64] He made this observation after a study of the Bengali-owned banks which did not enjoy any government help and had to compete with the quasi-governmental Imperial Bank in the *moffusil*. In fact, Sarkar appreciated their courage because 'the collapse of a few banks (by his count, seventeen) between 1914 and 1928 did not un-nerve the Bengalis'. He thought that the Bengalis were cool and composed and stoical. He went to the extent that joint-stock banks had become core to Bengal's middle class and the intelligen-tsia.[65] It opened up not only 'new ways of earning a livelihood' for Bengali middle-class youth, but also helped them earn the *bhadralok* identity.[66]

Even then, he pointed out that a modern banking system founded on a modern economy in India was yet to strike a firm root. The complete and sound banker was still rare. But he was definite about a change in that direction because the banking system in developed European economies had to undergo similar predicaments. That he set as a target to be achieved by the Bengali middle class. They had to get out of usury and get into modern banking for investing capital in productive enterprises, as the developed people in Europe had done. This vital shift would require the combined endeavour of 'legislative assembly, private commercial establishments, chamber of commerce, industrial associations and others' (e.g., artists' associations and peas-ant associations). The use of bank must become a habit for all.[67]

Alamohan Das (1894–1969), whom Benoy Kumar Sarkar praised in a short piece *Shaw-pnachek Alamohan* (Five Hundred Alamohans) in 1944,[68] was articulating another imperative. He wrote: 'I do not like business only for increased profit making. Social service must be the objective of business. . . . Profit making should be a secondary goal of business'.[69] But he disapproved of keeping money idle:

> It is never rational to keep money gained through profit idle; it is a sin, it is a social crime. I think that the ideal for each rich person (the capitalist) should be to re-invest again in business the money so gained, to expand it and thereby engage the labour power of an increased number of men for service to society.[70]

The capitalist path was to him the only way employment could be generated for Bengali youth. Not only was a new attitude to profit urgent, but a new institutional arrangement was also necessary. Alamohan in fact submitted a plan for eradication of economic misery of the people in Bengal to the Governor in Bengal in 1945. An impor-tant proposal related to capital for investment in industries.

> Compared to other provinces, it is very difficult to find money for industry. If such a guarantee could be given that those who would invest money in industry would definitely get 4 to 5 percent of interest continuously, there would be no dearth of money for industry. There would be adequate profit for the

rich because of such a guarantee for in interest between 4 and 5 percent, because they now invest money at a much lower interest.[71]

Alamohan's plan for restructuring of wages for labour was not at all generous. He advised that the wage of the worker in the lowest category be at least one-tenth of the monthly salary earned by the manger in the highest category among the directors. His concern was with improvement in worker's efficiency. He thought that wage would be sufficient to make them happy and comfortable and to induce them to enhance their efficiency.[72] His preoccupation with inequality of wealth was due to his firm belief that communism was able to strike roots in India because of this inequality. His strong apprehension was that unless this income inequality would be eliminated, no law would be able to prevent the spread of communism in India.[73] He was disappointed even by Nehru. Alamohan's position finds a resonance in the letter to Nehru by Nihar Bala Sett: the same fear of communism and an equal dismay with Nehru's ineptitude. But he was more interested in capital and profit than in a fair wage for the working class.

Although Alamohan wrote nothing about the role of banks, it was implicit in his thoughts on how to ensure enough capital for industrial growth of Bengal. The Bengalis were desperate for some quantum increase in money available for industrial financing. They needed a philosopher's stone, namely, the vital capital. Benoy Kumar Sarkar wrote:

> Whatever might be the increase in the Bengalees' capacity for capital, foreign capital particularly the British capital, and some American, German, Japanese and Marwari and Gujrati capital are absolutely needed in Bengal. The need for foreign capital will be there for some time more.[74]

He was categorical in his advice: 'The Bengalis with capital must learn to cooperate with foreign capital. Let the servants of Bengal be up and doing to increase the quantum of foreign capital (in Bengal)'.[75] Benoy Kumar Sarkar, the academic and Alamohan Das, the entrepreneur, were articulating a discourse in formation, a discourse in favour of capital-driven growth of Bengal. The discourse would appear to be committed to the welfare of the people at the bottom – the poor and the lower middle class. Looked at from another angle, it would be an expression of *swadeshi* in economy. These represented the desperate

32

needs of contemporary Bengal. But these merely laced a more fundamental advocacy of capitalism in the periphery, deeply integrated in
the capitalism–imperialism global chain. Were they oblivious of the
contradiction between their agenda for Bengal and the path to their
realization? Was it a deliberate ploy? For Benoy Kumar Sarkar, the
imperative for everybody across the social strata was to concede continuing dependency of the Indian economy,

> the peasant, the trader, the usurer, the merchant, the artisan,
> the bank employee, the insurance employee and others would
> do well to acknowledge that the Indian rupee would continue
> to be the tail of the British pound. There was room for gains
> for the peasant-the labour-the middle class-and-the rich in the
> movement for nourishment of the British empire and in the
> biased policy on imports and exports.[76]

Both Alamohan Das and Benoy Kumar Sarkar chose as the targets
of their discourse the Bengali middle-class youth in search for employment and identity.

> The way the Bengali nation has become active with objectiv-
> ity and this worldliness, towards securing the foundation of
> the development of the country and in enhancing wealth, that
> foundation would soon be the foundation of the new econ-
> omy of India. And, the world will learn to know India through
> the thinking [on economy] and programme innovated by the
> Bengalis.[77]

The Bengalis would lead; such was the collective self-indulgence. Was
it a search for self-belief? The men who owned and managed banks in
the early part of twentieth century and who showed enterprise became
almost folklore, eulogized for superior qualities in their own times.
'Enterprise' for wealth-making was hailed as if it were the only male
virtue which would bail out the Bengali people from misery and the
stigma of *chakri*, salaried employment. The best example of valorisation is Alamohan Das who became famous by the adjectival prefix,
Karmobir, that is, a courageous performer of great deeds. By his own
account, it was Acharya Prafulla Chandra Roy (1861–1944), who
coined the epithet for him.[78]

Quite a few individuals became exceptionally important in the
swadeshi impulse in creations of banks in Bengal: Dwarkanath Tagore

(Union Bank, 1829), Durga Charan Laha, Hiralal Sil and Patit Paban Sen (Calcutta Banking Corporation, 1863; later National Bank of India, 1864), Narendra Chandra Dutt (Comilla Banking Corporation, 1914), Jyotish Chandra Das (Bengal Central Bank, 1918), Batuk Dutt (The New Standard Bank, 1930; later Chairman, United Bank of India), Indubhusan Dutt and Dr. Shanti Bhusan Dutt (Comilla Union Bank, 1922) and Dhirendra Nath Mukhopadhyay (Hooghly Bank, 1932). Some of them were also celebrated for their qualities: thrifty (Narendra Chandra Dutt), hard-working (Bala Krishna Dutt), innovative mobile banking (Bala Krishna Dutt), rising above the demands of a happy family life (Bala Krishna Dutt), and not profit-maximizing (Bala Krishna Dutt).[79] There were tales of personal sacrifice also, like: Narendra Chandra Dutt (founder, Comilla Banking Corporation, 1914) giving up a prosperous legal practice, Indubhusan Dutt and Dr. Shanti Bhusan Dutt (founders, Comilla Union Bank, 1922) abandoning zamindari and legal practice respectively, Jyotish Chandra Das (founder, Bengal Central Bank [1918] moving out of a viable audit firm, Dhirendra Nath Mukhopadhyay [founder, Hooghly Bank, 1932]) giving up zamindari and politics.[80] All of them were praised for their enterprise and sacrifice. But the social history of the banking crisis in Bengal is silent about the names of the victims of failed enterprise. In keeping with the historians' duty as envisaged by Jacques Rancière, this research reconstructs the story of the abject sufferers.[81]

The Statesman, 18 February 1880, had observed on the opening of the Bengal Banking Corporation Limited (1866) with a share capital of Rs. 2 crore (20 million) in 1883, largely directed by Bengalis (probably failed by 1884):

> An Indian bank 'conducted strictly upon European principles of banking', while doing a purely Indian business and under Indian management, is an enterprise, the mere projection of which is a fact that may be regarded as the opening of a new economic era in this country. . . . It gives us great pleasure to announce that a movement (inducing people 'to deposit their little savings at a small interest') . . . has been started among the people themselves. A number of native gentlemen of good position and high character – men of education and well-known in Calcutta – have determined to start a bank, to be called, 'The Bengal Banking Corporation Limited'. . . . It has been suggested to us that the corporation will fail, because it is said, 'native gentlemen will not conduct it strictly upon

European principles of banking', and because 'natives will not trust natives'. We mention this merely to show our native friends what is the nature of the reproach which they have now an opportunity of showing to be baseless. We are hopeful that they will show this triumphantly.[82]

That was not to be.

Greedy men and greedy institutions

That was not to be because of some greedy men and their greedy institutions – the banks. The institutions which manage money are vulnerable to greed of men who control them. The ethos of the bank provides a perfect cover for corrupt practices on the part of those who are at the helm of the enterprise. The drive to raise capital for economic development of the people and the country did degenerate in some cases into desire for excessive profit. On the other hand, the lure of high interests from banks undermined moral restraints of the ordinary depositors. Bimala in Rabindranath Tagore's *Ghare Baire* thought as much when she observed: 'The urge to save money in the bank [set up by her husband] was very high. But for the precise reason for which the people's interest grew, the bank slipped through the high interest chasm and disappeared'.[83]

In certain kind of explanation of banking failure, there is a discernible intention not to blame it on greed only. A 'lack of banking knowledge on the part of the directors and the managers' and an absence of 'sane, sound and trained bankers' is often attributed the cause of the banking crisis.[84] But that was explaining the earlier collapses between 1913 and 1915. Even then, greed was hinted at in this kind of explanation. 'In some of the Indian Joint Stock Banks, the Bank officials took too much of the "loanable" money and invested in their own enterprises'.[85] 'It is a well-known fact the shareholders of a bank always hanker for large dividends and they induce the management to pick up precarious profit and a cheap popularity on an inadequate reserve'.[86] This applied to later failures also.

Failures of banks in India in recent years have been principally due to inefficient management, irrespective of whether the banks were managed by Europeans or Indians, as is borne out by the failures of the Alliance Bank of Simla and the Bengal National Bank. The inefficiency of management has been responsible in each case for bad investments ultimately bringing the banks to ruin. . . . Where banks come to grief for want of adequate liquid funds to meet an unforeseen demand for heavy withdrawals, timely help by the Central Reserve Bank providing rediscount facilities will enable them to avert failure.[87]

That was regarding the bank failures in late 1920s. For 1940s and the 1950s, the observation was

the inevitable reaction set in with the end of the war and in 1946 these banks could not attract fresh deposits. As their advances were generally sticky, they found it difficult to meet even moderate withdrawals. The conditions were aggravated by the communal disturbances, the postal strike, the Imperial Bank strike and finally by the stock exchange crisis.[88]

As an example of explanations which exonerate an individual for his moral lapse by placing the blame on crisis in the economy, we can quote Alamohan Das of Das Bank. He wrote in his autobiography:

An explanation

The readers have of course the right to know how and why disaster struck this unique progressive 'Das Bank' The popularity of the Das Bank was increasing so fast that in June, 1946, the money deposited by the people was nearly 40,000,000/- four crores of rupees. Of the 60 branches of the Das Bank 20 were in East Bengal. According to the policy of the Das Bank the deposits from an area would be invested only in that area. For this reason the deposit received in East Bengal was spent on industry and business in East Bengal itself. While the activities [of the bank] were going on smoothly, the public life in Bengal went topsy-turvy in almost all spheres under the sudden impact of direct struggles by the Muslim League in the month of August of the same year. Needless to say, the most of the industrialists and businessmen in East Bengal were Hindu. They became so scared by this sudden revolution in public life, they in large numbers started looking for shelter and employment in West Bengal and elsewhere. Even those who had their deposits in the branches of the bank in East

Bengal, they kept on demanding money from the Calcutta office of the bank. Observing their plight and in the hope that the public life in the country would again become peaceful after the crisis would be over, the Das Bank started giving them some amounts of money [against their deposits] from the Calcutta office itself.

But by this time, the depositors from East Bengal had extracted about 70 per cent of the deposits from the Calcutta office of the bank by exerting great collective pressure. At the other end the great amount of money invested in trade and commerce in East Bengal became unrealized because of political catastrophe. It is unnecessary to talk at length on this. On the whole, the Das Bank came to such a state of affairs because of sudden state revolution, that there was no other way than seeking the refuge in the honourable High Court.[89]

But, as subsequently found, Alamohan Das was evidently unscrupulous with regard to money granted to his bank to turn it around.

Of the total advances in the New Fund, those granted to two companies in which Shri. Alamohan Das, the bank's chairman is interested amount to Rs. 14.66 lakhs and form 97% of the total. This was done despite the fact that the liquidity ratio of the bank [10.4%] was very low.[90] In fact his manipulations for appropriation were astounding. Because high social esteem was bestowed on Alamohan Das and his likes, it is interesting to find how low they could stoop. This is what the RBI discovered purchase of a building at 12 Netaji Subhas Road, Calcutta, belonging to the Das Bank Limited by the Howrah Insurance Company Limited, Calcutta, at price of Rs. 759282.

As the amount involved formed about their half the total real assets of the purchaser company, and the companies in question have the same chairman, we felt that the purchase needed to be probed into. . . . It appeared that, to obtain the necessary cash to pay the Bank, the 'Howrah' sold, inter alia, its holdings in the shares of India Machinery Company Limited and Bharat Jute Mills Limited . . . the Howrah Insurance Company has stated that it has sold the above shares at their face values, whereas the market values of the above shares (as furnished by the company) at the time of the disposal were Rs. 39,968. . . . On the safe assumption that no prudent person would purchase any shares at a price many times higher than their market value, we thought that 'Howrah' might have sold the above shares to the Bank itself at their face values and repaid the proceeds of the sale as part payment towards the purchase of the property. In short we thought the sale of the above shares might have been merely a book adjustment and the shares were in effect exchanged with Das Bank Limited as a part payment. Neither the Bank nor the Insurance Company could be a loser by adopting such a course. On the other hand both the companies would be able to show their interchanged assets at 'cost prices' which are much higher than their intrinsic worth, and thereby able to show a far better financial position.

In view of the above, we called for the names of purchasers of the above shares. But we were stumped by the fact that the list did not include either the Bank or any of its directors. But even if the Bank is not the direct purchaser of the above shares, it is possible that the shares might have ultimately found their way in to the hands of the Bank, and the purchasers might have been merely nominees of the Bank.[91]

It was observed in a note in a secret statement on Das Bank dated 27/28 August, 1953:

The difference between the face value and the market value of the shares sold by the Howrah Insurance Co. Ltd. [Rs.2.70 lakhs] almost equals the profit made by the bank on the sale of the building [Rs.2.78 lakhs]. Taking the amount of profit made on the sale of the building the bank showed in 1952, for the first time since it suspended payment, a net profit of Rs. 2.95 lakhs.[92]

In many cases, personal greed was invigorated by professional help.

The M. D. Sudhin Datta (the Managing Director, the Calcutta Commercial Bank) used to take advice from very shrewd accounts experts such as P. K. Ghosh (RBI auditor) and Rangaswami (Editor, *Indian Times*) in keeping the books and in preparing balance sheets, weekly Reserve Bank statements.[93]

The indictment dated 16 August 1949 stated:

> It is clear that deliberate and extensive frauds, which are now before the Police, have been committed by the Managing Director accompanied by gross negligence on the part of the other Directors. The Inspecting Officer, in his confidential supplement . . . states that out of advances examined as much as 53 percent of the advances are wholly bad. Misappropriations by the Managing Director have been estimated in the region of Rs. 76 lacs whereas the outside liabilities total Rs. 159 lacs; apart from these amounts lost by breach of trust, Rs. 50 lacs are further shown as irrecoverable or doubtful assets.[94]

In fact, greed became the bond of a herd of unscrupulous persons.

> It would appear that the directors, particularly the Chairman Mr. Nirmal Chandra Chunder, would be involved in the pledge of the fixed deposit receipt with the Comilla Union Bank Ltd. – Rs. 22 lakhs, and the guarantee letter passed by the bank in respect of advances by the Comilla Union Bank Ltd. to the concerns of the Managing Director, Mr. S. N Dutta. In any case it is difficult to avoid the conclusion that every member of the Board of Directors is . . . responsible for the non-disclosure in the balance sheets of the years 1945, 1946 and 1947, of this contingent liability.[95]

We have no account of the high bank officials deliberating with each other on ways of defrauding. But we may recall Adam Smith cynical observation in his *Wealth of Nations* (1776) that 'people of the same trade seldom meet together, even for merriment and diversion, but the conversation ends in a conspiracy against the public, or in some contrivance to raise prices'.[96] His observations on the broad category of merchants and manufacturers also are illuminating.

> Their thoughts . . . are commonly exercised rather about the interests of their own particular branch of business, rather than about that of the society, [hence] their judgement, even when given with the greatest candour . . . is much more to be dependent with regard to the former of these two objects than with regard to the latter. . . . The proposal of any new law or regulation of commerce which comes from this order ought

always to be listened to with great precaution, and ought never to be adopted till after having been long and carefully examined, not only with the most scrupulous, but with the most suspicious attention.[97]

The herd of defrauding men sometimes had the family bond among themselves. They merely enlarged the network for convenience. Mark Granovetter, an economic sociologist, has observed: 'Force and fraud are most efficiently pursued by teams – "honor among thieves" – that usually follows pre-existing lines of relationship'.[98] The Bengal National Bank was 'one of the few outstanding institutions which resurgent patriotism created in the eventful years 1906–1907'. In its operations, it claimed 'the temptation to declare high dividends was firmly and consistently resisted'. But what was the real story?

> The bank became gradually a family concern. Young men without any qualifications found themselves in responsible positions simply because they were connected with the promoters and organizers of the bank. Five out of six directors became heavily indebted to the bank. One of them alone obtained a loan of Rs. 3 lakhs against no security of any kind. Two of the moving spirits made it their special concern to obtain unsecured accommodation for a host of their friends and associates. Most of the bank officers were content to have overdraft accounts for themselves without any security or insufficient security. The auditors were not forgotten; they received generous accommodation from the bank.[99]

Maybe, because defrauding had the support from collective cunning, there was meticulous planning about ways of projecting a normal and legitimate face of banking operations. The game would not be located except through painstaking inspection as one of the Bengal Bank Ltd. The inspection began in July 1945, was reopened in 19 December 1947 and completed by 18 February 1948. The Report observed:

> A feature of this Bank which overshadows all others is the practice of manipulation on a large scale. This is indicated by
>
> (i)   the large number of entries in various accounts on selected dates;
> (ii) the practice of splitting up loans of round sums in to several loans for smaller accounts;

(iii) loans repeatedly granted to parties despite previous dealings with these parties have been very unsatisfactory;

(iv) the practice of granting *(a)* loans against goods; *(b)* loans against bills; and *(c)* overdrafts against hypothecation in several cases for the purpose of apparently making inter-adjustments between those accounts or in other accounts;

(v) credit entries purporting to represent repayments by the borrowers in confusing fractions but ensuring that the total is a round sum;

(vi) the abnormal transactions between the Head Office and branches for a bank of this size . . . there are unlimited opportunities for making adjustments between the Head Office and its 23 branches. There are various ways in which these entries can be effected and so much scientific skill is brought to bear upon them that it will not be easy to detect them.

Further: 'The bank appeared to have provided funds for the purchase of its own share'. 'It appeared to have encouraged large scale speculative dealings in shares and provided the bulk of working capital to borrowers by lending on long term basis on hypothecation'.[100] In many cases, the imperative of keeping the relationship between the banker and the clients at an impersonal level was not followed. As Thomas Crump observes 'where the personal relationship between banker and client is allowed to override the bureaucratic norms, the result – which is often regarded as corrupt – may threaten the whole banking system'.[101]

If and when somebody detected unscrupulous practice, the bank officials made incredible claims. Take the case of the Calcutta Commercial Bank. (Table 1.3) The bank officials were confronted with

Table 1.3 Calcutta Commercial Bank deposits

Year	Deposits		Advances
	High	Low	Highest
1942 April	Rs. 33,88,000	Rs. 29,19,000	Rs. 21,80,000
May	34,44,000	30,31,000	20,64,000
June	47,05,000	33,47,000	23,53,000
July	40,09,000	28,45,000	24,15,000
August	42,86,000	24,98,000	23,51,000

'certain dubious fluctuations in the Bank's deposit figures as detailed below':

> When asked to explain these, the Bank replied that they could only attribute the sudden rise in deposits noticeable from the table above to the influx of money in some of their accounts, adding that it was 'quite likely that many of such receipts in several accounts coincided during the week under review recording noticeable rise in figures' and regretting their inability to analyse more critically the factors influencing these receipts. Obviously this is no explanation at all. . . . An examination of the Bank's balance sheets for the years ending the 31 December 1940 and 1941, as compared with the figures for the weeks immediately preceding and immediately following the year-end, discloses a regular practice on the part of the Bank to resort to window dressing.[102]

In the above-mentioned case, the accounts were fudged, but not altogether destroyed. But the managing director of the Pioneer Bank was desperate to hide, and apart from the fact that 'accounts (were not) kept properly', some pages of the cash book (were made) missing.[103]

The moral decay was profound. Was it a lack of information and insight into ways of the Indian bankers or a correct understanding when a Western scholar commended on their commercial morality?

> There can be no surer proof of the soundness of a people's moral condition, and of their habitual regard to truth in the transactions of life, than the prevalence of so much credit as is necessary to the existence of such a system of Banking. The native Bankers themselves are patterns of commercial morality. The dishonouring of a *hoondee* is an event of rare occurrence with them.[104]

Probably, it was a misreading of the state of commercial and professional morality. The art and science of defrauding was already deeply in the Bengali banking culture.[105] Maybe, the number of dishonest persons was small; maybe, the looting by the Englishmen in Bengal encouraged the immoral trend. They got away with it.

> We hear of defalcation to the amount of two, three, four and even twelve lacs of rupees in different offices; and yet, strange

to say, the sahibs in charge of these establishments suffer nothing from the circumstances. Had a Bengali been implicated in the matter, we would have had packs of police sergeants pursuing the supposed culprit and dragging him from the zenana to criminal jail by way of a prologue to something more fearful;[106]

Reverend John Marshman, explaining the fall of the Union Bank, blamed the 'folly and fraud' of its English directors: 'systematic extravagance living and wild gambling speculations . . . whose moral sense is depraved and whose habits are corrupted'.[107] By 1940s, the unscrupulous Bengali bankers had learnt how to get away because only a few of them suffered in the court of law.

This infected everybody dealing with other people's money as in insurance business. Benoy Kumar Sarkar was ecstatic about Bengali youth in insurance. He wrote:

The loan offices, or the Bengali 'cottage-banks' as they are called, are the new centres of renewal of Bengal. These centres have succeeded in adding to the fame of the Bengali people. Bengali youth have developed an expertise as insurance agents; they are earning an income, and also contributing to the country. The insurance agents represent the formation of a new business class and a new outlook. The success of the insurance agents as social reformers is priceless.[108]

However, his celebration was not well founded. Faith, trust and good sense have never been sufficient moral resources to stem economic crises due to unscrupulous behaviour of key financial players.

The greed of the individuals in positions of authority in the banks easily fed into the greed of the institutions. Probably both gained autonomy over moral limits of self-seeking which would destroy others and over the legal frame of appropriate institutional conduct. The connection between the personal and the institutional lay in the 'fact the shareholders of a Bank always hanker for large dividends and they induce the management to pick up precarious profit and a cheap popularity on an inadequate reserve'.[109] This led to offer of high interest to the depositors and the banks developed 'ruinous rivalry' over mobilizing deposits by paying a very high rate of interest to the depositors. This eventually 'forced the banks to entertain illegitimate business and this was one of the chief causes for the failure'.[110] The RBI observed:

Many of these banks (scheduled and non-scheduled banks owned and managed by the Bengalees) offered very high rates of interests to attract deposits, spent lavishly on advertisements and opened numerous branches even in the far off places, with the result that during the war when, due to inflationary conditions, the public had large surplus funds for investment, the banks showed remarkable progress. . . . The deposits of non-scheduled banks in Bengal rose from Rs. 4.87 crores in January, 1940 to Rs. 30.78 crores in August, 1946. The deposits of Bengalee scheduled banks also rose from Rs. 5.43 crores at the end of 1939 to Rs. 69.85 crores at the end of 1946. The additional resources were not, however wisely used. In the case of non-scheduled banks a scrutiny of their balance sheets . . . [and] inspections conducted under the Banking Companies [Inspection] Ordinance, 1946, disclosed that the financial position of many of these banks was unsatisfactory.[111]

Further, as a part of the rivalry among them, the banks set up a large number of branches. During the year ended 13 April 1949 the Comilla Union Bank Ltd., extended the sphere of its operations by opening six new branches, three of them at important centres outside West Bengal: Benares, Madras and Allahabad, which brings the number of the bank's branches to 40 in all of which 10 were situated in Pakistan.[112]

On a hindsight, the crisis in banking originated in institutional haste to expand business beyond organizational capability and in greed of men at the helm of the banking organizations who took advantage of lax regulation. Meticulous care was taken to create a modernist saving culture on the potential depositors by combining appeal to individual interest with the interest of the country; by arguing that *swartha* (self-interest) and *swadeshi* (patriotism) could be symbiotic; by invigorating instrumental rationality with the communitarian emotion; and, by reinforcing the authority of disciplinary knowledge with wise words of a literature, thereby creating a symbolic capital in the service of economic capital. The decay must have been initiated by a few greedy men in charge of greedy institutions. Could that be due to a moral void at the level of the community?

It is well known that the 1940s in Bengal were both tumultuous and tragic. In the contentious decade, Bengal underwent violence and death of enormous magnitude. The Dhaka riots in 1941,[113] the Quit India movement or the India August movement 1942, the Famine of

1943, the Tebhaga movement of 1946, the Calcutta Riots of 1946 – the 'Great Calcutta Killings'[114] – and the 1947 Partition of Bengal all in a way brought out the perversities of the colonial state, the politicians and the communities. Social bond and principles of fairness and justice were ruptured by political manipulations of identities and interests as well as by unfair administrative interventions. Throughout the decade, there was a series of working-class struggles. Happening in the midst of these momentous happenings were the run on banks, no less ruinous of lives of men, women and institutions. If finding a prominent place in newspaper reports and editorials is a measure of public anxiety, then the banking crisis was no less an expression of public concern about perversity of men in ownership and managerial positions, and inefficacy of the state. The swadeshi impetus for creation of banks obviously related formation of indigenous banks to the anti-colonial struggle, at least initially. But otherwise, the bank failures were out of the frame of the larger and the critical political events in the 1940s. As we treat this as a moral failure of the contemporary Bengali *bhadralok* as owners, managers and shareholders, we also need to acknowledge another round of moral failure during the Great Calcutta killings in 1946. Some became victims of an overriding sense of insecurity during communal tension, and tolerated, encouraged or participated in what were considered and condoned as acts of self-defence.[115] Taken together, indulgence in financial malfeasance and communal violence did indicate serious moral lapses on the part of the Bengali *bhadralok*.[116]

When we go by the 'book view' of norms imparted routinely to children in Bengali *bhadralok* families, the regime of moral control was fairly strong for the cohort of financial transgressors in the first part of the twentieth century. This is evidently based on biographical studies of even a small sample of the members of the community. But it is common experience also that despite the best exposure to morals in texts read at the school or at home, or moral stories heard at home and elsewhere, every society has deviants and delinquents, and nonconformists and rebels. Evidently, a moral regime is never founded only on reading or listening to moral texts early in life. If and when moral influences from other institutional sources correspond to the moral messages of the texts, the early moral lessons through the texts are reinforced. But even then, the sustainability of early moral training is not ensured. The lived experience of a young learner can contradict the textually set morality. In any case, nobody lives by morals alone. It appears that the moral defaulters in Bengal in the 1940s escaped the prohibitory moral net.

Still it is worthwhile to recall Bengali *bhadralok* engagement with the creation of a moral web to contain and control moral deviance. There was a virtual explosion in writing and publishing books on moral education for the very young readers both within the school curriculum and outside of it in the nineteenth century.[117] Both institutions like the Fort William College, the Calcutta School Book Society and the Vernacular Literature Society, and individuals like Ishwar Chandra Vidyasagar played a pioneering role in imparting moral education in the young of the Hindu middle class.[118] The *Kathamala* (1856) stories are well known.[119] In one of the stories, the picture of the fox coveting grapes in the tree beyond its reach could be the first but not the only visual introduction to the notion of greed. Next could be our reading of *Jataka*, India's oldest collection of stories, aided by visuals in the form of line sketches (with the refrain 'Too much greed is not good'). The editions of *Ramayana* and *Mahabharata* for very young readers contain implicit reference to grief due to indulgence in greed. Vidyasagar wrote *Mahabharata* (Introductory Part) (1860) and *Sitar Bonobas* (Sita's Exile to the Forest) (1860) in Bengali for young readers. Duryodhana's greed for royal power and Sita's desire for the golden deer brought grief to both. *Data-Karna* (Charitable *Karna*) and *Thakurmar Jhuli* (Grandmother's Bag of Stories) (1908) by Dakshina-ranjan Mitra Majumdar (1877–1957) in *The Sleeping Kingdom* (in Bengali) celebrates a prince who scrupulously avoids greed. Greed is at the centre of the narrative in *Alibaba* (1897) by Kshirode Prasad Vidy-abinod (1863–1927), a very popular three-act musical play, which draws on the fantasy of *Arabian Nights*. *Shishusiksha* (Children's Education) (in three Parts) by Madanmohan Tarkalankar (1817–1858) was written originally for school-going tender girls, to teach among other things, how to write compound words. In one example, it instructs a learner how to use a special sign on the seventeenth letter of the Bengali alphabet to indicate the *r*-sound. It locates this letter with the sign in a moral advisory which stipulates – actually imparts wisdom – that 'greed is the source of peril'. The pedagogy inserts the moral into development of cognitive capacity. In continuation of this is the pointer to the moral principle that 'you should not covet another person's things', in a section on Easy Reads in the book.[120] Moral training received by Bengali school-age children was not through the schools alone. The home was probably a more critical agent of moral education. We all recall the Bengali adage that whoever does not learn the fundamental principles of disposition and behaviour very early – by the ninth year – would not even in his or her old age. Incidentally,

Durkheim made a similar observation that 'if, beyond this second period of childhood – beyond school stage – the foundations of morality have not been laid, they never will be'.[121]

The comprehensiveness of a community's moral critique of greed is indicated, among other indicators, by the number of words used to denote greed. A famous Bengali thesaurus, *Monimanjusa*, lists six nouns and 16 adjectives which denote greed in Bengali.[122] Five more nouns and six adjectives are in a collection of Bengali synonyms.[123] Universally, words fall into disuse both in the colloquial as well as literary articulations. Whatever are the reasons for the turn towards linguistic economy, fewer words mean diminished capacity for cognition, and possibly less words to convey caution and moral indignation towards moral deviance. The same is in case of proverbs. Bengal had a rich repertoire of proverbs. The numerical estimates of proverbs in Bengali are interesting: 803 in 1832, 2,354 in 1868, 1,218 in 1890, 2,271 in 1893, 104 in 1898–1902, 1,000 plus in *c* 1917, 700 in 1930/31, 1,000 in 1935, 3,201 in 1836, and 1,829 in 1938.[124] There were eight Bengali proverbs focused on greed in 1946.[125] Evidently, a proverb has a deeper chain of reasoning a word cannot convey. A few which are still used include *lobhe paap, paape mrityu* (Greed is sinful, it leads to death). In 'vernacular painting' in the form of *Jom Pat* (scroll paintings on Yama, the Lord of Death) we have the goriest visuals of punishment for sins including greed.[126] Gaganendranath Tagore's hand-coloured lithograph, *The Fake Brahmin Dispensing Blessing for Lucre* (c1918) is a caricature of greed of the priestly class.[127] But even when the words and the proverbs lose their place in everyday language, or when the vicarious visual cognition of greed hibernates, their traces remain in collective conscience as well as in individual psyche. They usually re-surface in times of crisis. We recall moral anxiety of Fatima in *Alibaba* (1897) and of Giribala in *Parash Pathar* (1948) about fortuitous fortunes.[128] It is not impossible that individuals have a lurking fear of punishment. Scenes of hell in the last canto of *Mahabharata* have the same power; this power holds true for those who are disinclined to take risks in an improper financial venture or in any immoral indulgence.

What is interesting is that the time of moral censure of avarice was also the time of enticement for making money unrestrained by moral inhibition. In *churi bidya maha bidya jodi na pori dhara* (The art of stealing is great if one is not found out), can be read by some as an inducement with a caution. But there are a few proverbs which bring out indispensability of money, like: *arthe man, sare dhan* (Honour lies

47

in money one possesses, and the superiority of paddy lies in the quality of the fertilizer), and *taka taka taka/tomar shubhro baron chakra garon/tumi bine sab fnaka* (coin, coin, coin/your white colour and round shape/everything is void without you).[129] However, we do not have any reliable biographical account of moral education received or missed by the men whose restraint faltered in the 1940s Bengal.

Kaliprasanna Sinha (1841–1870) shows in his narratives in *Hutom Pyanchar Naksha* (1862) that the mid-nineteenth-century Calcutta *bhadralok* was fascinated by attractions of money. Different categories of the rich, the powerful and the educated had different ways of making money with no scruples about their lust for money.[130] So that they would not suffer from informal sanctions, but they just attributed normality to avarice. The categories of middle-class men engaged in unfair practices were: the 'old' constituent of the Western-educated class prone to unthinking imitation of ways of the Englishmen, the 'new' component of Western-educated class which was not predisposed to pretensions of the 'old' and orthodox traditionalists without the knowledge of English. To the 'new' category belonged those who had received social renown, many of whom were the followers of the Brahmo Samaj and were in service. The 'old' segment acquired their riches from land holding, brokering and business.

Dwarkanath Tagore (1794–1846), a Western-educated brahmin, is an interesting example in history of wealth-making and status-seeking: one who was rich being 'mercilessly efficient and business-like but not generous' as a zamindar, and also by his entrepreneurship, and esteemed for his contributions to the Bengal Renaissance. Curiously, he did not have any moral qualms for owning 43 whore houses in Calcutta. Incidentally, in 1829, he founded the Union Bank in Calcutta which crashed after initial success, following his death. Money-making was evidently becoming free from moral inhibitions. This probably created moral anxiety about individual character implicit in what Ramakrishna Paramahamsa (1836–1886) said as a renunciatory alert *taka mati, mati taka* (money is mud and mud is money).[131] The collapse of banks in the 1940s was rather close to this mid-/late nineteenth-century turn to money culture. In Western European history, Scottish Enlightenment is located as a time when greed extricated itself from moral censure and became reconceptualized as 'rational self-interest'.[132] Was the late nineteenth century and early twentieth century the 'Scottish' moment in Bengal money culture?[133] At one end, it had the economics books in the vernacular for young readers and the lay public; at the other, the early nineteenth-century Young Bengal, which subscribed to classical economics of, among others, Adam Smith. Further, his *Wealth of Nations* was a set text in the courses at the Haileybury College (1805) where the first formal chair in Modern History and Political Economy was created by the East India Company. The college was founded 'to train the Company's cadre of covenanted servants to be sent out to India'.[134]

It is well known that universally contraries – in this case, moralities and immoralities – coexist. In times of stress in public life, the contradictions are accentuated. To begin with, a few individuals become vulnerable to opportunities for deviant gains-making. Then it becomes infectious, and the resultant crisis deepens. Retrieving trust in banks became an imperative because of the vital place banking institutions occupied in Bengal's economy.

Notes

1 Sabyasachi Bhattacharya, *The Defining Moments in Bengal: 1920–1947* (New Delhi: Oxford University Press, 2014): xii; see also Chapter 7. A focus on the period is also in Tanika Sarkar and Sekhar Bandyopadhyay, eds., *The Stormy Decades: Calcutta* (New Delhi: Social Science Press, 2015). An earlier work is by Pranab Chatterjee, *Struggle and Strife in Urban Bengal, 1937–47* (Kolkata: Das Gupta and Co., 1991). Less scholarly but definitely authentic are the diary-like entries of excerpts from observations by intellectuals and political persons by an activist communist Amalendu Sengupta. See his *Uttal Challish Asampta Biplab* (Turbulent 40s, the Unfinished Revolution) (Kolkata: Pratibhas, 2006). The reminiscences of Abani Lahiri of the Tebhaga movement 1946–1947 is of the same quality; see Abani Lahiri, *Tirish Challisher Bangla* (Kolkata: Serriban, 2015).
2 Liaquat Ahmed, *Lords of Finance: 1929, The Great Depression, and the Bankers Who Broke the World* (London: Windmill Books, 2010): 14–15.
3 Ramachandran B. Rau, *Present-Day Banking in India* (Calcutta: University of Calcutta, 1922): 70, fn. 2; for an analysis of the banking crisis of 1913–1914, see Amiya Kumar Bagchi, *The Evolution of the State Bank of India, Volume 2: The Era of the Presidency Banks 1876–1920* (New Delhi: State Bank of India and SAGE, 1997): Chapter 17.
4 There is no mention of a bank in Bengal undergoing failure or liquidation in Table 6 and 12 in *Statistical Tables Relating to Banks in India With an Introductory Memorandum*, Department of Statistics, Calcutta (Calcutta: Superintendent, Government Printing, India, 1915 [2nd issue], to 1934 [11th issue]): 6–11.
5 *The Reserve Bank of India, Volume 2: 1951–1967* (New Delhi: Oxford University Press, 1998): 455.
6 Editorial, 'Liquidation of Banks', *The Amrita Bazar Patrika* of 24 April 1952; F 1339 Liquidation of Banking Companies (01.05.1951–16.07.1952), C 183 B [vol. I], RBI Archive.

THE INSTITUTIONAL CRISIS

7 The beginning of insurance in Bengal from 1865 and the proliferation of banks in Bengal under the swadeshi impetus have been pointed out by all scholars working on the Bengal economy in late nineteenth and early twentieth century; see Prathama Banerjee, 'A Social History of Banking in Bengal in the Late Nineteenth and Early Twentieth Century', Unpublished Notes on UBI History Project, CSSS Files: 19–21.

8 Appendix 1, Statistical Tables Relating to Banks in India and Pakistan, RBI, 1947: 102–132.
'The Registrar of Joint Stock Companies, Bengal, estimated that 850 to 900 non-scheduled banks were functioning in that Province, more than half of which were only loan companies and did not do any real banking business. Nearly 75 per cent of the non-scheduled banks had a paid-up capital of less than Rs. 75,000 and some even below Rs. 500. The deposits of this class of banks in Bengal had risen from Rs. 5 crores to Rs. 31 crores between 1940 and 1946; those of Bengali scheduled banks had increased from Rs. 5 crores to Rs. 70 crores during the same period'. *The Reserve Bank of India, Volume 1: 1935–1951* (Mumbai: RBI, 1970; rpt 2005): 727.

9 *The Reserve Bank of India, Volume 1: 1935–1951*: 436.

10 Quoted in Bagchi, *Evolution of the State Bank of India, Volume 2: The Era of the Presidency Banks 1876–1920*, Chapter 17: 484.

11 *The Reserve Bank of India, Volume 2: 1951–1967*: 453.

12 *The Reserve Bank of India, Volume 1: 1935–1951*: 723.

13 Confidential report, D (1)1d/- A. L. Q. C Pg.188A, File 1336, RBI Archive.

14 Mahesh Chandra Bhattacharyya, *Byabosai* (The Businessman) (Kolkata: Nityalal Sil's Library, 1920): 89.

15 1 lakh = 100,000; 1 crore = 10 million.

16 Blair B. Kling, *Partner in Empire: Dwarkanath Tagore and the Age of Enterprise in Eastern India* (Kolkata: Firma KLM, 1981): 225.

17 Extract from letter No. 372-CM dated the 13th June 1953 from Dr. B. C. Roy, Chief Minister, West Bengal, to Shri A. C. Guha, Deputy Minister, Finance, Government of India. C 183 VI F 1338, RBI Archive.

18 Letter to the Governor, RBI, Cal. from Pramatha Nath Mukherjee, President, the Nath Bank Employees' Association, 13 March 1950. C 266-vol. 1, F 1744, RBI Archive.

19 C 266-vol. 1, F 1744, RBI Archive.

20 *Capital*, 16 November 1950: 754–755.

21 F 1339: Liquidation of Banking Cos. (01.05.51–16.7.52) C 183B, vol. 1, RBI Archive.

22 Letter to C. D. Deshmukh, Finance Minister, Government of India, 8 June 1951. C 183 B, vol. 1, F 1339, RBI Archive.

23 Memorandum submitted by the Bengal Trades Association on the need for change of banking policy in West Bengal, to the Prime Minister of India, June. C 183-VI F 1338, RBI Archive.

24 Jayati Gangopadhyay, 'Aami Duronto Baishakhi Jhor', in *Tomaaro Geeti Jaagaalo Smriti* [in Bengali], vol. 2 (Kolkata: Pratibhaas, 2009): 173.

25 Rokeya Sakhawat Hussain (1880–1932), a remarkable Muslim feminist and a social worker in Bengal, lost a vital deposit for her fledging school, established in 1908, due to the failure of the Burma Bank in 1911. Abdur

Rauf et al., eds., *Rokeya Writing Collection* (Kolkata: Bishwakosh Parishad, 2006): 609.

26 Editorial, *The Amrita Bazar Patrika*, 11 March 1950, C 266-vol. 1, F 1744, RBI Archive.

27 A Letter to the Editor, *The Nation*, 20 March 1950, from Nalini Ranjan Mitra, Sudhanshu Bhusan Sur, and Phani Bhusan Biswas. C 183 V F 1337, RBI Archive.

28 M. S. Gore, 'India', in *The Role of Savings and Wealth in Southern Asia and the West*, edited by Richard D. Lambert and Bert F. Hoselitz (Paris: UNESCO, 1963): 196.

29 'In the initial phase (1946–1948) of the refugee flood, a preponderance of the refugees belonged to middle-class groups (the Bengali *bhadralok*), whose level of education was higher than that of the general population of West Bengal and who had been concentrated in service occupations and in trade before migrating'. Further, 55 per cent of refugee families were high caste and 13 per cent middle caste. Harold Lubek, *Urban Development and Employment: The Prospects for Calcutta* (Kolkata: Concept Publishing, 1982): 36–37.

30 C 183 IV F 1336, RBI Archive.

31 Ibid.

32 Pierre Bourdieu, Luc Boltanski, and Jean-Claude Chamoredon, *Bank and Its Customers: Elements for Sociology of Credit* (1963) analysed in Richard Swedberg, 'The Economic Sociology of Pierre Bourdieu', *Cultural Sociology 5*, 1 (2011): 67–82. doi:10.1177/1749975510389712

33 *Capital*, 16 November 1950: 754–755.

34 Indrajit Mallick, 'B. K. Dutt: A Development Banker from Bengal', in *Money and Credit in Indian History: From Early Medieval Times*, edited by Amiya Kumar Bagchi (New Delhi: Tulika, 2002): 207. Similar practices elsewhere and later have taken place. For example, Banco Azteca (Mexico, 2002) 'has the policy of visiting the homes of the applicants for credit in order to carry out "environmental" assessments'. Some extracts of an interview with an evaluator of the Banco Azteca narrates: 'Basically, we deal with people with low incomes. In general, they work in building and domestic service. The ideal customer does not have a pay cheque; he/she works per week or per day of whatever. Ideal customers do not progress a little bit more because they don't know how to save. Each time the company told me that we were fulfilling them their dream, I thought it was a bit exaggerated, but in the course of time my own experience showed me that it was true. Their dream is to have a TV and a DVD to watch movies. All this explains why the lower classes are the ones who really look after the credit. We call for a series of requirements: receipt and more than two years' seniority (the so-called labor roots), a service (for example, a proof of residence) and his/her ID card. We authorize the credit by means of "environmental" (evaluations). We study the status of the person. A person can live in a cardboard house but being orderly at the same time. This last says a lot of the applicant, as for matters of responsibility. Many times you realize the importance that people give to a credit or how much they desire it from the way he/she treats you. . . . I can assure you that I have cried with my clients, because we have left bad times apart. I can

even consider some of them my friends, because they help me and I help them'. See Ariel Wilkis, *Morality and Popular Finance: Moral Capital as a Kind of Guarantee*, https://estudiosdelaeconomia.wordpress.com/ . . . / morality-and-popular-finance-moral-c, accessed on 14 May 2017.

35 For the distinction between personal and institutional trust, see Ingrid Größl, Rolf V. Lüde and Jan Fleck, 'Genesis and Persistence of Trust in Banks', Department of Socioeconomics Discussion Papers, Macroeconomics and Finance Series, Hamburg University, 2013, www.wiso.uni-hamburg.de/repec/hepdoc/macppr_7_2013.pdf, accessed on 7 May 2017.

36 *Capital*, 23 February 1911, quoted in Bagchi, *Evolution of the State Bank of India, Volume 2: The Era of the Presidency Banks 1876–1920*: 484.

37 Rabindranath Tagore, *Ghare Baire* (The Home and the World) (1916), translated by Sreejata Guha, Introduction and Notes by Swagato Ganguly (New Delhi: Penguin Books, 2005): 15.

38 Bourdieu, Boltanski and Chamoredon, *Bank and Its Customers*, analysed in Swedberg, 'Economic Sociology of Pierre Bourdieu': 67–82. doi:10.1177/1749975510389712

39 Brajendranath Bandyopadhyay, compiled and ed., *Sambad Patre Sekaler Katha* (The Accounts of the Past in Newspapers), vol. 1 (1818–1830) (Calcutta: Bangiya Sahitya Parishad Mandir, 1932): 105–106, 107.

40 Ibid.

41 Narendranath Laha, *Subarnabanik: Katha O Keerti* (Subarnabanik: Discourse and Achievements) (Calcutta: Oriental Press, 1941): 82. The Subarnabanik community in Bengal traditionally deals in gold and in banking.

42 Ibid.: 56–57.

43 Ibid.: 100–101. The quote from John Dryden (1631–1700) *Annus Mirabilis 1666* (1667) in a publication in Calcutta in 1879 is interesting, although there is no clue what Amrita Lal Dey, an alumnus of Calcutta's Presidency College, wanted to convey.

44 *Prabasi*, January, 1944: 12.

45 S. K. Muranjan, *Modern Banking in India*, 3rd ed. (Bombay: Kamala Publishing House, 1952): 295–296.

46 Charles Stafford, 'Some Qualitative Mathematics in China', *Anthropological Theory* 10, 1–2 (2010): 81–86. doi:10.1177/1463499610365373. Stafford has worked in a folk version of qualitative mathematics in Chinese culture. Based on field research, he observes that 'numbers are rarely just numbers in China and Taiwan – neutral tools for description and evaluation. For they are central to some of the most important Chinese/Taiwanese cultural narratives, and an interlinked range of special uses of numbers is highly salient in everyday life'.

47 Tagore reportedly never charged for over 100 advertisements between 1889 and 1941 because it was a part of his nationalist agenda.

48 Arun Kumar Roy, *Tagore in Advertisement* (Kolkata: Rabindranath Tagore Centre, ICCR, 2011).

49 A Purānic deity, Lakshmi is the goddess of Love, Beauty and Prosperity. In pictures, she is usually painted in a bright golden colour. In popular perception, riches represent her blessings on a man, and a miserable man is 'forsaken by *Lakshmi*'. There are colloquial terms for both the possibilities. Kuvera is the god of riches, although never commanding Lakshmi's

popularity. It is because of his place in the Rāmāyana, that he is known. See W. J. Wilkins, *Hindu Mythology*, 2nd ed. (Kolkata: Rupa & Co., 1989): 127–133, 388–393. In recent times, popular websites guide believers in their worship of Kuvera.

50 A brief analysis of the endeavour to create a saving morality in Bengal in early twentieth century is in Banerjee, 'A Social History of Banking in Bengal in the Late Nineteenth and Early Twentieth Century': 21–22.

51 Narendranath Laha and Jitendranath Sen Gupta, *Desh-Bidesher Bank*, Hrishikesh Series no. 15 (Kolkata: Oriental Press, 1930).

52 Harishchandra Sinha, *Banglar Banking* (Banking in Bengal) (Calcutta: Calcutta University Press, 1939). It had a list of technical terms rendered in Bengali. Some of the late nineteenth- and early twentieth-century Bengali writings on elementary economics include *Artha Byabohar* by Rajkrishna Raychowdhury (Calcutta: Sanskrit Press Depository, 1875), *Arthaniti O Arthabyabahar or Elements of Political Economy and Money Matters in Bengal* by Nrisingha Chandra Mukhurji (Calcutta: New School-Book Press, 1875), *Naba Arthaniti* (New Economics) by Satyacharan Bidyabinod (Calcutta: Vedanta Press, 1885), *Arthaniti: Elements of Political Economy* by Jogindranath Samaddar (Howrah, Calcutta: Dhirendranath Lahiri, 1912) and *Daridder Krandan* (Tears of the Poor) by Radhakamal Mukhopadhyay (Calcutta: Giridranath Mitra, 1915).

53 Sinha, *Banglar Banking*: 192.

54 Atul Sur, *Takar Bazar*, Viswavidya Series, Viswabharati (Calcutta: Tapasi Press, 1948). Professor of Economics in Calcutta University, he wrote *Aamra Garib Kano?* (Why Are We Poor?) (Kolkata: Sahityaloke, 1984).

55 Mukhopadhaya, *Arthaneeti O Artha Byabohaar*.

56 Ibid.: 53.

57 Ibid.: 1.

58 Samaddar, *Arthaniti: Elements of Political Economy*. It is a reasonably correct conjecture that he reproduced in elementary exposition in his book the Ricardian ideas which shaped colonial economic policy in Bengal. David Ricardo's *Principles of Political Economy and Taxation* (1817) was translated by Sudha Kanta Dey, which was published in serial form in *Arthic Unnati* between 1928 and 1930; John E. King, David Ricardo (New York: Palgrave Macmillan, 2013); David Ricardo, *The Works and Correspondence of David Ricardo*, vol. 10 (Cambridge: Cambridge University Press, 1955). Samaddar was a great admirer of 'such peace-loving, fair-minded people as the British', and of Dadabhai Naoroji; and of the colonial economic policy in Bengal. He quotes the famous work ethic in Gita, chap. 2, verse 47: 'To work alone thou has the right, but never to the fruits thereof. Be thou neither actuated by the fruits of action, nor be thou attached to inaction'. In Lin Yutung, The *Wisdom of India and China* (New York: The Modern Library, 1942): 64. The book was published under the patronage of Maharaja Sir Manindra Chandra Nandy, the Cossim bazar zamindar.

59 Haridas Mukhopadhyaya et al., *Benoy Sarker-er Baithake: Bingso Satabdir Banga-Sanskriti* (In Benoy Sarkar's *Majlis*: Bengali Culture in Twentieth Century), vol. 2 (Kolkata: Dey's Publishing, 2003): 674–675.

60 Ibid. However, this observation by Sarkar cannot be sustained in the face of data on the marginalization of the Bengalis and the Armenians and the increasing dominance of the Marwari merchants in Calcutta, 1906–1920. See Bagchi, *The Evolution of the State Bank of India, Volume 2: The Era of the Presidency Banks 1876–1920*: 81–90.

61 Benoy Kumar Sarkar, '*Dakgharer Madhybitto Punjiwalaar Baarti* (Growth of Capital Owners in the Post Office)', in *Bartir Pathe Bangali*: 38–39.

62 Mukhopadhyaya et al., *Benoy Sarkar-er Baithake*: 834–835; he wrote 'The capital of the Bengal Central Bank, Comilla Union Bank, etc. have considerably increased after 1943 . . . [such] is likely to increase in the war years. Maybe, we could see Bengali banks with a capital of a crore of rupees within a few years'; and 'After the end of the war a large number of businessmen, traders, bankers, those in insurance business, merchants and factory managers are likely to be in trouble. There is a possibility of many failing. There is no doubt that a few would manage to remain viable. . . . However, every businessman need to be cautious': 835.

63 Sarkar, *Baartir Pathe Bangali*: 64.

64 Sarkar, '*Bangali-Parichalito Joint Stock Bank Samhuo* (The Bengali Directed Joint Stock Banks)', in *Baartir Pathe Bangali*: 115.

65 Ibid.: 122.

66 The Western educated, generally upper caste, though open to others who shared this education and values.

67 Sarkar, '*Bank-Byabosai O Bharater Adhunik Arthaniti*', in *Baartir Pathe Bangali*: 185–189.

68 Mukhopadhyaya et al., *Benoy Sarker-er Baithake*, vol. 2: 674–675.

69 Alamohan Das, *Amar Jibon* (My Life) (Kolkata: The National Press, 2001): 4.

70 Ibid.: 4–5.

71 Ibid.: 89.

72 Ibid.

73 Ibid.: 91.

74 Sarkar, '*Chaai Bideshi Punji* (Foreign Capital Needed)', in *Bartir Pathe Bangali*: 55.

75 Sarkar, '*Bideshi Punjir Amdanir Byabostha* (Arrangement for Import of Foreign Capital)', in *Bartir Pathe Bangali*: 92.

76 Sarkar, '*Chaai Bideshi Punji*', in *Bartir Pathe Bangali*: 54.

77 Sarkar, '*1945–50 saner Bangali* (The Bengalis of 1945–50)', in *Bartir Pathe Bangali*: 57.

78 Prafulla Chandra Roy was a Bengali academician, a chemist and entrepreneur. He was the founder of Bengal Chemicals & Pharmaceuticals, India's first pharmaceutical company. He is the author of *A History of Hindu Chemistry From the Earliest Times to the Sixteenth Century A.D. With Sanskrit Texts, Variants, Translation and Illustrations* (Oxford: Williams and Norgate, 1902).

79 Indrajit Mallick, 'B. K. Dutt: A Development Banker from Bengal', in *Money and Credit in Indian History: From Early Medieval Times*, edited by Amiya Kumar Bagchi (New Delhi: Tulika, 2002): 216.

80 Ibid.: 203–218.

81 Jacques Rancière, *The Names of History: On the Poetics of Knowledge*, translated by Hassan Melehy, Foreword by Hayden White (Minneapolis, MN: University of Minnesota Press, 1994). 'It is a scientific duty insofar as it restores to the domain of knowledge a body of fact lost through a negligence or enmity both scientific and political. And it is a political duty insofar as it contributes to the legitimation of the democratic program peculiar to the modern age by substantiating the claim of the anonymous masses and nameless poor to a place in history' (p. ix).

82 Bagchi, *Evolution of the State Bank of India, Volume 2: The Era of the Presidency Banks, 1876–1920*: 91–92, quoted in note 10.

83 Tagore, *Ghare Baire* (The Home and the World) (1916): 15.

84 Rau, *Present-Day Banking in India*: 80.

85 Ibid.: 82.

86 Ibid.: 87.

87 The Indian Central Banking Enquiry Committee, 1931, vol. 2, *Evidence* (Written) (Calcutta: Government of India, Central Publication Branch, Calcutta, 1931): 495.

88 Confidential Report from RBI to the Central Board on 31 January 1949, C 183, vol. 4, F 1336, RBI Archive.

89 Das, *Amar Jibon*: 83–84.

90 Summary of the Inspection Report on the Das Bank Ltd., Calcutta under section 35 of the Banking Companies Act, 1949, C 315, vol. 1, F 13772, RBI Archive.

91 Letter to G. Balasubramanian, Secretary, RBI, Central Office, Bombay, from A. Rajagopalan, Government of India, Department of Insurance, D.O. No. 37-IB(1)/52 dt. 19.8.53. C 315, vol. 1, F 13772, RBI Archive.

92 C 315, vol. 1, F 13772, RBI Archive.

93 Correspondence from O. P. Gupta, Under Secretary, Govt. of India, to Secretary, Home, Govt. of West Bengal, No. D. 591-F. 1/49, 25 January 1949, C 183, vol. 4, F 1336, RBI Archive.

94 C 22, F 1137 NAR, RBI Archive.

95 Inspection of the four Bengalee scheduled banks (Calcutta Commercial Bank Ltd., Mahaluxmi Bank Ltd., Noakhali Union Bank Ltd., Pioneer Bank Ltd. C 183, F 1336: 88–91) under moratorium inspection by the RBI, commenced on 16 December 1948, under section 3 of the Banking Companies (Inspection) Ordinance, 1946); the report, dated 16 February 1949, was submitted by Mr. L. K. Desai, Deputy Chief Officer, Department of Banking Operations, Bombay, who was deputed to Calcutta, to study the progress of the inspections.

96 Quoted in Mark Granovetter and Richard Swedberg, *Sociology of Economic Life*, 2nd ed. (Boulder, CO: Westview Press, 2001): 53.

97 Adam Smith, *The Wealth of Nations*, Books 1–3, ed. with Introduction and Notes by Andrew Skinner (London: Penguin Books, 1999): 358–359.

98 Mark Granovetter, 'Economic Action and Social Structure: The Problem of Embeddedness', *American Journal of Sociology* 91, 3 (1985): 492.

99 Muranjan, *Modern Banking in India*: 302.

100 The confidential letter to the Chief Officer, Department of Banking Operation, RBI, Central Office, SB 97/45, 10 August 1945. C 120, F 1285,
RBI Archive (10.8.1945–17.3.1954).

101 Thomas Crump, *The Phenomenon of Money* (London: Routledge and
Kegan Paul, 1981): 100.

102 Memorandum to the Committee of the Central Board, The Calcutta
Commercial Bank Ltd. From C. D. Deshmukh, Deputy Governor, RBI,
Central Office, Bombay, 22 September 1942. C 22 Calcutta Commercial
Bank F 1137 NAR, RBI Archive.

103 From the Diary of work done by the Deputy Governor (Mr. Mehkri)
during his visit to Calcutta 26 March 1950; C 183, vol. V, F 1337, RBI
Archive.

104 Northcote Cooke Chas, *The Rise, Progress and Present Condition of
Banking in India* (Calcutta: Bengal Printing Co., 1863): 15.
'A hoondee was a bill of exchange or cheque, peculiar to India, and
given between native bankers. It commenced with an invocation to
Ganesa, the god of wisdom. The bill then mentioned the mode and date
of payment. They had no stamp or legal authorisation, but instead the
hoondee's authenticity was guaranteed by certain mystic signs under-
stood by the bankers on both sides. Hoondees were still in use at the
time of the British occupation of India'. www.probertencyclopaedia.
com/browse/JH.HTM

105 The serious early cases of fraud include the fraud committed on the
Bengal Bank (1806) by Soobul Chunder Dey (a party) to the tune of
Rs. 40,000 in 1824, which was dismissed by the Supreme Court for want
of evidence; 'one of the most successful frauds ever perpetrated' on the
Union Bank (1829) by Mr. A. H. Sim, the Accountant of Rs. 64,000 with
collusion of the English and Bengalee ledger writers to falsify their book;
example: 'a payment of Rupees 592–1–4 was converted into one of 10,
592–1–4, and in the same way the other entries were falsified by prefix-
ing or altering one or more figures'. Chas, *The Rise, Progress and Present
Condition of Banking in India*: 101, 180, 181.

106 'The Bengali is a great thief; even the threat of hanging does not deter
him'. Editorial in *Gyandurpan*, 11 March 1848, quoted in *Bengal
Hurkaru*, 16 March 1848, reproduced in Kling, *Partner in Empire:
Dwarkanath Tagore*: 223.

107 In the *Calcutta Review*, June 1848, quoted by Kling, *Partner in Empire:
Dwarkanath Tagore*: 227.

108 Sarkar, *Bartir Pathe Bangali*: 5.

109 Rau, *Present-Day Banking in India*: 87.

110 Ibid.: 80.

111 Confidential Report from RBI to the Central Board on 31 January 1949,
C 183, vol. IV F 1336, RBI Archive.

112 *Capital*, 16 September 1949, p. 427.

113 'According to police report 2,519 households of 81 villages were attacked
and looted affecting 15,724 persons in these areas. The victims were pre-
dominantly Muslims in Dhaka and Hindus in the rural areas'. *Bangla-
pedia*, National Encyclopedia of Bangladesh, en.banglapedia.org/index.
php?title=Dhaka_Riot,_1941, accessed on 9 May 2017.

114 Five thousand to 10,000 death and 15,000 wounded in savage attacks and rape on poor Muslims and poor Hindus mainly, Claude Markovits, 'The Calcutta Riots of 1946', *Online Encyclopedia of Mass Violence* (5 November 2007), ISSN 1961–9898, www.massviolence.org/The-Calcutta-Riots-of-1946, accessed on 7 May 2017.

115 André Béteille has written about 'the Great Calcutta killings' in his memoir *Sunlight on the Garden: A Story of Childhood and Youth* (New Delhi: Penguin/Viking, 2012). Implicit in his narrative is the incidence of young people from the middle-class neighbourhood engaging the Muslim with violence and arson. So did Tapan Raychaudhuri in his *The World in Our Time: A Memoir* (New Delhi: Harper Collins Publishers, 2011).

116 Embezzlement by public officials in different ranks in late nineteenth century has been recorded in Judicial files in the State Archives. In some cases, native bankers were the victims.

117 Ashis Khastogir, '*Unish Shataker Bangla Boi* (Nineteenth-Century Bengali Books) (in Bengali)', in *Unish Shataker Bangali Jeeban O Sanskriti* (Nineteenth-Century Bengali Life and Culture) (in Bengali), edited by Swapan Basu and Indrajit Chaudhury (Kolkata: Pustak Biponi, 2003): 338–396.

118 Poromesh Acharya, '*Bangali Bhadraloker Shikkah Chinta: Unish Shatak* (Bengali Gentle Men's Thoughts on Education: Nineteenth Century) (in Bengali)', in *Unish Shataker Bangali Jeeban O Sanskriti* (Nineteenth-Century Bengali Life and Culture) (in Bengali), edited by Basu and Chaudhury: 227–253.

119 *Kathamala* contains translations of Aesop's fables – written in English by Reverend Thomas James – by Ishwar Chandra Vidyasagar (1820–1891). Strangely, the word greed (*lobh*) does not occur in the list of key words that follow each story, though it occurs twice in the very brief text and greed is used as an explanation of non-fulfilment of a desire. The word occurs in the lists of keywords following the stories: 'The Axe and the god of Water', where the word *nirlobh* (devoid of greed) is defined as *lobheheen* (without greed, devoid of desire) (p. 4), 'The Dog-bitten Man', where the word *lobh* is defined as *pratyasha* (longing) and *lalosa* (covetousness) (p. 59), and 'The Dog and Its Shadow', where the word *pratyasha* (longing) is defined as *asha* (expectation), *lobh* (greed) (p. 22).

120 Ashis Khastagir, ed., *Shishusiksha by Madanmohan Tarkalanar* (Kolkata: Pustak Biponi, 2003): 47, 50, 61.

121 Emile Durkheim, *Moral Education: A Study in the Theory and Application of the Sociology of Education* (1925), A New Introduction by Everett K. Wilson (New York: The Free Press, 1973): 18.

122 Jagannath Chakraborty, *Monimanjusa: Bengali-English Bi-lingual Thesaurus* (Kolkata: Book Syndicate, 2002): 394.

123 P. Acharya, *Sabdosandhan* (Search for Words) (Kolkata: Bikash Grantho Bhavan, 2003).

124 The estimates are given in a review of sources by Sushil Kumar De in his *Bangla Probaad* (Bengali Proverbs) (Kolkata: Ranjan Publishing House, 1946): 409–414. The years mentioned are the years of publications of compilations used by the author. Some of these are district-based counts.

125 Ibid.

126 Gurusaday Dutt wrote about this *pat*s of the indigenous Bengal school: 'Each *pat* or roll of multiple scrolls is like a moving picture gallery containing a series of pictures coming one after the other in which the development of a complete story from beginning to the end is depicted with wonderful force and vividness, while the story of each picture is melodiously chanted by the *patuas* in lyrical compositions of their own. The moral basis of art has always been kept steadily in view. Each *pat* ends with a picture of the court of the King of Death and the Last Judgment, and the artist invariably ends up chanting the eternal law of the ultimate triumph of virtue and the defeat and punishment of vice'. Gurusaday Dutt, *Folk Arts and Crafts of Bengal: The Collected Papers* (Kolkata: Seagull Books, 1990): 71–72. *Jom Pat* has a long history. Reference to *Jom Pat* is in the seventh-century Banabhatta's historical biography, *Harshacharita*. Amitabh Sen Gupta, *Scroll Painting of Bengal: Art in the Village* (Bloomington, IN: Author House, 2012). My exposure in 1950s was through a vendor who used to hang colourful *Jom Pat* along with pictures of deities from the iron railing of Sadharan Brahmo Samaj prayer hall (1878) on Cornwallis Street (now Bidhan Sarani), near *Thanthania Kalibari*. Typical of *pat* painting was a serial juxtaposition of forms of vice and commensurate punishment inflicted by Jom (Yama), aided by Chitragupta and Yamadutas. The serials I saw did not have any picture of rewards for the virtuous ones when they would be in heaven; see Ashoke Bhattacharya, *Baanglar Chitrakala* (Art in Bengal) (Kolkata: Paschim Bangla Academy1994): 92. *Jom Pat* has disappeared from such vendors' wares approximately from the 1970s. The space is taken over by pictures of Hindi film actors. What has possibly also disappeared from the Bengali psyche is the notion of after-life; and with it the metaphors of *swarga-sukh* (heavenly happiness) and *narak jantrona* (hellish anguish).

127 'In this caricature, a Hindu priest is represented as a demon-like creature, enormous in size with layers of skin around his neck and an evil expression on his face. He is shown performing purification for three women worshippers in exchange for a large bag of money which he holds in his right hand. On the money bag is the Bengali inscription "Rupee Goddess". To further highlight the hypocrisy of the Hindu priesthood, the priest is shown sprinkling dirt into the ritual container of holy water, hence the title of the print: "Purification by muddy water"', collections. vam.ac.uk/ . . . /purification-by-muddy-water-the-lithograph-tagore-gaganen, accessed on 6 August 2017.

128 Prasanta Ray, 'Conjugality in Times of Fortuitous Fortunes: *Alibaba and Parash Pathor*', Lecture, Department of Modern History, Calcutta University, 2009.

129 Krishna Dutta, *Probader Jhuli* (A Basket of Proverbs) (Kolkata: Levant Books, 2007): 14, 22.

130 Kaliprasanna Sinha, *Hutom Pyanchar Naksha* (1862), reprinted with annotation and editing by Arun Nag (Kolkata: Subarnarekha, 1990); see *The Observant Owl Hootum's Vignettes of Nineteenth-Century Calcutta*, by Kaliprasanna Sinha, translated from the original Bengali by Swarup Roy; A Black Kite book, published by Permanent Black, New Delhi, 2008; *Sketches by Hootum the Owl: A Satirist's View of Calcutta*,

translated by Chitralekha Basu, foreword by Amit Chaudhuri, illustrations by Sumitro Basak (Kolkata: Samya, 2012).

131 Swami Saradananda, 1398 B.E. (1991), *Shrishriramakrishna Lila Prasanga*, vol. 1, part 2 (Kolkata: Sadhakabhava, Udbodhan Karyalay, 1991). Narasingha P. Sil observes: 'As to *kanchana*, literally gold and symbolizing lucre, he had little qualms in leading a comfortable life or even buying personal property or gold ornament for his wife, while making a public confession of his adverse physical reaction at touching coins or sermonizing on the worthlessness of money: "money-mud, mud-money"'; Narasingha P. Sil, 'The Professor and the *Paramahamsa*: Martin Luther and Ramakrishna Compared', *Asian Social Science* 7, 5 (May 2011). doi:10.5539/ass.v7n5p3:. 5

132 Ryan K. Balot, *Greed and Injustice in Classical Athens* (Princeton: Princeton University Press, 2001): 18.

133 Reportedly, 'John Fergusson, then probably the largest and most capable merchant in Calcutta and an Ayrshire man, had provided for "hundreds of his countrymen, in so much that I might almost say, that all the inhabitants of Ayrshire have migrated to Bengal"'. 'On average [between 1808 and 1820], they constituted around 25 per cent of the European diaspora there, by far the largest group, apart from the English'. Indeed, the 'Scottish moment' may have begun one century earlier. G. K. McGilvary, 'The Scottish Connection With India 1725–1833', *Empire – Recherches en cours*, Numéros › 14, etudesecossaises.revues.org

134 Amiya Kumar Bagchi, 'The Problem of Colonialism in Classical Political Economy: Analysis, Epistemological Breaks and Mystification', *Studies in History* 12, 1 (1996): 105–136.

2

RETRIEVING TRUST

The banks, the state and the press

The banks

The crisis came in its full blast, and regaining the trust of the people became urgent for the bankers as well as the state and the economy. The bankers used the press to reassure their clients; individual banks issued press statements in vernacular dailies and collective efforts through newly created Consumers' Union. Take the case of the Bengal Central Bank Ltd. The news item claimed that it had enough funds to pay the depositors in cash – 107 per cent of deposit to be paid back on demand and 77 per cent of all deposits. It claimed total reliability because of its safe credit policy (*Ananda Bazar Patrika*, 10 May 1948). The bank publicly congratulated the directors for managing the bank efficiently (*Ananda Bazar Patrika*, 17 May 1948).

An advertisement announcing itself to be an effort to eliminate unfounded apprehension on the part of the depositors came out in *Ananda Bazar Patrika* on 19 May 1948. The Consumers' Union, with the help of a few (unnamed) popular institutions, started a movement. It took upon itself the duty to give the movement an appropriate form, by getting in touch with depositors in different bazars and trade centres to prevent the adverse reaction of rumours started by interested persons. The Union met the representatives of trade and commerce in the office of the General Traders' Association. The advertisement had a motto: 'The depositors' interests are the interests of the banks'. It was sponsored by a business house with a chain of sweet shops in Calcutta.

This was an attempt to impress upon the depositors that everything was under control as far as the banks were concerned and that the government created problems for the depositors. The banks issued newspaper clarifications from time to time. One such by the directors of the Bank of Commerce Ltd., Calcutta, on 10 May 1948, through the *Ananda Bazar Patrika*, shifted the blame on the government's sudden notification on 20 April 1948 eliminating the name of the bank from the list of scheduled banks. It claimed that as a result, the depositors started drawing money in a panic, forcing the bank to suspend its activities temporarily from 6 May. The directors were making all the arrangements to reopen the bank soon and were hoping that all the depositors would get a total repayment of their deposits. The depositors reportedly had withdrawn their deposits between 20 April and 6 May 1948. That the banks were reluctant to fulfill their public commitment of paying back the depositors on their demand was evident in the fact that the judiciary had to issue instructions to the banks to do so. Subsequently, the Bank of Commerce announced to its more than 8,000 depositors in Calcutta branches alone that arrangements would be made for repayment at the rate of 25 per cent to each depositor of Rs. 100. The depositors were requested to bring their cheque books and pass books. They were to be informed through newspapers about the dates of repayment according to their respective serial numbers and types of deposits (*Ananda Bazar Patrika*, 21 June 1948).

The retrieving act was driven also by a belief in a conspiracy against the Bengali-owned and Bengali-run banks by the non-Bengali businessmen. The government press note did not specify such people as responsible for 'despicable lies and scary rumours' about the Bengali banks. But many were convinced that men were hired to spread lies and rumours to create panic among the depositors. Such men were found creating a ruckus in front of some banks in Calcutta. Had they been successful in their aspersions, the Bengal economy would have been surely ruined because much of the Bengali economic growth was due to the sincere cooperation among the Bengali banks. The banks also gained from the growth in industry and commerce. Without denying the role of the non-Bengali business community in Bengal's growth, the *Ananda Bazar* 17 May 1948 editorial titled 'The duty of the Bengali banks', believed that the directors and the managers of the Bengali banks must be united among themselves against repugnant lies, dreadful rumours and ruckus in front of Bengali-run banks by a section of malicious non-Bengali men. Because, it was their wisdom, combining with the good sense of many depositors, that foiled the conspiracy. That some unscrupulous men could indulge in such behaviour was due to RBI removing the Bank of Commerce out of the schedule which set off the panic of the depositors and its subsequent silence and inactivity when the Bengali-run banks became vulnerable. Since there would be the possibility of such challenges in the future, Bengali management must learn from this experience and follow those principles which would strengthen the banks. The editorial, however, did not categorically mention the requisite principles (*Ananda Bazar Patrika*, 17 May 1948).

The state

What about the fledging post-colonial state? Did it engage in retrieving the trust of the ordinary depositors in banking? It persisted with the adiaphoria of the colonial state.

The colonial administration of the British imperial state used to blame the ordinary depositors as the spoilers of an insecure balance between cash reserve and a frenzied withdrawal of deposits. This is evident in the report of the Indian Central Banking Enquiry Committee in 1931. It consulted the members of the elite like P. R. Srinivas and C. S. Rangaswami, editor and managing editor, *Indian Finance*, Calcutta, on 29 September 1930. Their observations in no way conceded the mismanagement and fraudulent behaviour of the bank owners and their higher officials. They pointed out 'the proverbial shyness of the Indian depositors' which combined with certain developments like the economic slump during the great depression. This heightened public nervousness led to a decline in profit. This diminished a bank's capacity to pay dividends, which in turn made the depositors nervous. They further mentioned public vulnerability to 'the mere whisper of a rumour or even a very vague or mischievous report' which provoked 'a raid on his account and this necessitates banks keeping a very large liquid position. This would stand in the way of making "large profits"'. Subsequently, the depositors, would lose confidence in banks. In no way was the moral failure of the managerial class conceded. But the purpose of setting up the 1931 Enquiry Committee was more to secure the interests of trade and commerce rather than of the salaried and low-earning depositors, who eventually formed the Consumers' Union. Ironically, even the ill-paid bank accountant, Subrata, in Narendranath Mitra's short story and in the later film *Mahanagar* by Satyajit Ray, snubbed an anxious prospective depositor's inquiry about a run on Subrata's bank through his brusque suggestion that the client could open an account elsewhere.

The merchant community referred to larger developments in politics to account for the banking crisis, thus exonerating the moral responsibility of the managerial elite. This is brought out in the response by the Indian Chambers of Commerce to a question in the questionnaire framed by the RBI. It observed:

> The inevitable reaction set in with the end of the war and in 1946 these banks could not attract fresh deposits. As their advances were generally sticky, they found it difficult to meet even moderate withdrawals. The conditions were aggravated by the communal disturbances, the postal strike, the Imperial Bank strike and finally by the stock exchange crisis.[1]

The elite evidently had no sympathy for the depositors. The Chambers of Commerce was consulted by the Enquiry Committee. In response to the question: 'Have you any suggestions to make for the regulation of expeditious liquidation and advance payment to depositors in case of failure of banks?', the Chamber observed:

> The Chamber considers that the regulation of expeditious liquidation is a matter for the Court and, so far as the question of advance payment to depositors is concerned, this must depend on the circumstances of the case and in particular on the assets expected to be available.[2]

The Chambers was naturally unwilling to implicate the bank officers in bank failure. That was in 1935. Not much changed in the post-1949 Banking Companies Act (amended in 1950) in favour of the depositors. The failure of the Calcutta High Court to frame the necessary rules to speed up liquidation process and to provide the necessary stuff heightened public anxiety about recovery of deposits lost. It is reported that 'of the eighty-two banks that suspended payments in Bengal during 1947–1950, only thirteen banks working under the schemes of arrangements had made "small payments" to their depositors'.[3]

Threatened with an irretrievable collapse of banking and its grave consequences for the Bengal economy, calming the nerves, re-calming the people should have become very urgent for the state and the merchant community. In view of that, the Dominion Parliament was prodded into an intervention in the Bengal banking crisis mainly at the behest of Arun Chandra Guha, an MP in the Dominion Parliament. In his three questions, he wanted to know from the Dominion Parliament on 2 September 1948 (1) the names of the banks closed down after the [Second World] war; (2) whether it was true that despite the banks becoming non-functioning, the managing agent, the managing director, the manager and the other officers were receiving their monthly salaries; and (3) whether the government was aware that if they were paid their salaries, that was against the interests of the depositors and the shareholders. He could extract an answer only to the first question. The same report named 24 banks suffering liquidation after the second world war, nine banks whose application for liquidation were pending with the High Court, and nine banks had applied for it to the Court (*Ananda Bazar Patrika*, 5 September 1948).

The next best thing the government could do was to issue a press note on 14 May 1948, requesting the depositors not to pay heed to the irresponsible and malicious rumours spread by people with ill-intentions (*Ananda Bazar Patrika*, 15 May 1948). If the rumour would continue to be effective, this would lead to a possible collapse of banking in Bengal and the economy of Bengal. A more authoritative request came from a statement by 'the prime minister of Bengal', as the chief minister of a state was then called, Dr. Bidhan Chandra Roy. The request was addressed to the depositors so that they should not pay any heed to rumours nor start withdrawing their deposits from the banks. He thought that eventually even the large banks would not be able to withstand the run. This would help nobody. The prime minister's concern again was about the viability of the economy of the country. Banking was an institution which rested on public trust. He argued that creation of trust took time, but once lost it would take many years to revive public trust. The onus was shifted primarily to the depositors, and not to the authorities. Dr. Roy drew on his expertise in pathology to point out that scare was an outcome of physical discordance and used this as an analogy to reflect on the health of the economy. His instructions to the banks prohibiting them from using the money of the depositors to set up any industry or to directly manage came last in his exhortation. So that the banks could be protected from the adverse consequences of industrial recession, he entrusted the Reserve Bank (1935) with the task of examining the activities of the banks and to advise them because 'poor depositors' valued the approval of the Reserve Bank as a security of their deposits. He advised that the depositors, the banks and the Reserve Bank need to act in unison (*Ananda Bazar Patrika*, 28 September 1948).

Apprehending that the issue of press statements might not suffice, the prime minister of Bengal and the deputy governor of the RBI paid visits to five of the banks suffering from runs on them on 23 September 1948 (*Ananda Bazar Patrika*, 23 September 1948). The RBI functionary made it clear that the Bank had started giving financial advances to the beleaguered banks because protecting the interests of the depositors was considered to be its duty. Drawing public attention to the fact that these steps were producing positive results in terms of retrieving public trust, he pointed out that the tendency to panic withdrawal had considerably diminished. He argued that even a secure bank would collapse due to continuous withdrawal of deposits. Again, the ordinary depositors were advised against heeding to rumour and causing run on banks. But it took the opportunity to exonerate itself in the face of public dismay in what people thought to be an abdication of its responsibilities (*Ananda Bazar Patrika*, 23 September 1948). It is significant that the National Chamber of Commerce thought the same way. However, the deputy governor of the RBI maintained that the four banks, which failed, despite the provision for applying to the RBI for financial support, did because either they did not avail the opportunity or took only one-third of the support extended by the RBI (*Ananda Bazar Patrika*, 24 September 1948). The merchant community's reaction was various. For example, a group of 34 business from Chittagong thought

> whatever might be the cause of their [banks'] failure, a man in the street here believes that had the Reserve Bank cared to know whether the banks were submitting correct weekly statements and also inspected at least some of these scheduled banks even for once in several years, that would have been a sufficient check to the management and thousands of our unfortunate country men could have been saved from financial collapse and starvation and that the Reserve Bank is accused of lethargy, red tape, neglect and shortcoming of the Reserve Bank in this respect they make the Government responsible.[4]

They were morally outraged that the banking mess 'reduced thousands of poor men of very small means to street beggars and that among them are East Bengal Refugees, students, helpless widows, orphans, and so on, and the thousands of employees of banks and business firms'. Some other merchants shared the anxiety but readily announced through the popular press their trust in the ability of the government and its principal regulatory institution, the RBI, to re-establish control over banking crisis. The latter was categorical in pointing out the undue anxiety of bank collapse was very harmful for a trading centre like Calcutta. Both expressed their trust in the RBI. Thus, projecting a return to normality was a tactics typical of the merchant community's management of public discontent. When the crisis in banking abated, it even wanted punitive measures from the RBI. The executive committee of the Bengal Traders' Association wrote:

> The Committee earnestly requests the Reserve Bank of India to appoint a Board of Liquidators to look in to the affairs of the closed-door banks and take necessary steps to give the depositors the dues and penalize the persons found responsible in running these banks down, or misappropriation of the assets of these Banks in any form.[5]

Some banks however played a blame game by shifting the onus on a faulty or hasty decision by the government as in the case of the Bank of Commerce Ltd. This was a part of their individual effort to regain depositors' trust.

An announcement

> The Directors of the Bank of Commerce regrets to inform the depositors, the share-holders and associated individuals and well-wishers that the Indian government has eliminated the name of the Bank of Commerce form the list of the scheduled banks through a sudden notification on last April 20th. As a result the apprehensive depositors in large numbers started to withdraw their deposits every day.[6] For this reason the Directors have been compelled to temporarily suspend all banking activities. But they are making arrangements for re-opening the bank very soon and they hope that each depositor will get back the whole of the amount they had deposited.
>
> Directors, Bank of Commerce Ltd., Calcutta[7]

The Bank of Commerce did not stop with the expression of an intention to reopen its normal activities to regain public trust. It explained the unjustified report on the part of an inspector of the RBI which prompted the government to think that the bank would suffer due to a possible devaluation of its assets in Pakistan. Thus, it implicated the government for its plight. But it was happy that the government did not prohibit acceptance of new deposits or continuation with the other activities of the bank; and no charge of dishonest action was levelled against any director. The bank exonerated itself of any responsibility for the run on it. It was triggered by the adverse reaction on the part of the clearing house which it had duly communicated to its members. The 'news', according to the hindsight of the bank, soon reached the people to induce them to panic withdrawals. The bank had the support of its depositors who gathered in meeting. They unequivocally criticized the RBI for inflicting grave injustice to the bank by removing it from the schedule. Their request to the bank was that it should appeal to the appropriate authority and do what was necessary itself to return to its previous viability. What was far more important was that the depositors present in that emergency meeting pledged that nobody would withdraw more than 25 per cent, which would not be more than Rs. 5,000, from the amount lying with the bank on 6 May 1948, in the next four months. They insisted that the bank should convene a meeting of all depositors to keep them informed about its actions. To maintain liaison, the meeting set up a committee of four depositors (*Ananda Bazar Patrika*, 18 May 1948). Even then, the bank made a public pronouncement that it would take some time to realize the money due to it and the security to be in a position to pay up all its debts. It also appreciated the judiciary's permission to keep on hold repaying the depositors for four months. However, when the judiciary instructed it to return deposits on 8 July 1948, it issued a public notification, stating that to begin with it would return deposits of Rs. 100.00 or less. Because of more than 8,000 of such cases in its Calcutta office, it would notify about dates when select groups of depositors would be paid. Only after this round of payments, depositors with more than Rs. 100.00 as deposit would be paid back 25 per cent of their amount with the bank. The bank even worked out a schedule for repayment to the depositors, which was announced through the vernacular press (*Ananda Bazar Patrika*, 15 August 1948). This was to impress upon the clients that it was determined to be an efficient institution.

The Calcutta National Bank (estd. 1935, liquidated 30 April 1953) chose a somewhat contentious path while reacting to regulation by the RBI when it served a notice on the Calcutta National Bank Ltd., prohibiting receiving fresh deposits with effect from 14 May 1951. S. M. Bhattacharyya, chairman of the Board of Directors issued a press statement contesting RBI's allegation that the bank failed to keep minimum balances with the RBI. 'He said that not only had the bank enough resources to pay back all deposits in full, but he expected that the shareholders would also get their money back in case of liquidation of the bank'.[8] But the bank had already lost its credibility because of an adverse report by an inspection: 'the bank had resorted to considerable manipulations of accounts with a view to writing off bad debts, depreciation and losses in shares and debentures and losses due to forgery and fraud, etc'.[9] It had to pay Rs. 39.28 lakhs as dividend to the depositors.

Such assertions by beleaguered banks were invigorated by the acknowledgement of their critical role in trade and commerce. 'A Ditcher's Diary' observed:

> Each of the five banks (about to be amalgamated) named in the scheme – the Bengal Central Bank, the Comilla Banking Corporation, the Hooghly Bank and the Calcutta National Bank – has an important record of service to the business community and each has played significant role in financing the trade and industry of the Province.[10]

The interest of trade and commerce had to be protected at any cost. This is what the deputy governor, RBI, wrote:

> The Board after having considered the situation arising out of the suspension of payment by the Nath Bank Ltd., Calcutta, and the consequent run on other banks, and being of the opinion that a special occasion has arisen making it necessary and expedient that action should be taken under sub-section (1) of section 18 of the RBI Act for the purpose of regulating credit *in the interests of trade, commerce and industry*' [italics added].[11]

The RBI to which the defrauded men and women looked up for support did not come forward to give them any relief. It was more focused in restoring institutional discipline so that the afflicted banks would regain their momentum. This was catering to the needs of the economy and the merchant community. Take the case of the Nath Bank depositors' appeal to the governor, RBI, and dated 14 March 1950. The RBI conceded that

> The depositors' pleading for the intervention of the Reserve Bank for the amalgamation of the Nath Bank with the other four banks as neither liquidation (n)or scheme of arrangement extends any hope for the depositors. No action on our part, however, appears necessary at this stage.

Their frantic letter and telegrams went unheeded.

The Reserve Bank was not keen to help the 'poor depositors' who lost their deposits because of moral failure and inefficiency of the management of a bank. It observed:

> The Reserve Bank of India neither interferes in nor settles disputes arising out of transactions between banking institutions and members of the public. . . . If a bank refuses to honour its obligations the proper procedure for you to adopt is to consult your legal advisers in the matter. You may, if you so desire, refer the matter to the Registrar of Joint Stock Companies, Bengal.[12]

But how could a lower-middle-class depositor access judicial help?

The RBI in fact had a more legally unassailable position on the question of the loss suffered by the depositors. It maintained:

> The West Bengal Government suggested that whether the RBI had any moral or legal responsibility in the matter or not, it should assist banks in difficulties to enable them to pay off their depositors by taking risk to the extent of Rs. 50–60 lakhs. In this connection it should be borne in mind that the loss to the Reserve Bank is borne by the tax payers all over India as the profits of the RBI are transferred to the general revenues of the Government of India. We shall, therefore, have to consider whether there is any justification for the depositors' losses being made good to the cost of the general taxpayer. If the depositor had placed

his money in an unsound bank, it could be argued, assuming that the depositor is an innocent person, that there is no justification for the transfer of the loss from one innocent person, i.e. the depositor, to another innocent person, i.e. the tax payer. In actual practice, however, many of the depositors would not be absolutely innocent. . . . If a depositor puts his money in an unsound bank because he is lured by the higher rate of interest, he should have no cause for complaint if sometimes his money in his principal is lost. It would also not be possible to find out how many were lured by higher rate of interest, etc. If, therefore, an attempt is made by us to assist even unsound banks in difficulties, we would be encouraging the depositors to place their money in such banks and incidentally be instrumental in lowering the standard of banking. If the public feel that we are assisting unsound banks, they will have no incentive to choose better banks even at the cost of loss of some interest. It would, therefore, appear that the depositors of unsound banks will have to learn how to invest their money at their own cost.[13]

The moral responsibility for the loss by the depositors was promptly shifted to their vulnerability to greed – greed for a greater interest against their deposits – on the part of the management of a bank; as if the losing depositors were rightly served for being tempted by offer of large interest by banks, for not being cautious! The depositors were made responsible another way:

If we are not hopeful of the bank's survival even with our assistance, it is obvious that we shall be lending money to the bank to make payment to the extent of 16 annas in the rupee to those depositors who withdraw their deposits from the bank while it continues to function, while the remaining depositors, who are not aware of bank's financial difficulty or unable to withdraw their deposits because they are payable after sometime, may get little or nothing.[14]

It is interesting that advertisements, books and monographs written to motivate the potential depositors never alerted them about the possible insecurity of their deposits.

The RBI was determined to look the other way about the immorality of the superior bank officers even when it had become a public issue. Its stand was again unambiguous.

> Mr. Guha [an M. P.] has suggested that in respect of misfeasance or malfeasance, etc., of directors, the delinquent members of the ex-management should be called up on to prove their innocence and that therefore suitable amendment in the law should be made accordingly. Mr. Guha seeks to introduce a novel principle of law that an Ex-Director, Manager, or Secretary of a bank which has given in to liquidation is guilty of breach of trust unless proved innocent. This would make it difficult for banks to secure experienced personnel for their Directorate and Management and we are not in favour of this proposal.[15]

Mr. Guha was unrelenting. He insisted on a favourable resolution of the problem. He wrote:

> This [non-submission of any returns or reports to the Registrar, Joint Stock Companies by 146 non-scheduled banks] is scandalous state of affairs. This should be stopped at the earliest. It is no use citing legal and technical difficulties. We shall have to do something to remedy this situation.[16]

But the RBI could not be motivated. When it came to helping the banks, the government was willing (Table 2.1). However, almost nothing percolated to the ordinary depositors.

The RBI was generally silent about the victims from the middle class in official documents like, Local Board Minutes, the Imperial Bank of India, Bengal Circle (1940–1943, 1949–1950). The five pages Questionnaire for Expediting Liquidation proceedings against banking companies did not include any question regarding the interests of the ordinary depositors. The Questionnaire was prepared by the RBI at the suggestion of GOI in August 1951.[17] No opinion was sought from the ordinary lower-middle-class people although the various Chambers of Commerce, bank managers and shareholders' associations were duly consulted.[18] The RBI did not compel the banks to pay back the creditors because it thought that the rules governing its activities would not allow such a proactive role (Tables 2.2 and 2.3).

Table 2.1 Advances to Bengali banks since 4.8.1948 (in lakhs of rupees)

Name of the Bank	Date of Advance	Amount	Section of Act	Security	Balance Outstanding	Remarks
Bengal Central Bank	11.9.1948	65	17(4) (a)	Government securities	1.30	At concessional rate of 2% p.a.
	20.9.1948	50	"	"	"	
	23.9.1948	99	"	"	"	
	15.12.1948	08	"	"		
Calcutta National Bank	21.9.1948	20	"	"	Nil	
	23.9.1948	01	"	"	"	
	4.10.1948	0.5	"	"	"	
	24.11.1948	08	"	"		
Comilla Banking Corporation	18.9.1948	25	"	"	2.25	At concessional rate of 2% p.a.
	20.9.1948	75	"	"		
	21.9.1948	50	"	"		
	6.12.1948	90	"	"		
Dinajpore Bank	24.9.1948	04	"	"	04	
Hooghly Bank Ltd.	4.10.1948	05	"	"	Nil	
	6.10.1948	2.5	"	"	"	
Nath Bank	20.9.1948	12.5	18 (3)	Market shares	60.4	
	21.9.1948	6.8	"	"	"	
	21.9.1948	18.4	"	"	"	
	22.9.1948	8.0	"	"	"	
	4.9.1948	1.8	"	"	"	
		5.0	"		"	
	missing	20.0	"	Title deeds	"	

Pioneer Bank				
4.8.1948	1.67	"	Marketable	2.82
9.8.1948	0.42	"	shares	"
20.8.1948	0.40	"	Gold	"
31.8.1948	0.20	"	ornaments	"
31.8.1948	0.05	"	Marketable	"
3.9.1948	0.18	"	shares	"
8.9.1948	0.36	"	Bills	"
9.9.1948	0.27	"	"	"
13.9.1948	0.14	"	"	"
			Shares	
			"	
			Overdraft	

Table 2.2 Banks not paying dividends to their creditors (Assam and Calcutta)

Name of the Bank	Date of Liquidation	Total Liabilities
Aryan Bank Ltd.	20.3.1950	Rs. 14,97,491.00
Assam Corporated Bank Ltd.	16.6.1948	Not available
Associated Bank of Tripura Ltd.	19.12.1949	24,12,000.00
Bank of Calcutta Ltd.	14.2.1949	94,07,239.00
Beleghata Bank Ltd.	8.8.1949	4,18,164.00
Bengal Associated Bank Ltd.	31.3.1951	98,778.00
Bengal Bank Ltd.	12.12.1949	44,47,764.00
Bogra City Bank Ltd.	12.12.1947	10,42,664.00
Citadel Bank Ltd.	11.7.1949	1,91,104.00
City Bank Ltd.	11.4.1949	6,28,312.00
Comrade Bank Ltd.	21.11.1950	1,96,602.00
Continental Bank of Asia Ltd.	27.8.1947	20,93,535.00
Darjeeling Bank Ltd.	10.2.1948	25,43,000.00
Dhakuria Banking Corporation Ltd.	20.9.1948	5,76,566.00
East Bengal Commercial Bank Ltd.	20.9.1948	5,81,874.00
Eastern Traders Bank Ltd.	28.2.1949	14,68,570.00
Kuver Bank Ltd.	6.8.1948	Not available

File no. C183B, vol. V: Liquidation Proceedings of the Banking Companies, F 1343 (11.3.1953–11.7.1953) RBI.

Table 2.3 Banks paying dividends to their creditors in Calcutta (among 68 banks all over India)

Name of the Bank	Date of Liquidation	Liabilities as on the Date of Liquidation	Liabilities So Far Paid	Remarks
Calcutta Commercial Bank Ltd.	22.11.1948	Rs. 3,10,44,596.00	Rs. 2,87,523.00	Paid to preferential creditors only
Nath Bank Ltd.	27.3.1950	3,37,90,800.00	15,61,048.00	Including preferential creditors at Rs. 47,895.00

File no. C183B, vol. V: Liquidation Proceedings of the Banking Companies, F 1343 (11.3.1953–11.7.1953) RBI.

The press

The role the both the vernacular and the English news dailies, played in connection with the bank crisis, fits Benedict Anderson's conceptualization of 'print capitalism'. The press had its job like carrying alluring bank advertisements, reports on the banking crisis and publishing government press notes. This was standard everyday journalistic work. But it was engaged also in creation of a critical public, which contributed to the formations of democracy within the colonial frame.

> Of all Britain's non-settler dependencies, it was first in India that a flourishing modern press developed. The first Indian daily paper was the *Calcutta Journal* established in 1819 by British radicals and Indians who attacked the corruption and monopoly of the East India Company, lending an air of critique, sarcasm and controversy to the Indian press that it has never lost.[19]

That explains its cautionary as well as critical interventions. The depositors provoked into hasty withdrawal of their deposits were cautioned against vulnerability to rumours spread by 'interested' persons. They were advised to seek objective information regarding actual conditions in banks they had deposited money before deciding to withdraw their deposits. They had their right to withdraw their deposits and invest their money to another bigger bank. But they would earn the same rate of interest. However, smaller banks would be unable to invest their money in business which would eventually damage the stock market and trade and commerce. These exhortations by the press harped on the imperative of the national development and of serving the interests of the 'thousands of investors' were cited in. But it was admitted that it was not unusual for ordinary depositors to be apprehensive of loss of their hard-earned money deposited in banks because of mismanagement of banks. The critical position was prompted by moral outrage at the failure of the banks due to corruption and inefficiency of the management. The *Amrita Bazar Patrika* editorial on 11 March 1950 represented the mood.

> The desirability of helping the creditors of the suspended banks will not perhaps be denied by any right-thinking person. The bulk of the creditors of these banks comes from the middle class which has been the hardest hit by the present

economic distress. . . . How would one wish that the culprits whose negligence, inefficiency and dishonesty sent to rack and ruin thousands of families which had placed their earnings into the custody of the bankers in good faith, would be brought to book swiftly and effectively and be given exemplary and deterrent punishment, so as to restore a healthy morality in the banking world . . . the despair and the tears of distressed persons are bound heavily to react on the wellbeing of the state. This is peculiarly true of banks like Nath Bank, Pioneer Bank . . . whose creditors comprise a considerable section of the refugees from East Bengal where in fact the banks had originated. The relief and rehabilitation of the refugees have already put a heavy drain on the central and the state exchequers. But it is forgotten perhaps that this strain on the resources of the state, already reaching a breaking point, is bound to increase a thousand fold, if the hitherto solvent refugees comprising thousands of creditors of these banks are rendered destitute for want of effective scheme for the immediate distribution of their divisible assets.[20]

The press was critical also of the way the liquidation process was conducted by the authorities. A letter to the editor, the *Amrita Bazar Patrika*, by one Amiya Nath Sanyal is a clear indictment:

depletion of funds (due to a wrong policy on settling case arising out of liquidation process) available ultimately for distribution among the unfortunate depositors. A good portion of the said wastage could have been prevented if only the Rule-making authority had taken a little trouble to frame rules for a speedier and cheaper mode of realizing claims of this Banking Companies in liquidation.[21]

The *Amrita Bazar Patrika* persisted in its public duty by giving press coverage of both the crime and the criminal proceedings against some banks. A report on 18 April 1950 observed:

It is clear that deliberate and extensive frauds, which are now before the Police, have been committed by the Managing Director [the Calcutta Commercial Bank Ltd.] accompanied by gross negligence on the part of the other Directors. The Inspecting Officer, in his confidential supplement . . . states that out of the advances examined as much as 53% of the advances are wholly bad. Misappropriations by the Managing Director have been estimated in the region of Rs. 76 lakhs whereas the outside liabilities total Rs. 159 lakhs; apart from these amounts lost by breach of trust, Rs. 50 lakhs are further shown as irrecoverable or doubtful assets.

The same edition of the newspaper reported: 'Judge takes cognizance of Nine Separate Cases. Hearing of Calcutta Commercial Bank Defalcation case Begins' and eight persons were accused by police 'on charges of conspiracy, falsification of accounts and misappropriation of the funds of the bank amounting to one crore of rupees'. There was a note of regret about the moral decay of a bank which 'was started in a very humble way . . . with only 300 shares'.[22]

Maybe the voice of the press in moral support to the losers was probably heard by those in the authority positions, but the commensurate actions were not forthcoming. A lengthy editorial in *Amrita Bazar Patrika* in 1952 explained the plight of the ordinary depositors.

a banking concern goes in to liquidation, the depositors in most cases do not get any return in the shape of dividends from the assets of the bank. The reasons are many. First, the assets usually do not cover the amount of depositors. . ..

Secondly, liquidation is a costly process owing to the complicated legal procedures . . . and in the long run it is found that legal and various other expenses swallow up a large portion of the realised funds.

Thirdly . . . liquidation proceedings take a very long time which change the character of the assets and cause comparatively heavy establishment costs.

When the Banking Companies Act was amended in 1950, the hope was held out that under the provisions of this Act, the Reserve Bank of India would take up the liquidation proceedings of the failed banks and the legitimate interests of the depositors would be safeguarded. . . . Of all the states in India, West Bengal has unfortunately suffered most in the respect of the liquidation of banking concerns and the middle class people of this state lost a major portion of their savings as a result of bank failures. . ..

But the ordinary depositors will wonder why the Reserve Bank should not be saddled with some responsibility at least for failure of the Scheduled Banks. People deposited their hard-earned money with the Scheduled Banks in the full knowledge that the Reserve Bank, after carrying on periodical inspections, has certified their credit-worthiness. . . . This implies the obligation that if the bank suspends business on any account the Reserve Bank, after realizing the assets, should pay off the depositors in full and leave a surplus of at least Rs. 5 lakhs for the benefit of the shareholders. The affected depositors can hardly feel satisfied with the argument that the Reserve Bank cannot discharge its obligations owing to legal complications. . . . If an amendment of the existing laws can enable the Reserve Bank to come to the rescue of the depositors, our legislators should see to it that it is done without delay.[23]

The records show that only a very few paid dividends on liquidation (Tables 2.2 and 2.3). We have already noted the Reserve Bank advising every adversely affected person that 'If a bank refuses to honour its obligations the proper procedure for you to adopt is to consult your legal advisers in the matter'.[24] The rich and the well-placed exactly did that (Table 2.4).

The outcomes of the legal suits are not well known. But they could at least access the state institutions for amelioration of their loss. They could make a procedure for redress operational. It consisted of empowering the judiciary to take note of impropriety by the management of a bank. Mr. P. S. Mokashi, Central Office, Department of

Table 2.4 Legal suits by the rich and powerful shareholders/mortgagees of Nath Bank in liquidation in 1950s[25]

Serial No.	Names Individuals and Firms	Identity
1	Harihar Chakraborty	
2	H.S.M. Isahaque	
3	Purshottam Chaube & Co.	
4	R.C. Ghosh & Co.	Stocks and shares
5	Fani Bhusan Banerjee	
6	Subodh Kumar Dutta	Businessman
7	Basanta Lal Murarka and others	Businessman

Serial No.	Names Individuals and Firms	Identity
8	Santosh Kumar Biswas	Businessman
9	Hariprasad Ganeriwala	Businessman
10	Sheikh Mazahar Elahi	Proprietor, Messrs Bullion & Shares Financiers
11	Govind Das Bhatter	Stocks and shares
12	Basant Kumar Banerjee	
13	Jatindra Nath Mitra	
14	Joybeb Khan	
15	Pranesh Chandra Ghosh	Businessman
16	Gopal Chandra Dey	
17	Bhim Chandra Mukherjee	Working for gain at N. I. C. Co.
18	Pratap Narayn Vajpeyi	Businessman
19	A.C. Dey & Co.	Stocks and share broker
20	Naba Kumar Dutt	Businessman
21	Ranajit Das Gupta	Tea merchant
22	Dwijendra Nath Mukherjee	
23	Pulak Krishna Roy Menoka Tea Estate & Gopal Krishna Tea Estate H.S.Ms Ishaque & another Mrs. A. Das & another	Tea merchant
24	Jogendra Kumar Mozumdar & another	
25	Chundmull Batia	
26	Scientific Glass Works, Mangal Chakraborti, Shyam Sundar Swaika and others	
27	Sharkarlal Ruia Bengal Dal Mill and Jewanmull Satyanarain	
28	Harendra Nath De	
29	Nripendra Chandra Bhattacharjee and others	Stock and share dealers
30	Sailendra Kristo Dutt Jagaldaga Colliery	Coal merchant
31	Satyendra Nath Misra	
32	Ashoke Banerjee	

Banking Operations, Bombay, wrote to S. K. Sen, deputy secretary to the Government of India, Ministry of Finance, Department of Economic Affairs:

> As regards the question of taking penal action against those responsible for the failures of banks, it may be stated that Section 45c of the Banking Companies Act has prescribed special provisions by which the court is empowered to take cognizance of and try in a summary way any offence alleged to have been committed by any person who has taken part in the formation or promotion of the company which is being wound up, or any part or present directors and officers.[26]

For those impatient about regaining their lost deposits, the use of cunning was an easier way out. We have already referred to how the rich managed to make up their losses by hook or crook. What about the low earners and the vulnerable? Before reconstructing their helpness, we need to add that there was no protest organized by political parties, particularly the 'Left' parties. Only a feeble civil society critique of avarice was articulated through theatre and literature.

Protests

The lone voice of pleading and protest within the parliamentary frame was of Arun Chandra Guha (1892–1983) who represented the Indian National Congress in the Indian Parliament in two consecutive terms from 1957. Earlier, he was a member of the Constituent Assembly in 1949. His sympathy for the middle-class victims of bank 'runs' derived from his revolutionary idealism. He was thrice jailed (1916–1918, 1923–1928 and 1930–1938) by the British administration for his participation in violent politics in Bengal as a member of the *Jugantar Dal*. He wrote *First Spark of Revolution: The Early Phase of India's Struggle for Independence, 1900–1920* (1971). His 'Cooperation as Remedy' (1963) followed his grief due to the unrealized socialist project.[27] 'Revolution', 'Socialism' and 'Cooperation' were the keywords in his political discourse. His sympathy for those who suffered due to collapse of banking was only natural. That he took an initiative of institutionalizing banking and finance in the agricultural sector as a minister of state (finance) under C. D. Deshmukh, the then Union finance minister, explains his knowledge of banking in Bengal.

What about the CPI and the other Left parties like Forward Block and Revolutionary Socialist Party? The silence on the part of the CPI members in the Parliament is noteworthy. The party had six members from West Bengal in the first Lok Sabha constituted in 1952.[28] It had also developed strong organizational base in the state at the time.[29] That was, in part, due to their success in drawing the urban Bengali middle class in it agitational fold. But this was focused on larger issues of anti-colonial struggle and working-class rights, and not on bank failures. It was not that the party did not know about a spate of bank failures in mid-1940s. It knew that 'Banks [were] rolling down their shutters'. They also condemned 'unscrupulous activities of . . . bankers', in the sketchy reconstruction of the history of the bank employees' movement.[30] What is significant is that the CPI did not use the Parliament as the institutional space for protest. But bank gates were sites for its larger class politics. This is testified in one autobiographical narrative by Chitta Maitra, a distinguished organizer in Kashipur National Carbon Workers' Union in the early 1940s:

> I lost my job trying to organize a strike in the National Bank in 1945. I used to deliver lectures using a tube brought from Kashipur at the bank gate. Employees' associations had just started coming up. Middle-class employees did not want to join movements as they were scared to lose their jobs.

Kiran Shankar Roy, the owner of the bank, mocked at his revolutionary zeal saying:

> You are a communist; you don't want any exploitation. We do exploit [the employees]. Hence, you wage struggles against me as much you can. Why should you waste your time doing your job? You have used a tube to deliver your speech. Does anybody do that in front of a bank?[31]

Maybe that provoked many like Chitta Maitra to go for a bigger struggle. They did. The Imperial Bank of India Staff Association (1920) organized the first major strike in 1946: a 46-day strike between 1 August and September 1946 in the Bengal Circle in 300 branches and pay offices involving 6,100 employees, although the strike in Calcutta was not total because of police atrocities on the employees.[32] The condemnation of the repression by Jyoti Basu in his speech on 14 August 1946, in front of the Bengal Assembly gate in 'a gathering of the students' community, striking employees and public' was probably the first significant involvement of the communists in the banking sector employees' struggles. Gita Mukherjee was the other communist who participated in the protest process.[33] But racial discrimination rather than class exploitation was the main reason of their struggle. The estimate of discrimination was as follows: 'Monthly pay bill of 6,100 employees – Rs. 2,70,000/- i.e. avg. Rs 44/- per head (excluding D.A.) But that of only 42 white officers (lords) – 85,000/- i.e. avg. Rs. 2,260/- (exclg. D.A.). So the ratio 1: more than 51'.[34] In the list of demands which led the employees to the massive strike, there was no mention of employment security. The bank employees themselves might not have apprehended a series of bank runs. In the film *Mahanagar*, based on Narnedranath Mitra's original story *Abataranika*, Subrata, the accountant in New Bharat Bank Limited gives a curt reply to a question from a prospective client who wants to know whether one or two 'runs' have taken place in the bank recently. Subrata turns cynical and says that 'the Bengali people are prone to rumours; it is not difficult for them to make a bank fail by spreading rumours [about unviable financial conditions]'. The New Bharat Bank suspends payment soon and the brusque accountant is beaten in front of the bank gate by an irate crowd afraid to lose their deposits. We can flashback to the scene in *Mahanagar* when the prospective account opener explains his anxiety about bank 'runs' by saying that he has only a meager amount for saving which he cannot afford to lose due to a bank failure. The clients were anxious, but the bank employees were unsuspecting about an impending collapse or they thought – as did Subrata – that their bank would survive one or two runs. Even if the bank employees would have an inkling of an impending collapse, the oath of secrecy would prevent them from sharing such information with their clients. Any breach of the rule of secrecy would make an employee liable to be dismissed 'without notice or payment in lieu of notice'.[35] Some bank employees must have lost their jobs as their banks went into liquidation. But that was overlooked by the CPI as well as by Arun Chandra Guha, probably because their size was miniscule. Towards the end of the 1930s, only 3,467 persons were in bank employment, which was less than 1 per cent of the employees in certain selected but important industries in Bengal.[36]

This might explain why in the chronicles of events between January and July 1946, by Amalendu Sengupta, himself a communist and a meticulous observer of political turmoil in the 1940s in India, agitation due to bank 'runs' do not figure at all.[37] What about the staff associations? Could they apprehend collapse of 43 banks between 1947 and 1949? They occasionally came across cases of fraud and malfeasance. But probably they had no inkling of the catastrophe for the depositors, shareholders and themselves. They did not protest as much they pleaded with the authorities through their own staff associations. No strike was reported in the print media.

Civil society

Given the fact that the depositors of the liquidated banks did not take part in protest activities, that the state was largely adiaphoric, and that the political Left was silent, did the banking crisis go unnoticed by everybody? What about civil society's response to the crisis and its victims, particularly the lower-middle-class depositors? Whatever moral critique the illicit money-making practices by the unscrupulous individuals in 1940s and 1950s provoked, that took the form of performing arts – theatre mainly. It must be admitted that there is no definite clue that the playwrights and directors of theatre groups were consciously articulating their moral angst. But a connection between crisis and creativity is universal.[38]

Dukhir Iman (The Honesty of a Poor Man), a three-act play written and directed by Tulsi Lahiri and first performed in 1946 in Srirangam of Sisir Bhaduri, depicted a slice of Bengal's rural life during the Bengal famine with strong condemnation of black marketing and hoarding. The critique was inset in the narrative on communal amity as in his *Chhera Tar* (Snapped String) (1950). It was written by Tulsi Lahiri in the regional dialect. Considered to be the 'first really people's drama' after *Nildarpan* (1872 in National Theatre), it was about the victims of greed of merciless money-hunters. Close on its heels came *Kalo Taka* (Black Money), a three-act play written by Sachindranath Sengupta (1892–1961),[39] a nationalist and moralist playwright, and performed on December 20, 1947, in Minerva, a theatre hall in Calcutta. Jawhar Ganguly and Swarajubala Devi, the two prominent actors of the time, performed the leading roles. It also offered a powerful critique of immoral ways of money-making by the 'black-marketers and the others of their tribe' during the famine: the black-marketers gaining 'one thousand rupees against every man dying due to the famine'. This was in fact the estimate of John Ackroyd Woodhead's report which one character in the play used to castigate the culprit. Both the plays had nothing to do with bank failures. But greed for money and the consequent immiserization of common people connect the two plays with the financial scandals in early twentieth-century Bengal.

For the Bengali middle class, the next encounter with avarice was in Rajsekhar Basu's *Parash Pathar* (1948).[40] It reached the middle-class home easily through graphic serials in *Ananda Bazar Patrika* in 1948. It is not a story of a money-hunter. It is about power of money fortuitously received, which first lessens the moral discomfort of a middle-aged lower-middle-class Bengali couple; then, cleanses their early inhibition to make it easy for them to use the new resources for social climbing until the male protagonist's adventures in alchemy begin to undermine both the local and global economies and their moral composure. Bank failure was one such damage. But in the interlude between initial incomprehension of the power of the philosopher's stone and moral panic, there was the free play of avarice. Chance (possession of the stone) was replaced by calculation. Two Bengali proverbs convey how avarice gains autonomy from moral control: *labhe lobhe bare* (Gains Stimulate Greed) and *lobher chokhe chak chakani* (Greedy Eyes Shine). Cine goers will recall the signature poster of Satyajit Ray's film *Parash Pathar* (1958), which shows the principal protagonist's eyes wide open and shining at the prospect of fortune the chance possession of a philosopher's stone would create.

What *Parash Pathar* shares with *Kalo Taka* and *Dukhir Iman* is the eventual recovery of the moral self. Common in the stories is also an attention to the morally impermissible ways of making money, which was so visible in the war years and during the tragic Bengal famine. Between the two plays and the short story – that is, between the rural (*Dukhir Iman*) and the urban (Calcutta) settings (*Kalo Taka, Parosh Pathar*), between the use of grim narratives in the two plays and satire in the short story, lay the middle class's understanding of the immoralities of wealth-making in early twentieth-century Bengal. We may add to it the film *Alibaba* (1937) by Madhu Bose. For the agonized Bengali middle-class men and women, there was reckonable possibility of conscientization.[41] True, the power of a moral message by itself does not conscientize a receiver. The fact that the best theatre performers were playing the critical roles and the best playhouse was the venue must have drawn theatre lovers to these plays. In the absence of previews peculiar to our times, the storylines could be unknown to them till they watched the plays. But the titles of the plays (*Dukhir Iman, Kalo Taka*) could be evocations of their implicit empathy for the victims, and of commitments to moral positions represented by certain characters in the plays.

Middle-class theatre goers encountered a moral scrutiny of a banker's immoral indulgence for the first time in the period under study
in Sombhu Mitra's 1949 Bahurupee production, *Sedin Bangolakshmi
Bankey* (On that day in Bangolakshmi Bank) (1949) performed on
8 November 1954 in Calcutta. The script was based on a translation of Anton Chekov's one-act play *The Anniversary* (1891)[42] by Ajit
Gangopadhyaya.[43] The Chekov play contained 'a biting exposure of
the private banks in Russia', and more.[44] We have no clue whether
Sombhu Mitra had the Bengal banking crisis in mind when he chose
the play; no clue either whether his audience could connect the play
with the crisis. The form of the play was farce – vaudeville which takes
it close to the comic and the satirical in *Parosh Pathar*. We have no
idea whether that interfered with location of the moral critique by the
audience as it might have done in case of the song–dance–hilarity of
Alibaba. But there is one stark similarity between the Chekov/Gan-
gopadhyaya texts and Narendranath Mitra's *Sahridaya* (1956): the
principal protagonist (Shipuchin/Samaresh in *The Anniversary/Sedin
Bango Lakshmi Bankey* and Suropati in *Sahridaya*) was misleading
the depositors about financial ruin of the bank, and appropriating
their savings even when the bank was on the brink of collapse.[45]

Understandingly, such moral critique of immoral financial practices indicative of a perverse money culture did not reach the level of
criticism from the writers, playwrights and artists of the famine. The
famine sketches by artists in Bengal and literary representations were
far more powerful moral censure of dehumanization produced by the
'money-hunters'.[46] What about the way of collective action?

Notes

1 Confidential Report from RBI to the Central Board on 31 January 1949;
C 183, vol. 4, F 1336.
2 The Indian Central Banking Enquiry Committee, 1931, vol. 2, *Evidence*
(Written) (Calcutta: Government of India, Central Publication Branch,
Calcutta, 1931): 477.
3 Gopalan Balachandra, *The Reserve Bank of India: 1951–67, Volume 2 of
History of the Reserve Bank of India* (Mumbai: Reserve Bank of India):
457.
4 Letter to His Excellency the High Commissioner of India in Pakistan,
Camp – Chittagong, 14 April 1949; from Shri Jogesh Chandra Sen and
others (34 signatories) File No. C 183 B, vol. IV: 'Banking Crisis in West
Bengal', File Acc. No. F 1336 (4 January 1949–28 February 1950).
5 Observations by the Executive Committee in the Memorandum submitted by the Bengal Traders' Association on the need for change of Banking

Policy in West Bengal, to the Governor [RBI], May 1951. C 183-VI, F 1338, RBI Archive.

6 The depositors reportedly withdrew their deposits between 20 April and 6 May.

7 *Ananda Bazar Patrika*, 10 May 1948.

8 *Capital*, 17 May 1951: 691.

9 Report of Inspection of the Calcutta National Bank, June 1949. C 183-VI, F 1338, RBI Archive.

10 *Capital*, 30 March 1950: 303.

11 Memorandum to the Central Board: Banking situation in Calcutta from N. Sundaresan, Deputy Governor, RBI, 18 February1950, B-2, File No. 1336.

12 Letter No. DBO 1905/NSB 65/47 dt.15 September 1947, to Pragdas Mathuradas of Belka Bank Limited from T. K. Ramasubramaniam, Deputy Chief Officer, Department of Banking Operations, RBI.NB 172 F 491 NAR, RBI Archive.

13 From D. G. (M), 28 January 1949, Confidential Report from RBI to the Central Board on 31 January 1949. C 183, vol. 4, F 1336.

14 Letter from O. P. Gupta, Under Secretary (GOI) to Secretary, Home, Govt. of West Bengal, 25 January 1949. C 183 B, vol. 4, F 1336 (4 January 1949–28 February 1950).

15 D. O. No. DBO. Liq 326/C. 183B-52, 11 July 1952: Letter to Mr. Sen, Dy. Secy., Ministry of Finance, Dept. of Economic Affairs, from A. R. Thanawala, Central Office, Department of Banking Operations, Bombay. C 183b, vol. 1, F 1339, RBI Archive.

16 A. C. Guha, 15 June 1953, from Office of Deputy Minister, Finance [G].

17 DBOD C 183, vol. 1, F 1339, 1 May 1951–16 July 1952.

18 Summary of opinions on the Banking Companies Bills 1948 from the various chambers of commerce, bank managers, and shareholders' associations 90, vol. 18, F 1611 AR, 30 August 1948–19 October 1948.

19 C. A. Bayly, 'Indigenous and Colonial Origins of Comparative Economic Development: The Case of Colonial India and Africa', *Policy Research Working Paper 4474* (The World Bank Development Research Group Poverty Team, January 2008).

20 Editorial, *Amrita Bazar Patrika*, 11 March 1950, C 266, vol. 1, F 1744, RBI Archive.

21 Letter by Amiya Nath Sanyal, *Amrita Bazar Patrika*, 24 May 1952, C 183 B, vol. 1, F 1339, RBI Archive.

22 C 22, F 1137, RBI Archive.

23 *Amrita Bazar Patrika*, 24 April 1952, editorial 'Liquidation of Banks'. Arun Chandra Guha himself had written a letter to the minister of finance, Government of India, in June 1951. C 183 B, vol. 1, F 1339, Liquidation of Banking Companies, 1 May 1951–16 July 1952. See also, *The Reserve Bank of India*, vol. 2: 1951–1967: 456–457; C 183 B, vol. 1, RBI Archive.

24 Ibid.

25 Sources:

(1) C 57 (44) F 33608). (2) C 57 (43) F 33607. (3) C 57 (42) F 33606. (4) C 57 (41) F 1610. (5) C 57 (40) F 1609. (6) C 57 (39) F 1608. (7)

C 57 (38) F 1607. (8) C 57 (37) F 1606. (9) C 57 (36) F 1605. (10) C 57 (35) F 1604. (11) C 57 (34) F 1603. (12) C 57 (33) F 1602. (13) C 57 (32) F 1601. (14) C 57 (31) F 1600. (15) C 57 (31) F 1599. (16) C 57 (29) F 1598. (17) C 57 (28) F 1597. (18) C 57 (27) F 1596. (19) C 57 (26) F 1595. (20) C 57 (25) F 1594. (21) C 57 (24) F 1593. (22) C 57 (23) F 1592. (23) C 57(4) F 1565. (24) C 57 (5) F 1566. (25) C 57 (7) F 1567. (26) C 57 (7) F 1567. (27) C 57 (12) F 1572. (28) C 57 (14) F 1574. (29) C 57 (17) F 1578. (30) C 57 (18) F 1579. (31) C 57 (21) F 1590. (32) C 57 (22) F 1591.

26 D. O. No. DBO 318/C 182–51: Correspondence from P. S. Mokashi, Central Office, Department of Banking Operations, Bombay to S. K. Sen, Deputy Secretary to the Government of India, Ministry of Finance, Department of Economic Affairs. C 183-VI F 1338, RBI Archive.

27 'Cooperation as Remedy', *Kurukhestra* in 1963, reprinted it A. R. Desai, *Rural Sociology in India* (Mumbai: Popular Prakashan, 1969): 484–488; *First Spark of Revolution: The Early Phase of India's Struggle for Independence, 1900–1920* (New Delhi: Orient Longman, 1971); *India's Struggle, Quarter of Century, 1921–46* (New Delhi: Publications Division, Ministry of Information and Broadcasting, Govt. of India, 1982).

28 Some of them like Hirendra Nath Mukherjee were remarkable parliamentarians.

29 Joya Chatterji, *The Spoils of Partition: Bengal and India, 1947–1967* (Cambridge: Cambridge University Press, 2007): 278–282.

30 *An Outline on the History of Bank Employees' Movement*, The CPI-dominated AITUC had its count also: 'During 1913 to 1917 and on the Impact Immediately After World War I – 600 Banks. During World War II – 365 Banks and Immediately After Independence at Least – 45 Bank, Totaling 1010 as Per Modest Assessment', www.befi.in/library/05.pdf, accessed on 15 May 2017.

31 Amalendu Sengupta, *Uttal Challish Asampta Biplab* (Turbulent Forties, Unfinished Revolution) (Kolkata: Pratibhas, 2006): 109, 346.

32 *An Outline on the History of Bank Employees' Movement*.

33 Amiya Bagchi, *The Evolution of the State Bank of India, Volume 3: The Era of the Imperial Bank of India: 1921–1955* (New Delhi: State Bank of India and SAGE, 2003): 490.

34 Ibid. For more accurate and relevant data, see Table 7.1 (Monthly Pay of clerical staff of the Imperial Bank of India, Calcutta): 468 and Table 7.1 (Supervising staff in the Imperial Bank of India, 1921, 1926 and 1943): 506, *The Evolution of the State Bank of India, volume 3*; ibid.: 491: the disparity was not on racial lines only. It was lower than that offered by the RBI and the Bank of India also. For the details of the context and the aftermath of the 1946 strike, see ibid.: 482–498.

35 Ibid.: 452, 468.

36 See, Iftikhar-UlAwwal, 'The Problem of Middle Class Educated Unemployment in Bengal, 1912–1942', *IESHR* 30, 1 (1982): 35 (Table 2: Consolidated Figures of Employment in Certain Selected Industries in Bengal, 1939).

37 Sengupta, *Uttal Challish Asampta Biplab*: 146–148; 343–344.

38 This connection has been reconstructed in Amit Kumar Gupta, *Crisis and Creativities: Middle Class Bhadralok in Bengal c 1939–52* (New Delhi: Orient Blackswan, 2009).
39 Sachindranath Sengupta 'believed that a dramatist must have a mission to fulfil'. [The reference for this quote is Mohan Lal, *Encyclopaedia of Indian Literature: Sasay to Zorgot* (New Delhi: Sahitya Academy, 1992): 3920]. That inspired him to compose the play about the hoarders and black-marketers: 'the spectacle of a degraded humanity'. See Sushil Kumar Mukherjee, *The Story of Calcutta Theatre, 1853–1980* (Calcutta: K. P. Bagchi, 1982). Sachindranath Sengupta also wrote *Rastra-Biplab* (Revolution) (performed in 1944), *Swadhinatar Sandhane* (In Search of Freedom) (performed in 1947) and *Ei Swadhinata* (This is Freedom) (1949).
40 This is shown in an illustrative sketch by an unintroduced artist in the serialized version of Rajsekhar Bose's Bengali short story *Parash Pathar* (The Philosopher's Stone) in *Ananda Bazar Patrika* in the same year it was published (1948). In it, the male protagonist is first amazed by the power of the stone, then scratching his head in indecision, then telling his wife about the prospect of good life which excites her, eventually both becoming busy making gold out of their everyday utensils. See *Ananda Bazar Patrika*, 10 October 1948: 11. For an English translation of the story, 'Parash Pathar' (translator unstated), see, *Not All in Fun: A Selection From Tales by Parashuram (Rajsekhar Bose)* (Calcutta: Indian Publishing House, 2000). For the Bengali original, see Dipankar Basu, ed., 'Parash Pathar', in *Parashuram Galpo-Samgra* (Collection of Stories by Parashuram) (Kolkata: M. C. Sarkar and Sons Pvt. Ltd., 1992): 294–300.
41 Conscientization as conceptualised by Paulo Freire, *Pedagogy of the Oppressed* (New York: Continuum, 2000).
42 Anton Chekhov, *The Anniversary*, https://ebooks.adelaide.edu.au/c/chekhov/anton/plays2/chapter14.html, accessed on 15 May 2017.
43 Ajit Gangopadhyay, *Nirbodhe Osedin Bangolakshmi Bankey* (Calcutta: Shankar Pustakalaya, 1954).
44 Vera Gottlieb, *Chekov and the Vaudeville: A Study of Chekov's One-Act Plays* (Cambridge: Cambridge University Press, 1982).
45 Prasanta Ray, 'Naamer Sandhaane' (In Search of Names), Susobhan Sarkar Memorial, 2015, organized by Itihas Sansad, West Bengal and Department of History, Presidency University, Kolkata.
46 The album by Nikhil Sarkar on the Bengal famine contains the agonizing sketches and paintings by Ramkinkar, Zainul Abedin, Somnath Hore, Chittaprosad Bhattacharya, Sudhir Khastgir, Gobardhan Ash, Atul Bose, Paritosh Sen, Gopen Roy, Bhabesh Sanyal, Prankrishna Pal, Sunil Madhav Sen and Gopen Roy. See Nikhil Sarkar, *A Matter of Conscience: Artists Bear Witness to the Great Bengal Famine of 1943* (Kolkata: Punascha Publication, 1998). Among the poets, Birendra Chattopadhyaya (*Strange Fragrance of Rice*) deserves a mention; see his *Selected Poems*, translated by Robert Hampson and Sibani Raychaudhuri, illustration by Bijan Chaudhury (Kolkata: Thema, 2013). See Sabyasachi Bhattacharya, *The Defining Moments in Bengal: 1920–1947* (New Delhi: Oxford University Press, 2014): 289–292.

3

THE VICTIMS

The loss

One becomes curious to know the amount – if not the exact, the approximate – lost by the savings' or current account holders in the fragile banks in view of a consensus that the lower middle class, including the refugees, suffered immensely. An answer to the question 'Who lost and how much?' presupposes information on who were saving in banks which suffered runs on them. Unfortunately, there is no authoritative indication of how much money the ordinary depositors lost due to the collapse of the banks where they had their deposits. A definitive reconstruction of the aggregate amount of money in the form of lost savings is impossible. The reasons are obvious: bank records do not mention one's class location; and class location itself is a problematic exercise.[1] There is a dearth of data on personal savings during the period 1930–1940. This could be because, as the National Council on Applied Economic Research (NCAER) observed, 'The saving (or investment) of a single individual or a household, though very important in determining the economic welfare of the individual or the household, possesses little economic significance at the aggregate level'.[2]

This premise among economists invisibilizes the individual saver. Because of the non-availability of records of the banks which suffered runs, we are left with only the possibility of a conjectural exercise towards location of practice of saving distinctive of a middle-class fraction; and, the amount of money lost by individuals. This is despite the fact there were claims with regard to the amount lost both in the press, in political representations, in collective petitions by the depositors and the bank employees and in their personal communications. These claims, as far as the amount is concerned, are more figurative than definitive. These were by a grieving Nihar Bala or a combative Member of Parliament, Mr. Guha, or a humane editor. The 'ordinary depositor', a term used in petitions, press reports and parliamentary discussions, is not a legal or official category though he or she is a real entity. He or she could be anybody: a salaried employee or a wage earner or a self-employed person, an unemployed person, a retiree in lower or middle ranges of the middle class, or one who has inherited some money. Nothing else by way of his or her financial liabilities, earnings and savings in any form is in public knowledge. Given the non-availability of records of individual depositors, it is difficult for a researcher to estimate individual loss so that an average can be worked out. Public deliberations in the press, discussions in the Dominion Parliament, the reports of various banking enquiry committees and the observations by men in state structure, all had to go by collective names like 'ordinary depositors' or 'middle class' or 'refugees'.

A possible route to a surmise would be to make conjectures about how much such people might have saved after spending on the necessities. It is a good guess that they did save, even if the amount would be meagre. But this was also in the form of Provident Fund or insurance, and not in all cases, savings in banks only. This seems to be the case from whatever data are available. We have no firm clue. Some individuals might not have considered savings in three different institutions – Provident Fund, insurance and bank – as separate choices regarding how to set apart money after essential expenses, which was in many cases administered surplus for future use. Proportions were in probability calculated. Even money 'earned' under one could be re-saved in another, like shifting money received on maturity of an insurance could be put in a savings bank account. But it appears that the lower middle class saved only a small fraction of the total amount they earned any way in banks. But what is numerically small is not negligible because even setting that apart for saving must mean a regime of under-consumption. They must have known that it was paltry but hoped it could be something to fall back up on in contingencies in future. This is how savings connects the present with the future. It is an appropriate example of Bourdieusian 'saving morality', an ethos which requires that 'people should save before they buy anything' and 'should be ascetic and not enjoy anything before they buy it'.[3] In all the middle-class family budget surveys, drawing on savings over a past period was cited as a source of income.[4] This made the loss due to bank liquidation a great loss, particularly for the lower middle class.

The refugees

Let us take the case of the refugees because their loss provoked various demands for justice. From among the two million who came over to West Bengal following riots in 1946 and in 1950, 'the rich brought some properties. But their number and how much they brought are unknown'.[5] This research is interested in those at the other end of the class spectrum: those without any land of their own and those without employment at the time of migrating to West Bengal: the lower middle class and the poor (Table 3.1). 'Unemployment' stands out as a powerful push factor between 1935 and 1950.

They, in all probability, did not bring much money when they came to West Bengal; if some of them did, it must be very small amount for contingent expenses in their place of destination. A majority of them lacked the qualifications and skills and the social capital to make a significant income through employment, permitting savings in any form. Even in early 1950s, significantly high numbers were seeking jobs. 'Unemployment rates in the early years of 1950s were low for ordinary migrants, quite high for original residents and extremely high (over 35 per cent) for displaced migrants from East Pakistan. The situation of the educated unemployment was already a crisis'[6] (Table 3.2).

True, many had come from East Bengal before the communal eruption there, and everybody was not struggling for a minimum foothold. For example, the upper middle class comprising very few who sold their immovable property in East Bengal or acquired the exchange

Table 3.1 Causes of migration in different periods

Causes	1935–1939	1940–1946	1947–1950
No land to cultivate	03.8	03.8	02.8
Unemployment	49.7	41.8	32.3
Prospects of better employment	17.4	18.3	09.8
Lack of educational facilities	04.4	03.4	01.3
Communal factors		05.2	52.2
Transfer in service		0.57	0.65
Proximity to relations etc.	18.4	23.1	10.8
Others	03.1	02.6	0.3

Source: S. N. Sen, *The City of Calcutta* (Calcutta: Bookland Pvt. Ltd., 1960): 199; based on Table 3.2. 'Causes of Migration in Different Periods, 1957–58'.

Table 3.2 Distribution of persons seeking employment in early 1950s (persons in thousands)

All Classes Combined	
West Bengal	287.2
Refugees	99.0
Middle Class	
West Bengal	178.6
Refugees	69.2

Source: Survey of Unemployment in West Bengal, 1953, vol. ii, Part 1, Table A (12): 27.

value of their property there and invested the money in private industries in West Bengal, and a sizeable educated middle class were eagerly accessing the new opportunities created by the government.[7] Joya Chatterji has summed up the situation:

In the first wave of Hindu refugees to cross over into West Bengal . . . the overwhelming majority were drawn from the ranks of the very well-to-do and the educated middle classes, with assets and skills which they could take with them across the border and, in many cases with kith and kin on the other side. Of the 1.1 million Hindus who had migrated from the east by June 1948, about 350,000 were urban bhadralok; anther 550,000 belonged to the rural Hindu gentry. Many of the rest were businessmen.[8]

They must be the persons who saved money in banks, some of which collapsed.

The poor Hindu peasants, sharecroppers or agricultural labourers who migrated late between the end of 1949 and early 1950, and who constituted 40 per cent of all the displaced persons who came over to West Bengal were in the dire need for support. They did not carry any disposable property into West Bengal because they had none. In fact, they arrived as destitutes. They obviously had some occupational skills. About the same time, 'more than 100,000 artisans' with occupational skills (making bangles, tailoring, weaving) came to West Bengal.[9] They concentrated in cities and towns as did eventually the peasant migrants. Many of them were very hard working, earning in more than one way. They might have saved a little for their uncertain future; but may be not in banks.

Those among the poor and lower middle class who did not have relatives already in West Bengal and who came after the first wave of arrivals had to settle down in government camps. Their number, 55,337 between July and October 1948, was significant though much less than those admitted to such camps in 1950 and 1951.[10] Their number increased to 70,000 by the end of 1949.[11] At the end of 1950, it became 200,331. Those in government camps would not have any reckonable surplus even after compromising on the necessary expenses to be any position to save. The dole amount for an adult staying in a camp for an old migrant was Rs. 13.00 per month; Rs. 15.00 in cases where mixed doles, that is, part cash, part ration, was given. Clothing allowance was Rs. 16.00 annually. Although the camp inmates enjoyed certain facilities like accommodation, water supply, sanitation, lighting, medical help and primary education for free, they had to buy food in the market.[12] If the conditions of the displaced persons in camps from 1950 onwards would be any indicator, these poor migrants were leading a very miserable life. 'The amount of dole and the money which they were getting were not sufficient to meet their daily expenses not to speak of giving education and medical help to the children'.[13] For upper-caste men unwilling to do manual work, the average income of those in Jirat (Hooghly, West Bengal) camp was Rs. 10.1 anna; for the lower-caste men ready to do any kind of work, it was Rs. 11.13 anna. In Azadgarh colony (Tollygunge, West Bengal), average per capita income was Rs. 3.20 for upper-caste men and Rs. 2.86 for the lower-caste men. For their meagre income, they would do anything: 'at present they are anyhow eking their livelihood by running petty shops, hawking goods, working as petty hands in neighbouring mills and factories. Some engage in manufacture of basketry, profession of making drums and earthen ovens'.[14] 'They followed such trades as peddling of glasswares, brasswares, clothes and vegetables, etc., or were employed in industries or offices, drawing very poor salary, or followed such professions as those of barber, carpenter, furniture polishers etc'.[15] A part of their earning would be taken as monthly subscription from the plot-holders in Azadgarh. The vendors too would have to pay daily rents to the administrative committee for selling vegetables, fish and other things in the market within the colony.[16] It is not impossible that they still managed to save a very small amount. After all, the forced migrants must have had a height-ened sense of insecurity which would prompt them to save incremen-tally. It was their loss due to banking failure which became a moral issue for the sympathetic others.

There are studies on occupational shift between past occupations in their home country and after arrival and settlement here in West Bengal (Tables 3.3 and 3.4). Such shifts were associated with a fall in income in the category of lowest earners.

These also suggest who were earning a reasonable income. For example, 'The middle classes have successfully rehabilitated them-selves by small trade or employment as skilled labour in factories in east Calcutta. Many found employment in pharmaceutical, chemical

Table 3.3 Percentage distribution of migrants from Pakistan by occupations followed before migration and after migration

Occupation Class	Percentage Following Occupations under Col. (1) before Migration	Percentage Following Occupations under Col. (1) after Migration	Per Capita Annual Income (Rs.) of Migrants in West Bengal after Migration
(1)	(2)	(3)	(4)
Agriculture	10.2	08.2	391
Cottage industry	02.6	02.8	577
Caste profession	01.4	01.2	595
Learned profession	01.5	01.2	910
Trade	05.7	04.8	877
Skilled labour	00.1	00.1	955
Unskilled labour	00.4	02.1	400
Services	03.5	05.9	1034
Other occupations	01.1	01.1	651
No occupation	73.5	72.6	. . .
All classes	100.0	100.0	Rs. 722
Number of individuals	(2143228)	(2143228)	

Source: State Statistical Bureau (West Bengal): Report, 1951 – Tables 16 and 18: 38, 40.

Reproduced in K. B. Pakrasi: *The Uprooted: A Sociological Study of Refugees in West Bengal*, Table A (Calcutta: Editions Indian, 1971): 145–46.

Table 3.4 Distribution of refugee–migrant families by income group before and after migration

Income Group (Rupees per month)	Families before Migration (percentage)	Families after Migration (percentage)
(1)	*(2)*	*(3)*
1–50	09.8	31.9
51–100	30.3	36.4
101–250	41.6	25.5
251–500	13.5	05.1
501–1000	03.5	00.9
Above 1000	01.3	00.2
Total	100.0	100.0
(Number of families)	(429272)	(429272)

Source: State Statistical Bureau (West Bengal): Report, 1951:9.

Reproduced in K. B. Pakrasi: *The Uprooted: A Sociological Study of Refugees in West Bengal*, Table B (Calcutta: Editions Indian, 1971):146.

and engineering workshops. The educated were employed in schools and offices'.[17] In the better placed middle-class spectrum were those who came because of 'fall in income from land proprietorship in East Bengal' and 'were in learned professions, bureaucratic services, banking and commerce' after coming to West Bengal. They probably saved in banks. The 'fisherfolk, agriculturalists and others who hardly owned any land' in their home country 'tried to settle down as skilled gardeners or fishermen on the outskirts of the city'. They could be better off than those in government refugee camps or in the colonies. The latter were so economically insecure that they categorically expressed that they expected from the government opportunities for secure earning (Table 3.5).

The income they managed to earn was meagre, given the limited scope available in the local post-war economy. We have some idea of their income (Table 3.6), but no clue whether they earned enough to save in banks. May be some of them did. If they lost due to the banking crisis, the loss was severe in the context of a history of more grievous loss in course of forced migration, and of their income insecurity after arrival in West Bengal.

Table 3.5 Financial needs of male and female refugee subjects in Jirat and Azadgarh, West Bengal, India

Residential Locality: Jirat	Needs in India	Percentage
Male	Means of livelihood	84.3
	Financial help (including business loan)	74.5
Female	Regular financial and other help from the government	100.0
	Permanent source of income and good financial condition	34.6

Residential Locality: Azadgarh	Needs in India	Percentage
Male	Financial help from government	77.0
	Means of livelihood and good financial condition	23.0
Female	Financial help and good financial condition	64.6

Source: Studies in Social Tensions among the Refugees from East Pakistan, B. S. Guha Memoir 1, 1954, Tables 15, 17, 6 and 8: 27, 28, 65 and 66 respectively.

Note: They had mentioned other needs also.

Table 3.6 Income of refugees in Jirat and Azadgarh (in rupees)

Residential Locality: Jirat	Average Weekly Family Income	Average Per Capita Income	Average Weekly Income in East Pakistan before Migration
Upper Caste	10.1.0	NA	53.0.0
Lower Caste	11.13.0	NA	27.8.0

Residential Locality: Azadgarh	Average Weekly Family Income	Average Per Capita Income	Average Weekly Income in East Pakistan before Migration
Upper Caste	19.0.0	3.20.0	NA
Lower Caste	16.13.0	2.86.0	NA

Source: B. S. Guha, *Studies in Social Tensions among the Refugees from East Pakistan*, B. S. Guha Memoir No. 1, 1954 (New Delhi: Department of Anthropology, Government of India, Government of India Press, 1954; Calcutta: 1959); Tables 9 and 3: 14 and 130.

The lower middle class

What about the Bengali middle class as such in the 1940s? As we move
from the refugees to the lower middle class in Bengal, we obviously do
not treat the two categories as mutually exclusive. Evidently, we now
examine the plight of a larger class segment. We have few reports from
the data which were collected with some rigour:[18] *A Sample Survey of
After-Effects of the Bengal Famine;*[19] *A Short-Term Enquiry into the
Living Conditions of the Bengali Middle-Class 'Bhadralok' with a
view to Estimating a Minimum Wage;*[20] *A Study of Expenditure Patterns of Calcutta Middle-Class Family Budgets;*[21] *World War II and
the Consumption Pattern of the Calcutta Middle Class;*[22] *Report on
an Enquiry into the Family Budgets of Middle-Class Employees of the
Central Government;*[23] *Report of the Comparative Cost of Living in
the Different Towns of West Bengal during November 1950;*[24] and
*Family Budget Enquiry in 23 Towns of West Bengal including Cal-
cutta, 1950–51* (Table 3.7).[25] Among all these enquiries, only *A Sample Survey of After-Effects of the Bengal Famine* had a singular focus
on rural Bengal. Taken together, they provide reliable insights into the
financial status of the urban Bengali middle class, mainly its salary-
earning segment. This is despite, as noted by the Indian Economic
Enquiry Committee of 1925, the middle and upper classes in India
'resenting' 'enquiries regarding their income and expenditure'; and
despite the difficulty of working out a 'precise definition of the term
'middle class' by specifying upper and lower income limits' because of
'the existence of a large body of clerical workers with a rather low
basic salary (as low as Rs. 30 per month in some cases) who, nevethe-
less, demanded inclusion in this class'.[26] They were clerks in employment of the Central government or in Bengal government employment.[27]
But in the latter case, the 'inferior staff' in Bengal government
employment – those in the lowest income class (Rs. 0–35 per month) –
was also included in the Bengali middle class as were those employees
in the highest (Rs. 76–150 per month). However, the 'Rs. 35 upwards'
group was the *bhadralok* benchmark.[28] When 'Rs. 76–150' was the
terminal income range for the Bengali middle class in this inquiry,
Rs. 500 was set as the end of the spectrum of income drawn by the
contemporary middle class – the principal earner being in Central government employment.[29] The difference is possibly due to difference in
pay bands in central and state governments.

In another survey on the consumption pattern of the Calcutta
middle class, the largest concentration of middle-class families was

Table 3.7 Surveys of family budgets in 1940s and early 1950s

Name of the Survey[1]	Surveyor	Period of Data Collection	Place of Data Collection	Unit of Study	Sample Size (number of families or family budgets)
A Sample Survey of After-Effects of the Bengal Famine of 1943	Indian Statistical Institute, Calcutta[2]	1944 June to 1945 February	386 villages in 41 sub-divisions of rural Bengal	Family	15,769 families
A Short-Term Enquiry into the Living Conditions of the Bengali Middle Class 'Bhadralok' with a View to Estimating a Minimum Wage[3]	Provincial Statistical Bureau, Bengal	1946 April–May	Dacca, Rangpur, Brahmanbaria, Bankura	Family budget	1,328 (1,200 government employees with basic salary up to 'about Rs. 150' per month + 'salary earners' of other institutions and professional men of similar income levels)
World War II and the Consumption Pattern of the Calcutta Middle Class	Indian Statistical Institute, Calcutta[4]	1939 and 1945	Calcutta	Family budget	1,160 for 1939 estimate and 1,750 for 1945 estimate
A Study of Expenditure Patterns of Calcutta Middle-Class Family Budgets	Indian Statistical Institute, Calcutta[5]	1945	Calcutta	Family budget	1,785

Report of the Comparative Cost of Living in the Different Towns of West Bengal during November 1950	West Bengal State Statistical Bureau	1950 September to 1951 February		Family budget	6,086
Family Budget Enquiry in 23 Towns of West Bengal Including Calcutta, 1950–51	West Bengal State Statistical Bureau	1950–1951	23 towns	Family budget	6,373

1 All the surveys focused on income and its various sources, and expenditure on different items of consumption.
2 P. C. Mahalanobis, Ramakrishna Mukherjee and Ambika Ghosh, Statistical Laboratory, ISI. K. P. Chattopadhyay, Head, Department of Anthropology, Calcutta University did the pilot survey, and also guided the field work for the larger project. The report *A Sample Survey of After-Effects of the Bengal Famine of 1943* was published in *Sankhyā*, 7, part 4, 1946: 337–400.
3 Followed by *A Supplementary Note* to the Report, 1946.
4 S. Bhattacharyya, Statistical Laboratory, ISI.
5 S. Janardhan Poti, Statistical Laboratory, ISI.

thought to be in Rs. 51–100 to Rs. 201–250.[30] Thus middle-class location in terms of both income and expenditure rested on claims by the principal earner in the household and cut offs by researchers in the academia. As for the cut offs in survey reports, income and expenditure classes were used in statistical narratives, which, with a little liberty, can be taken as indicators of locations along a middle-class spectrum – proxy for 'lower' or 'upper'-middle-class fractions.[31]

Who could save during and after the Bengal famine and the Second World War? *A Sample Survey of After-Effects of the Bengal Famine* – a survey of rural Bengal – found:

> about seven lakh families in rural Bengal had probably suffered a lowering of economic status and decrease in earning as a consequence of the famine. Adopting 5.4 as the average family size of the family in rural Bengal (as estimated from Census 1941) the total number of persons whose economic position seriously deteriorated (and in many cases possibly reduced to semi-destitution) was about 38 lakhs.

It also found that about 2.4 lakh rural families (2.3 per cent of the total) had prospered.[32] There is however no estimate of their prosperity. It is a safe guess that they saved and invested in banks. Since 'middle class', or for that matter 'class', was not a category which guided this survey, there is no way it can provide any hint as to what happened to the rural middle class. But it does implicitly refer to classes when it sums up the impact of the famine:

> The poorer sections of the community, especially landless labour, fishermen and village craftsmen, were most severely affected and many were rendered destitute; the middle groups who had land of their own and other assets were naturally less vulnerable while the upper stratum remained immune and sometimes even prospered.[33]

Further,

> The effect of famine was not only destitution on an unprecedented scale but the lowering of the economic level of a large number of people who before the famine had some assets by selling which they succeeded in escaping total destitution but whose earning power was appreciably decreased.[34]

About 'seven lakh families (6.8 per cent of the total number in rural Bengal) had suffered a deterioration of economic status during the famine'.[35] Perhaps a small fraction of such families managed to save in very small amounts in banks.

What about the middle class, particularly, salaried segments in Calcutta? The following are the main observations on the basis of two family budget surveys of the middle-class people in Calcutta carried out by the Indian Statistical Institute in 1939 and in 1945.[36]

(1) 'The largest concentration of middle-class families is in the expenditure groups of Rs. 51–100 to Rs. 201–250, forming 68.5% and 63% of the total number of families sampled in 1945 and 1939 respectively'.

(2) 'About 63% of middle-class families surveyed in 1939 and 69% . . . in 1945 were, on the average, found to be spending nearly ⅔ and ¾ of their total expenditure on food, fuel and rent which together constitute what is called the necessary group'.

(3) 'In 1945, proportionally less of the family budget is allotted to clothing and miscellaneous items. Thus even the small percentage of 8.1% for clothing in 1939 is reduced to only 4.7% in 1945, i.e. a reduction by half and the percentage expenditure on miscellaneous, diminished from 27.4 to 20.8 as between the two years'.

(4) 'In order to meet a proportional increase of about ⅓ and ⅕ in respect of food and fuel expenditure, an average middle class family in 1945 had to reduce its expenditure on clothing and miscellaneous by about ½ and ¼ respectively'.

(5) 'A fall about 25% in the proportional expenditure on miscellaneous (*mainly medicine and educational expenses, not luxury items*), the conclusion that a fall in the standard of living of the middle class of Calcutta has occurred between 1939 and 1945 would not be unwarranted'.

(6) 'Cost of living has arisen out of all proportion to the expendable income'.

Equally significant is the fact that the incidence of deficit family budget was of high order: 77 per cent according to a comprehensive survey.[37] In these circumstances, except for the upper end of the middle-class spectrum, the other fractions of the class presumably saved a meagre amount of their surplus left after their necessary expenses, contributions to Provident Fund and insurance, and purchase of assets, in banks.[38] (Table 3.8)

Table 3.8 Expenditure on insurance and Provident Fund in Calcutta 1950–1951

Monthly Expenditure Levels (in rupees)				
Rs. 1–Rs. 100	Rs. 101–200	Rs. 201–Rs. 350	Rs. 351–Rs. 700	Rs. 701 and above
Rs. 1.47	Rs. 5.63	Rs. 9.47	Rs. 9.35	Rs. 13.02

Source: Table W (1.2): Percentage expenditure on the different items of consumption by different expenditure levels, Centre – Calcutta, *Family Budget Enquiry in 23 Towns in West Bengal including Calcutta, 1950–51*, Government of West Bengal State Statistical Bureau, West Bengal Government Printing Press, Alipore, West Bengal, 1954: 95.

Conjecturally observing, a little more than meagre could be saved by those who constituted 23 per cent of families with surplus budget;[39] or, those who had income beyond salary,[40] or a reckonable percentage of those families at the lowest expenditure level in 1935 becoming capable of expending little more in 1945 due to 'a general rise in money earnings',[41] or, those in government employment enjoying a larger average monthly income compared to those in non-government jobs.[42] Even then, the clerks in the employment of the Bengal government were extremely hard-pressed. It was claimed in All Bengal Ministerial Officers' Conference in 1945 that many clerks found it difficult to continue to save even a small amount and 'stopped contributing to Provident Fund, stopped paying Insurance premium and had to "contract debt to keep the wolf from the door"' The fact that there was a 'low rate of increase in real income throughout the colonial period and particularly in a period of 58 years between 1880 and 1930' must have already weakened their financial position.[43]

These are discrete data sets which do not allow a firm inference regarding who saved in banks and who lost due to run on banks. Given the fact that some of the inquiries on middle-class conditions of living, the samples consisted of those in government employment which would explain their propensity to save money in their secure Provident Fund. 'The middle-income salaried population probably has some savings, but the bulk of such savings are invested in provident funds and life insurance'.[44] However, to re-state the basic argument here, the little amount saved in banks – and lost due to bank collapse – was exceptionally significant because the loss upset a painstaking process of building up feeble financial security in the face of contingencies, particularly for the lower middle class including the refugees. How small could be their savings in banks which they lost because of the 'runs'? We can have at best a conjectural answer, given unavailability and inaccessibility of the necessary data.

The data on saving close to the period chosen are in two reports: *A Short-Term Enquiry into the Living Conditions of the Bengali Middle Class 'Bhadralok' with a view to Estimating a Minimum Wage* and *Family Budget Enquiry in 23 Towns of West Bengal including Calcutta, 1950–51*. The unit of analysis is the same, namely, the family. But in case of saving, it is the individual in the first report. The choice of the salary level (Rs. 36 to Rs. 75) is because the '*bhadralok* really commences his career from Rs. 35 upwards'. Incidentally, this group also represents 'younger men'.[45] Despite the fact that contributions to Provident Fund and insurance are listed under 'expenditures', these represent savings, though obviously not in banks (Table 3.9). However, beyond a suggestion of propensity to save (in Provident Fund and insurance) being greater in the youthful years, there is no hint as to their saving in banks. The expenses on insurance premium and Provident Fund decreased with age. In the absence of a matching series of income whereby the amount left in the hands of an individual employee after his total expenses (including that on insurance and Provident Fund) could not be calculated. That would have enabled a firm conjecture about a possible savings in banks.

The other clue regarding savings comes from 1950–51 data on family budget in Calcutta and 22 other towns in West Bengal (Table 3.10). This inquiry covered 'the menial and the middle-classes of people at Calcutta and Asansol'. Their ratio is not stated. However, only the data relating to those on the Rs. 101–Rs. 200–Rs. 350 monthly expenditure groups in the sample of family budgets were subjected to statistical analysis because these constituted 56.33 per cent of the total number of budgets examined. The other expenditure levels were Rs. 1–Rs. 100, Rs. 351–Rs. 700 and Rs. 7001 and above. Apparently, the middle-class segment is represented in this data set.

That some segments of the urban Bengali middle class could save must be due to larger family income from sources other than salary (Table 3.11). The reported other sources of income included total allowance and travelling allowance, gratuity and pension, trade and industry, profession, agriculture and dairy, cottage industry, rent/interest/loan received, savings and sale of cattle/lands, help from outside and other occupation, and other sources. The Report considered these to be 'doubtful sources' but conceded that 'the income really exist(ed)'.

Table 3.9 Total monthly expenditure in rupees at each age of an average employee corresponding to the Rs. 36–Rs. 75 salary level 1944 June to 1945 February***

Age	All Expenditures Except Insurance and Provident Fund	Column 2 Minus Expenditure on Sons 21 Years Old and Above	Column 3 Plus Insurance Premium*	Column 4 Plus Provident Fund (to the Nearest Half Rupee)	Contribution to Insurance ** Col.4 − Col.2	Contribution to Provident Fund Col.5 − Col.4	Total Contribution to Savings in Insurance and Provident Fund	All Expenditures Including Insurance and Provident Fund Col.2 + Col.8	Expenses on Insurance and Provident Fund as Percentage of Total Expenses
1	2	3	4	5	6	7	8	9	10
22	45.68	45.68	45.68	...	00.00	00.00		45.68	
23	46.40	46.40	46.40	...	00.00	00.00		46.40	
24	47.23	47.23	47.23	...	00.00	00.00		47.23	
25	48.30	48.30	52.30	55.5	04.00	03.20	07.20	55.50	12.97
26	49.64	49.64	53.64	57.0	04.00	04.36	08.36	58.30	14.34
27	50.93	50.93	54.93	58.5	04.00	03.57	07.57	58.50	12.94
28	52.77	52.77	56.77	60.5	04.00	03.73	07.73	60.50	12.78
29	54.43	54.43	58.43	62.0	04.00	03.57	07.57	62.00	12.21
30	55.73	55.73	59.73	63.5	04.00	03.77	07.77	63.50	12.24
31	57.79	57.79	61.79	65.5	04.00	03.71	07.71	65.50	11.77
32	59.24	59.24	63.24	67.0	04.00	03.76	07.76	67.00	11.58
33	61.25	61.25	65.25	69.5	04.00	04.25	08.25	69.50	11.87
34	62.93	62.93	66.93	71.0	04.00	05.07	09.07	72.00	12.60

35	65.14	69.14	65.14	73.5	04.00	04.36	08.36	73.50	11.37
36	67.53	71.53	67.53	76.0	04.00	04.47	08.47	76.00	11.14
37	69.93	73.93	69.93	78.5	04.00	04.57	08.57	78.50	10.92
38	72.57	76.57	72.57	81.5	04.00	04.93	08.93	81.50	10.96
39	75.12	79.12	75.12	84.0	04.00	04.88	08.88	84.00	10.57
40	77.68	81.68	77.68	87.0	04.00	05.32	09.32	87.00	10.71
41	80.38	84.18	80.18	89.5	03.70	05.32	09.12	89.40	10.20
42	82.78	86.34	82.34	91.5	03.56	05.16	08.72	92.50	09.43
43	84.95	88.30	84.30	94.0	03.35	05.70	09.05	94.00	09.63
44	87.31	90.34	86.34	96.0	03.03	05.66	08.69	96.00	09.05
45	89.56	92.15	88.15	98.0	02.59	05.85	08.44	98.00	08.61
46	91.66	93.62	89.62	99.5	01.96	05.88	07.84	99.50	07.88
47	93.23	94.33	90.23	100.0	01.10	05.67	06.77	100.00	06.77
48	94.92	95.14	91.14	101.0	00.22	05.86	06.08	101.00	06.02
49	96.13	95.47	91.47	101.5	-00.66	06.03	05.37	101.50	05.29
50	97.18	91.57	91.57	97.5	-05.61	05.93	00.32	97.50	00.33
51	97.49	91.15	91.15	97.0	-06.34	05.85	-00.49	97.98	-00.50
52	97.09	90.07	90.07	95.5	-07.02	05.43	-01.59	98.68	-01.61
53	96.52	88.85	88.85	94.5	-07.67	05.65	-02.02	98.54	-02.05
54	94.95	86.75	86.75	92.0	-08.20	05.25	-02.95	97.90	-03.01
55	93.50	84.75	84.75	90.0	-08.75	05.25	-03.50	97.00	-03.61

Source: A Short-Term Enquiry into the Living Conditions of the Bengali Middle Class 'Bhadralok' with a view to Estimating a Minimum Wage: 19.

* For a 25 years' endowment policy for Rs. 1,000 from the age of 25 years to 49 years.

** My estimations in Cols. 6 to 10 are based on the previous columns.

*** Data collection period: 1944 June to 1945 February.

Table 3.10 Average monthly savings per family, 1950–1951 (in rupees)[1]

Place	Average Monthly Income per Family Excluding the Sale of Assets[2]	Average Monthly Expenditure per Family Excluding Money Expended Towards Insurance and Provident Fund and Purchase of Assets	Average Monthly Expenditure on Insurance and Provident Fund	Average Monthly Savings per Family	Average Monthly Savings per Family as Percentage of Average Monthly Income per Family Excluding the Sale of Assets
1	2	3	4	5	6
Calcutta	370.29	333.54	13.08	36.75	9.92
23 Towns including Calcutta	229.00	214.24	6.04	14.76	6.45

Source: Average monthly savings per family is the difference between average monthly income per family excluding the sale of assets and average monthly expenditure per family excluding money expended towards insurance and Provident Fund and purchase of assets. This is adapted from Table S (8A): Average Monthly Savings per Family by Centres in *Family Budget Enquiry in 23 Towns of West Bengal Including Calcutta, 1950–51*, West Bengal State Statistical Bureau, 1954: 64.

1 Data collection period: 1950–51.
2 The average number of earners per family for all the towns was 1.46; for Calcutta, 1.49.

What we are not certain about is that the saving beyond saving in insurance and Provident Fund – even buying re-saleable assets – was in the form of bank deposits. Going by the expansion of banking during the period, it is a safe guess that it was by way of saving in banks. The proliferation of advertisements by the banks suggests that the bank owners and managers were aware that they could mop up the surplus income. Saving close to 10 per cent of monthly family income (Rs. 370.29) in Calcutta and an average of nearly 7 per cent for the average monthly income (Rs. 229.00) in 23 towns appears to be considerable. But the amount of money presumably saved in banks and lost due to banking collapse anytime anywhere may not signify the intensity of the sense of loss on the part of a loser. The sense of the

Table 3.11 Sources of income beyond salary for middle-class employees in four towns other than Calcutta,[a] 1945–1946

Pay Level	Rs. 1–35			Rs. 36–75			Rs. 76–150			All Levels		
Office	Govt.	Non-Govt.	Total	Govt.	Non-Govt.	Total	Govt.	Non-Govt.	Total	Govt.	Non-Govt.	Total
Total salary	27.07	23.20	26.33	59.66	53.95	58.08	100.91	92.81	99.66	53.19	50.52	56.54
Total family income	128.90	118.66	124.56	212.78	182.17	204.55	259.12	226.56	254.80	192.93	170.00	188.00

a Dacca, Rangpur, Brahmanbaria and Bankura.

Source: Adapted from Table 20: Family Budget Enquiry of Middle Class Employees, 1945–46: Average Monthly Income (in Rupees) per Family by Sources in A Short-Term Enquiry into the Living Conditions of the Bengali Middle Class 'Bhadralok' with a View to Estimating a Minimum Wage: 71.

loss must be a function of a number of contextual variables. Money saved in middle-class families is either earmarked for meeting social obligations which include marrying daughters or for future contingencies. More moderate the means, less the number of earners, greater the dependency burden, greater the despondency that some obligations will be compromised, greater is the sense of loss; greater is the grief.

Apart from the salary-earning segment, the middle-class businessmen in both East and West Bengal also suffered due to runs on banks or protracted liquidation process. Arun Chandra Guha observed: 'Bengal being pre-eminently a middle-class state, this collapse of almost all banking facilities has reduced small industrialists, traders and businessmen, being mostly from the middle class, to a state of idleness and penury'.[46] At the same time, the Bengal Trades Association affiliated with Bengal National Chamber of Commerce wrote to the Prime Minister of India in the same vein. An interesting fraternity based on 'consciousness of kind'[47] – 'innate collective feelings of similarity and belonging' developed among middle-class factions.

Notes

1 An exception was a savings bank for jute workers set up in Baranagar in 1884 by Sashipada Banerjee, in which case the class identity could be known. In the early years of labour movement in India, Sashipada Banerjee published a journal titled *Bharat Shramajivi* (Indian Labourers) in 1878 from Kolkata, exclusively devoted to the labourers. This journal started expressing the labour problems for the first time. He also founded an institute in 1880 to spread primary and hygiene education among the workers. A similar effort was initiated by Meghaji Narayan Lokhande in Bombay in 1898. He also started a journal, named *Deenabandhu* (Friend of the Poor) in Marathi. It is difficult to date the end of such philanthropic efforts. Obviously, such banks do not come within the purview of this monograph. Banerjee's bank for the working class is comparable to the National Girobank run by the British General Post Office (1968). Originally, it was a banking system based on direct transfer of accounts. It is reported that the banks in England did not seek savings from the working class, and even the lower middle class, because of unprofitability. For Giro banking see Thomas Crump, *The Phenomenon of Money* (London: Routledge & Kegan Paul, 1981): 6, 98–99. Widespread People's Savings Bank in Western Europe in early twentieth century has been pointed out in Louise D. Brandeis, *Other People's Money: And How the Bankers Use It* (New York: Frederick A Stokes Company, 1914): 214–216.

2 National Council of Applied Research, *Saving in India* (Calcutta: NCAER, 1961): 6.

3 The other ethos is signified by 'credit morality', 'a hedonistic type of morality'. The distinction between the two was worked out in the context

of French society in 'The Bank and Its Customers: Elements for a Sociology of Credit' by Pierre Bourdieu, Luc Boltanski and Jean-Claude Chamboredon (unpublished), see Richard Swedberg, 'The Economic Sociologies of Pierre Bourdieu', *CSES Working Paper Series*, Paper 52, 2009; Nina Bandelj and Frederick F. Wherry, eds., *The Cultural Wealth of Nations* (Palo Alto: Stanford University Press, 2011).

4 *A Short-Term Enquiry into the Living Conditions of the Bengali Middle Class 'Bhadralok' With a View to Estimating a Minimum Wage*, p. 71. Also, *Family Budget Enquiry in 23 Towns of West Bengal, Including Calcutta, 1950–51*, West Bengal State Statistical Bureau, 1954, Table 8 (12), p. 76. But in neither case, there is any indication of such savings being in banks.

5 Aditi Chatterji, *Ethnicity, Migration and the Urban Landscape of Kolkata* (Kolkata: K. P. Bagchi, 2009): 43.

6 Ibid.: 89.

7 Abhijit Das Gupta, 'The Puzzling Numbers: The Politics of Counting Refugees in West Bengal', *South Asian Refugee Watch* 2, 2 (December 2002).

8 Joya Chatterji, *The Spoils of Partition: Bengal and India, 1947–1967* (New Delhi: Cambridge University Press, 2007): 115; Prafulla K. Chakrabarti, *The Marginal Men* (Kalyani: Lumière Books, 1990): 1.

9 Chatterji, *The Spoils of Partition*: 115, 123.

10 Chakrabarti, *Marginal Men*: 2–3: Tables 1, 2 and 3.

11 Ibid.: 15.

12 Ibid.: 469–470.

13 B. S. Guha, *Studies in Social Tensions Among the Refugees From East Pakistan*, B. S. Guha Memoir No. 1, 1954 (Department of Anthropology, Government of India, Manager of Publications, Delhi, Government of India Press, Calcutta, 1959): 13. Understandably, when identifying their needs in India, most of men and women highlighted their financial needs. (Men: 84.3 'means of livelihood', 74.5 'financial help including business loan'; Women: 100.0 'regular financial and other help from the government', 34.6 'permanent source of income and good financial condition': 27–28.)

14 Ibid.: 53.

15 Ibid.: 59.

16 Ibid.: 52.

17 Chatterji, *Ethnicity, Migration and the Urban Landscape of Kolkata*: 92–93.

18 However, almost all the surveys admitted that they could not reach the ideal standards of enquiry they set for themselves.

19 P. C. Mahalanobis, Ramakrishna Mukherjee and Ambika Ghosh, Statistical Laboratory, ISI. K. P. Chattopadhyay, Head, Department of Anthropology, Calcutta University did the pilot survey, and also guided the field work for the larger project. The Report: 'A Sample Survey of After-Effects of the Bengal Famine of 1943' was published in *Sankhy* 7, part 4 (1946): 337–400.

20 Provincial Statistical Bureau, *Bengal: A Short-Term Enquiry into the Living Conditions of the Bengali Middle Class 'Bhadralok' With a View to Estimating a Minimum Wage* (Calcutta: Bengal Government Press, 1946).

It was followed by A Supplementary Note in the same year. This comes closer to this research on a number of accounts like the period of its data collection (1944–45 and a focus on the middle-class *bhadralok* with a salary of Rs. 35 per month.)

21 S. Janardhan Poti, 'A Study of Expenditure Patterns of Calcutta Middle-Class Family Budgets', Statistical Laboratory, Indian Statistical Institute, Kolkata, *Sankhyā*: 7, part 4 (1946).

22 S. Bhattacharyya, 'World War II and the Consumption Pattern of the Calcutta Middle Class', *Sankhyā*: 8 (1947).

23 *Report on an Enquiry into the Family Budgets of Middle-Class Employees of the Central Government* (Delhi: Government of India Publications Branch; Shimla: Government of India Press, 1949), A Government of India survey.

24 West Bengal State Statistical Bureau, *Report on the Comparative Costs of Living in the Different Towns of West Bengal During November 1950* (Calcutta: West Bengal Government Press, 1955).

25 West Bengal State Statistical Bureau, *Family Budget Enquiry in 23 Towns of West Bengal Including Calcutta, 1950–51* (Calcutta: West Bengal Government Press, West Bengal, 1954). This survey covered 'the menial and middle classes of people at Calcutta and Asansol': 5. Statistical analysis was made on 56.33 per cent of family budgets showing a monthly expenditure between Rs. 101 and Rs. 200 and Rs. 201 and Rs. 350.

26 *Report on an Enquiry into the Family Budgets of Middle-Class Employees of the Central Government*: iii.

27 *A Short-Term Enquiry into the Living Conditions of the Bengali Middle Class 'Bhadralok' With a View to Estimating a Minimum Wage.*

28 Ibid.: 4.

29 *Report on an Enquiry into the Family Budgets of Middle-Class Employees of the Central Government*: iii.

30 Bhattacharyya, 'World War II and the Consumption Pattern of the Calcutta Middle Class': 197.

31 *Family Budget Enquiry in 23 Towns Including Calcutta, 1950–51* refrained from 'choosing arbitrarily the classes of people for whom indexes could be prepared, such as, upper classes, middle classes, working classes etc., the [State Statistical] Bureau has defined, purely on statistical basis, expenditure levels for which the indexes were expected to be different from one another'. *Family Budget Enquiry in 23 Towns Including Calcutta, 1950–51*: Preface.

32 *A Sample Survey of After-Effects of the Bengal Famine of 1943*: 371.

33 Ibid.: 342.

34 Ibid.: 365. See also Tarakchandra Das, *Bengal Famine (1943): As Revealed in a Survey of the Destitutes in Calcutta* (Calcutta: University of Calcutta, 1949).

35 *A Sample Survey of After-Effects of the Bengal Famine of 1943*: 370.

36 Bhattacharyya, 'World War II and the Consumption Pattern of the Calcutta Middle Class': 197, 198 and 200. See also Dipankor Coondoo, 'Everyday Consumption and Level of Living: Economists' Approach', in *Pratyaha: Everyday Lifeworlds: Dilemmas, Contestations and Negotiations*, edited by Prasanta Ray and Nandini Ghosh (New Delhi: Primus 2016): Chapter 13.

37 *Report on an Enquiry into the Family Budgets of Middle Class Employees of the Central Government*: 51.
38 Saving in Provident Fund would be normal for those in government employment. The samples in some major enquiries were drawn from them. See *Report on the Comparative Costs of Living in the Different Towns of West Bengal During November 1950* (Calcutta: West Bengal Government Press, 1955).
39 Ibid.
40 See Table 20. 'Family Budget Enquiry of Middle Class Employees, 1945–46', in *A Short-Term Enquiry into the Living Conditions of the Bengali Middle Class 'Bhadralok' With a View to Estimating a Minimum Wage*: 71.
41 Bhattacharyya, 'World War II and the Consumption Pattern of the Calcutta Middle Class': 198.
42 See Table 20, *A Short-Term Enquiry into the Living Conditions of the Bengali Middle Class Bhadralok*: 71.
43 Dalia Chakrabarti, *Colonial Clerks: A Social History of Deprivation and Domination* (Kolkata: K. P. Bagchi & Company, 2005): 62, 56.
44 M. S. Gore, 'India', in *The Role of Savings and Wealth in Southern Asia and the West*, edited by Richard D. Lambert and Bert F. Hoselitz (Paris: UNESCO 1963): 216. Gore continues to observe: 'Both these sources [Provident Fund and Life Insurance] are tapped by the government for investment in the public sector. It would appear, therefore, that industrial capital in India is still from the business classes'.
45 *A Short-Term Enquiry into the Living Conditions of the Bengali Middle Class 'Bhadralok'*: 4.
46 C 183 B, vol. 1, F 1339.
47 Franklin Henry Giddings, *The Principles of Sociology: An Analysis of the Phenomena of Association and of Social Organization* (London: Macmillan and Co., 1896): 16–20.

4

THE LOSERS' RESPONSES

The victims of a bank collapse anywhere anytime are a heterogeneous group comprising loanees, shareholders, depositors and employees. Some of them have or find the means to recover from the resultant monetary loss. Some find it difficult, even impossible. This second category is usually referred to by expressions, as noted earlier, like the 'ordinary depositor' and the 'middle class'/'lower middle class'; in some usage as 'ordinary middle-class depositor'.[1] Going by the salary earned, the bank employees, particularly those in the category of office assistants/clerks and of the menial staff, belonged to the middle class/lower middle class. Reckoning with this category is important because many of them suffered a threefold loss: loss of employment, loss of savings and loss of face. These positional adjectives are implicit in another collective noun 'refugee', a category of victims we examine here. The women, whose stories of sufferance due to the same banking crisis we reproduce here, also belong to the category of 'ordinary middle class'. But this class location was unimportant because their loss was in the sphere of an intimate relationship. The entire episode involved the early twentieth-century multi-layered Bengali *bhadralok* community.

Universally, the losers' first response is to come together and gather in the public space in front of the locked bank, and express their individual and collective anxiety about the fate of their savings and about the quality of life. The sense of panic becomes infectious. One of the early representations of this is the illustration in Frank Leslie's Illustrated Newspaper, 4 October 1873: 'The Panic – Run on the Fourth National Bank', No. 20 Nassau Street, New York, 4 October 1873. The wood engraved print shows men huddled together and conversing with each other, and some of them trying to reach the first-floor office of a bank.[2] For the banking crisis in Bengal in the 1940s, we have a nearly similar representation in Satyajit Ray's film, *Mahanagar* (The

Big City) (1963). In both, the front space was the site for expression of a wide range of emotions: anxiety, fear, anger and despondency. After this first spontaneous collective reaction, the vulnerable stakeholders took recourse to various interventions, as it is everywhere every time.

We first turn to the lower-rank-holding employees and the ordinary depositors. The more numerous middle class, particularly its lower fractions, tried a number of ways to bring their loss to the attention of the relevant authorities. Some of these were collective efforts; some were individual representations of collective dismay and anger. None was politically inspired although at least one politician took the lead. There were no processions, strikes or sit-ins or violent reactions against the greedy men, the greedy institutions and an inept state. A strike was proposed by all bank employees in 1948, which was immediately criticized for being politically motivated and against the interests of the nation. This was following the call by the Central Bank of India employees for a one-day strike. Dr. Suresh Chandra Banerji, the President of the West Bengal Provincial Congress Committee, condemned the move as harmful for society. If undertaken, he thought, this would destroy the Bengali middle-class intelligentsia. The small Bengali-run banks where the middle class deposited their savings would be in deep crisis. He was confident that those Congressmen who believed in establishing socialism in a rule-bound way, would not join the August 14th maidan rally in support of the proposed strike (*Ananda Bazar Patrika*, 15 August 1948). There were only complains made to some appropriate authority. In fact, in a few cases the complainants chose to remain anonymous as in a letter to His Excellency the High Commissioner of India in Pakistan by 34 unnamed individuals from Chittagong on 14 April 1949. This has already been referred above.[3]

An example of collective representation by the depositors is the letter by the depositors of the Nath Bank. They, as the petition claimed, were representing the depositors of other failed banks also. The crisis became the initiator of a new bond, a bond among the defrauded clients. We have already noticed the formation of such sentiments among the traders, probably small traders. There was a pronounced concern for 'the lower-middle-class people, refugees from East Bengal, minors and widows and a few charitable and educational institutions'. There was a special mention of the interest of the Bengali depositors in East Bengal because the bank (along with four other banks to be amalgamated) had its origin in erstwhile East Bengal. Hence the bond among the victims of bank failures was much more widespread. The 'hard lot' was just about the only measure of the diminishing standard of living for the victims. The connotation of the terse estimate – hard lot – is not lost in the light of middle-class family budget surveys for a fair idea of a sense of insecurity overwhelming the hapless people.

The disempowering impact of loss of deposits based on a life's incremental savings was not confined to a fall in standard of living. They were helpless in the face of some 'influential debtors induc(ing) a group of depositors in favour of liquidation while the old management and interested employees try to form a rival group and the group which can secure majority votes carry the day'.[4] We have already noticed how debtors used their social position and networks to deny the faltering banks the funds they needed to meet their obligations to the depositors. Yet they could think of no other solution than amalgamation. As the Nath Bank management claimed: 'The bank has been urged by its numerous depositors to press with the Reserve Bank the question of its amalgamation with the other four banks in West Bengal'.[5] Suropati Chakraborty, the founder-chairman of *Deshlaksmi* Bank in Narendranath Mitra's *Sahridaya* was similarly requested by his employees to opt for amalgamation when his bank was facing closure. That would have secured the savings of the ordinary depositors and the livelihood of the poor employees. But he did not yield because that would diminish his domineering position and expose his misdeeds. Despite apprehensions about the eventual adversity, the Nath bank union appealed to the governor of the RBI for the same solution.

> It is your good self who only can bring about this amalgamation by compelling the other units (Nath Bank's co-bankers). Most of them, we believe, will come down to save from this calamity the interests of their fellow East Bengal refugees who form the majority of the creditors of the Bank. This amalgamation will strengthen the faith in banking among the people of Bengal, maybe of India, and save forty thousand of creditors from ruin.[6] The bank union was proud of the bank as it felt that the Nath Bank has played the role of Dadhichi in Hindu mythology who expressed his veneration to the gods by giving up his own life to save others; the bank played a similar role by deciding in favour of amalgamation.

Such interventions were not by the Nath Bank employee's union alone. Many other bank employee unions did the same though the employees had no idea of their future after amalgamation. The employees' associations of the Comilla Banking Corporation, the Bengal Central Bank,

the Comilla Union Bank and the Hooghly Bank in a joint letter pointed
out that 'none of the employers has so far discussed with us the future
set-up of service conditions and security of service in four amalgamating
banks'. However, they were confident that the 'employees' association
know the drawbacks of the existing institutions and can help in proper
reconstruction of the Banks to safeguard national interest.[7]

The offending banks were known to the employees' associations. The
Calcutta Clearing Banks Association 'black listed' them.[8] But this did not
enable them to extract from the state a positive response. This is amply
proved by the futility of the appeal by the Nath Bank depositors as indicated by the official note on the petition by the Nath Bank depositors.[9]

The Governor,
Reserve Bank of India,
Camp – Calcutta.
Dated, Calcutta, the 14th March, 1950.

Dear Sir,

We the undersigned depositors of Nath Bank Ltd., for ourselves
and echoing the sentiments of other depositors of that Bank and
similar other suspended banks beg leave to request you to consider the hard lot of depositors amongst whom there are lower
middle class people, refugees from East Bengal, minors and widows and a few charitable and educational institutions too.

It is our bitter experience that after the failure of many banks
in Bengal neither liquidation nor scheme of management could
bring real benefit to the depositors for reasons of which we do
not like to dilate here.

There are defects and pitfalls in the process of liquidation and
scheme of arrangement is worked out by or under the influence of
old management, and the depositors having no other choice left
to them accept one or other as unavoidable evil, and it is common
experience that influential debtors induce a group of depositors
in favour of liquidation while the old management and interested
employees try to form a rival group and the group which can
secure majority votes carry the day.

Now that the Reserve Bank has given its blessings to the scheme
of amalgamation of 4 principal Bengalee managed banks we
take this opportunity especially when you have pleased to come
to the spot to have first hand information, to appeal to you to
include Nath Bank Ld, (and if possible similar other suspended

banks) in the scheme of amalgamation. In this context we beg to draw your kind attention to the Editorial of the Amrita Bazar Patrika dated 11.3.50 which represents the views of the depositors and the general public (cutting enclosed).

We hope our appeal will not be treated as merely sentimental. We have much weightier reasons.

The scheme of amalgamation under the aegis of the Reserve Bank to be successful and for restoring lost confidence of depositors in Bengal should be extended to Nath Bank Ltd, especially in view of the fact that this bank (Nath Bank) and three out of 4 amalgamating banks have their origins in East Bengal and have got many common depositors and constituents.

We hope our appeal will receive due and most sympathetic consideration at your hands.

Yours faithfully,

Nandalal Banerjee
47/1 Garihat Road
Snigdhendu Basu
16B Bepin Pal Road
Bhabesh Mukherjee
171 A R. B Avenue
J. N DasPurkyastha
23 Janak Road
Ananatadev Dutt
22, South End Park
P. C Chatterjee
Bamunpara Lane, P. O Howrah
KrishnaLal Nath
P. O. Kasba
Suresh Ch Saha
Dacca Dairy, Lake Market
Ajit Chakraborty
Bally, Howrah
Jgendrachandra Choudhury
110/1 Amherst Street, Calcutta

> Note: The depositors' plead for the intervention of the Reserve Bank for the amalgamation of the Nath Bank with the other four banks, as neither its liquidation nor scheme of arrangement extends any hope for the depositors. No

action on our part, however, appears necessary at this stage.
22 March 1950
Source: C266-VOL. 1 F 1744, RBI Archive, Pune, India

So the victims remained uncertain of recovery of their loss.

There was hardly any individual representation on the part of the ordinary depositors. In 1948, two letters to the Editor were published in the Bengali news daily *Ananda Bazar Patrika*. There is no clue whether the letter writers were depositors who had lost their personal savings. But the writers had in mind the necessity of a vigorous and trustworthy banking system in Bengal rather than their own individual loss. However, both the letters reveal an ethnic bias against the non-Bengali community nurtured by many Bengalis then.

Sir,

The reasons why the sphere of banking is in distress today are different and hence the [re]organisation of the Bengali-run banks is needed. Because of closing down of some Bengali-run banks from time to time in the last few months, it is difficult for even the well-directed Bengali-run banks to do business outside of this province, and the expansion of non-Bengali run banks day by day in Bengal is also evident. I think that, in these circumstances, the functioning [Bengali-run] banks need to be amalgamated with each other. If that would take place, then a few immediate benefits are possible, like (1) the financial condition of these banks will be on firm foundation, and (2) trustworthiness [of the banks] to the people will easily resume.

But the amalgamation envisaged above will be possible only when associated directors will give up a little of their self-interest. In the interest of the nation, I request the concerned authorities to think over this proposal.

Sri Alok Kumar Ghosh

24 Strand Road,
Calcutta
Ananda Bazar Patrika

May 11, 1948

The second letter was cynical about the outcome of the empowerment of the RBI in re-invigoration of the Bengali-run banks, which was upper-most in the Bengali mind.

117

Respected Sir,

At last the central government has granted certain special powers to the Reserve Bank by ordinance. Thus empowered, the reserve Bank can henceforth render help to the imperilled banks, and make necessary arrangements to revive those banks which are in distress because of incompetent management.

In spite of that, after the closure of four Bengali-run scheduled banks in the last two weeks, there are enough reasons to doubt to what extent this ordinance can bring around the Bengali-run banks.

When, the prospect of Bengali-run banks has become bleak because of the non-co-operation of banks run by non-Bengalis on the one hand, and the depositors' indiscretion on the other, then we need enormous mental strength. Now the Reserve Bank is ready to lend to the Scheduled banks against adequate security. Consequently, now the imminent crisis probably will be overcome. But we shall have to adopt new plan to gradually revive the weak banks and use them for the prosperity of the nation. Even now, no single Bengali-run bank can compete with a non-Bengali-run big bank; but a few together can. So the main way to avoid the crisis is to create a new powerful bank. Such an arrangement will help regain the trust of the depositors. We think that one excellent bank in India will be created if the capital, deposit and efforts of four to five banks will be amalgamated. Hence we want that rather than remain emaciated after losing the general trust, the Bengali-run banks should be amalgamated to find their appropriate place in the all-India competition.

Sri Kalipada Bagchi

Baharampur
Ananda Bazar Patrika

September 25, 1948
Upper-most in their mind was the task of retrieval of trust in Bengali-run banks and, fundamentally in themselves – rather than recovery of their own financial loss.

The three women

Monetary loss is the usual indicator of fatality of bank disasters. This is not without reason. But it is also true that such disasters in their adverse consequences take the victims to a moral abyss, much beyond a diminishing of access to life chances available in the market. As the victims, the forced migrants and the middle-class figure in official records, political representations, editorials and news coverages, personal petitions and researches in the academia. Needless to say, the categories – the forced migrants and the middle class – are not exclusive. But the sufferings of women as intrinsically women deserve a special attention. Women bear a cost even when they do not lose money because a bank falters. The 'cost' is suffered in private places like home and household, and thus it remains outside of public reckoning. To make sense of it, we need to move beyond 'the economists' intellectual domain' and conceive money as social and cognize

> domestic money – which includes wife's money, husband's money, and children's money . . . a special category of money in the modern world. Its meanings, uses, allocation, and even quantity are partly determined by considerations of economic efficiency, but domestic money is equally shaped by changing cultural conceptions of money and of family life as well as by power relationships, age, and gender.[10]

Usually, women's victimization remains unnoticed because of 'androcentric blinders'.[11] A study on forced migrants in Bengal which opened up space for a separate listing of what women refugees want the state to provide to them is an exception.[12] Given the mention of the refugees and the middle class in available reports and representations, we need to focus on them in any conjecture on the loss suffered by them due to bank failures. But we need to remember that a few charitable institutions and schools also suffered financial loss.

In search of the victims of bank run, we now move from categories to characters. We stay still within the frames of unobtrusive data, though move away from statistics to texts. The location of the characters – the three women – has been somewhat serendipitous, particularly the characters in literary texts. The attention is on three women: Sujata, Arati and Nihar Bala. The first two are the protagonists in two novellas – *Sahridaya* and *Abataranika* by Narendranath Mitra, the last one being the basis of Satyajit Ray's film *Mahanagar*.[13] Unlike Nihar Bala,[14] Sujata and Arati are fictional characters. But they are not unreal. The author wrote in his preface to the English translation of *Abataranika*:

> About three years before India was partitioned and Bengal was divided into two parts, refugees from East Bengal were

flocking into Calcutta, searching for shelter and a means of livelihood. . . . I was quite close to many such families and it was, no doubt, my intimacy with them that inspired me to write . . . a story called 'Abataranika'. . . . About three years ago I transformed this story into a short novel [*Mahanagar*].[15]

Of the three, only Nihar Bala lost her deposit due to collapse of a bank. In her letter to Jawaharlal Nehru – that is why she has found a place in archival records – the loss beyond her savings is not evident, but implicit. She was active in public space like the categories of the victims analysed above, because to both the state was the institution to be looked up for succour. Its failure to provide that made it an object of critique for both. She also chose the same mode of petition – in her case – to the highest functionary of the post-colonial Indian state. Sujata is the daughter of an excessively ambitious banker, Suropati, typical of the times in Bengal: a flurry of entrepreneurial adventures. Arati is the wife of a poorly paid bank employee, who becomes a working woman much against the wishes of her in-laws and the mis-givings of her helpless husband, Subrata. Greedy Suropati mismanages his bank, and eventually shuts it down. A vulnerable Subrata loses his job because his bank has a 'run'.

While the struggles of Sujata and Arati are primarily in the pri-vate sphere of home, Nihar Bala contends with the prime minister of the country. Patriarchy is not merely an undefined context in all the three 'stories'. Because, the tragedies that engulf the women are due to moral collapse of intimate men in their lives: Suropati with his greed, ambition and lack of scruples; and Subrata with his challenged masculinity. Nihar Bala's story is different because there is no male protagonist because it does not have a familial setting. Her story is located beyond the family institutional site, that of the state. She is not like a feminist now who perceives the state as a male institution. If one chooses to gloss over the differences, the three texts – Nihar Bala's petition and the two novellas – can be seen as one story only: of a run on the banks and ruin of existential conditions and sensibilities; and of woman's agency brought out by contingencies, not of their creation.

All the three women are different from the usual stereotype of weak, vulnerable and submissive human beings. They continuously contend with men in the household (Sujata), men in the household and the workplace (Arati) and men – powerful men – in the public domain (Nihar Bala). In their moral engagement, they all win: Sujata preventing her father from a gory act of shooting his employee whom his daughter admires, dying a victim of a man's (father's) reckless-ness and follies of few other men, but exonerating all of them before her death; Arati protesting a racist slur on a colleague by her male employer, and giving up her job on which only everybody including a jobless husband depends. Morals of the two women have not been vitiated by any base human proclivity; Nihar Bala mustering courage to warn the premier with the possibility of the rise of the communists if the state would continue to ignore the plight of the common deposi-tors due to liquidation of banks. They refuse to be dismissed as frail victims. They tell the stories of many trapped in the same predicament.

Among the three women, Nihar Bala Sett of Sukhchar in 24-Par-ganas, West Bengal, is the only one who counts and recounts the loss suffered by 'many persons of middle-class people' – by her understand-ing, 'several thousands of West Bengal middle-class people' – between 1945 and 1950 in terms of money: 'more than Rs. 150,000,000'. There is no indication of the basis of her estimates, though. But the way she writes the numbers clearly suggests that, to her, the number of victims and the amount lost by them are exceptionally large. She is correct about the middle class being hard hit by the collapse of the banking system. This Bengali middle class was already under severe stress. *Capital* made the point:

> Many observers of economic conditions in this country have pointed to the effect of soaring prices of consumer goods and increased taxation during and since the war on the middle class, whose saving capacity previously supplied the invest-ment market with a supply of funds which now seem to have disappeared; and have suggested an important shift of income to industrial and agricultural labour.[16]

This middle class lost whatever little they had managed to save in the banks which discontinued business.

From: Sm. NiharBalaSett.*

P.O. Sukhchar, 24-Parganas, West Bengal.

22.4.1952

To: Hon'ble Sri J. L Nehru,
Premier of Indian Government,
India, New Delhi.

Sub: Liquidated Bank's case

Dear Sir,

I beg to draw your kind attention on the following facts for favour of your kind consideration and requested to take action on the following facts at your earliest convenience:

1   Perhaps you are aware of the facts that how many Calcutta Banks with their average 30 to 40 branches had been liquidated by the Hon'ble High Court, Calcutta in between the year 1945 to 1950 and perhaps you are also aware that how many persons of middle class people had suffered in this Bank crisis, where more than Rs. 150,000,000/- had been lost.

2   In many cases the official liquidator had been appointed by the Hon'ble High Court, Calcutta – but our present laws are such that it is only become good boom period for the officers of the above as there is section mentioned by the Assistant Registrar, High Court that if any one complains against the Official Liquidator then he must file a petition in the Law of Justice at High Court for redress though these officers are under the Officials of Hon'ble High Court.

3   Many sufferers have asked our Government to intervene and to expedite the Liquidated Banks' A/C, but to their surprise the settlement is a myth. Nobody understands the real cause of this unusual delay. People asked to work more by our beloved leaders of the Government but who sleeps and who works is a great question here.

4   Is it not a fact that our present leaders are mere a show boy in the hands of mystic laws and are allowing themselves to be played by their I.C.S and B.C.S officers? Or shall we understand that these leaders have got no such moral courage to ask explanation from these officers mentioned thereto or shall we understand that these leaders are only make propagandas for the sake of rich people of India, or shall we understand that these leaders are cordially welcoming Communism within our country or shall we understand that the leaders of our Government are so morally blunt as every free nations have the right to change the implicated laws in the House of Parliament and the same time the leaders can help the sufferers and make themselves to be proved as a worthy person to all his subject.

5   Here it is cleared that there is none in this Free India who can
    change or amend the laws of court as we are a lay man in law
    or laws we do not know the complication of laws or we do
    not know the Philosophy or Human Science so we will not to
    be able to give you our suggestions about the defect of laws –
    the leaders in our mind as like 'ALNESKER' who wanted to
    build castle in the air but they are not perhaps aware of the
    reality of the facts.[17]
6   Do you know how many amount of rupees (Rs. 150,000,000/-)
    had been lost from the vast population of middle class? Per-
    haps you are not aware that several thousands of West Ben-
    gal middle class people had been compelled to face a worst
    position than that of East and West Pakistan Refugees – there
    is a help, aid and support of these East and West Pakistan
    Refugees but Alas!!! There is no help and support for middle
    class people and thus you are depriving your own subject and
    the result perhaps you are not aware. . . .
7   Our leaders of India is very afraid of communism but a lay
    man in rural area will surely say that we have lost our money
    in the Bank though it was scheduled and affiliated by the
    Reserve Bank of India, which is only meant for the Big Pandas
    who are only know how to squeeze the poors and sufferers –
    but alas Big Pandas are sleeping with oil in their nose – a case
    has been proved in the speech of Sk. Abdullya of Kashmir and
    who can say what is written in our fate but these leaders are
    welcoming communism which is the Worst Fate of India.
8   We are afraid of communism but we shall be compelled to
    join our hands with hope that we may get some active help
    from the above as we have appreciated the National Congress
    men in the past.

    Under the circumstances, as we expect a better thing from you
so we are placing our grievances for an immediate action failing
which we shall lose our confidence on you.
    As a lay woman in writing a letter to you I beg to be excused
for any such matters which may pinch you but the case is a very
very true – but if you are late only God may tell what is written
in our fate.
    Anxiously awaiting the favour of your kind confirmation and
thanking you in anticipation at an earliest date.

Copy forwarded to the:

Hon'ble Dr. Harendra Kumar Mukerjee, Governor of West Bengal, Calcutta.
Hon'ble Dr. B. C. Roy, Premier of West Bengal, Calcutta.
Hon'ble Sri. Joty [Jyoti] Bose, M.L.A., Calcutta.
Hon'ble Dr. Shyama Prosad Mukerjee, of 77, Ashutosh Mukerjee Road, Calcutta.
Leader of the opposition group [group] in the Council House, Calcutta.

. . . . . . for favour of their information and requested to save us, from the hands of these calamity.
Yours faithfully,

Sd. (NIHAR BALA SETT.)
* F 1339: Liquidation of Banking Cos. (01.05.51–16.7.52)
[C183B, vol. 1]

Nihar Bala was a middle-class woman from West Bengal, and not a refugee from East Pakistan. In most of the representations to the state by politicians and in newspaper reports on the banking crisis, the plight of the refugees from East Pakistan is highlighted. Nihar Bala did not appreciate this. She decided to represent the Bengalis from the western part of Bengal. She regretted in her letter to the Premier:

Perhaps you are not aware that several thousands of West Bengal middle class people had been compelled to face a worst position than that of East and West Pakistan Refugees – there is a help, aid and support of these East and West Pakistan Refugees but Alas!!! There is no help and support for middle class people and thus you are depriving your own subject and the result perhaps you are not aware. . . ..

She seemed to be slow in coming out of the colonial mind-set because she still located herself as a subject, and not a citizen which she had become in the post-colonial constitutional order. But her political wit was robust because a little later in her letter she expressed her apprehension of the rise of the communists as 'the result perhaps you are not aware' as if she was holding out to the most powerful authority the possibility of being out-stripped by the communists. She believed that 'Our leaders of India is very afraid of communism'.

She wrote in English, mainly in poor English. But to her, English was the language of the powerful and the officialdom as well as of those who wanted to contend with such power. She had a keen sense of the ways of the powerful, the ministers and the bureaucrats, and of the possible political fall-out of growing economic crisis in Bengal and in India. She wrote to the 'Premier', 'Hon'ble Sri J.L Nehru', because she realized the futility of appealing to the local leaders.[18] Did she dismiss them as only of a secondary reference, because she forwarded a copy of the letter to them, did not write to them? In any case, that points to her understanding of the limitations of the sub-national power structure in Bengal: 'Dr. Harendra Kumar Mukerjee, Governor of West Bengal', 'Dr. B. C. Roy, Premier of West Bengal', 'Sri. Joty Bose, M.L.A', 'Dr. Shyama Prosad Mukerjee, of 77, Ashutosh Mukerjee Road, Calcutta' and 'Leader of the opposition groop [sic] in the Council House'. Her audacity to write to the highest power-holder of the country was bred out of dismay and desperation.

What did Nihar Bala lose apart from her money? She lost her trust in public authority, in fact the new found post-colonial authority. What struck her was the power of the new legal regime. She sensed it but was not in a position to fully comprehend the laws. But she was definite that the laws, instead of helping the distressed, contributed to their misery. To her, even the leaders, who could re-structure law (to help the victims of financial fraud), seemed to be as powerless as the common people. 'Here it is cleared that there is none in this Free India who can change or amend the laws of court'. It is evident in the question she raised:

> Is it not a fact that our present leaders are mere a show boy in the hands of mystic laws and are allowing themselves to be played by their I.C.S and B.C.S officers? . . . or shall we understand that these leaders are cordially welcoming Communism within our country.

She was confused by the ways of the authorities:

> In many cases the official liquidator had been appointed by the Hon'ble High Court, Calcutta – but our present laws are such that it is only become good boom period for the officers

of the above as there is section mentioned by the Assistant Registrar, High Court that if any one complains against the Official Liquidator then he must file a petition in the Law of Justice at High Court for redress though these officers are under the Officials of Hon'ble High Court.

She had contempt only for public institutions: 'a lay man in rural area will surely say that we have lost our money in the Bank though it was scheduled and affiliated by the Reserve Bank of India'.

She was apparently unwilling to be a passive sufferer because she spelled out the next course of action: 'We are afraid of communism but . . . we may get some active help from the above as we have appreciated the National Congress men in the past'.

Nihar Bala was a private person because she was silent in her letter of how the loss of her financial security had created disorientation in her intimate relationships. She was appalled by the plight of the middle class in West Bengal, to which she belonged. For her, it was a public issue to be addressed to a public institution only. Her civility ('I beg to draw your kind attention') was a matter of formality rather than a restraint on a host of her negative emotions. She was unyielding although she talked of destiny – her and the nation's. The stories of Sujata and Arati disclose another order of loss, but within their intimate circles of relationships. Nihar Bala loathed the sloth and the complicity of the state and its powerful incumbents. Her indictment of the unscrupulous banks responsible for ruining the lives of the people in her class and the community was implicit.

Bank failure does not produce economic insecurity for Sujata. It hurts her deeper – at the level of her sensibility. She eventually loses more – her life. Her misery is not directly because of the failure of a bank. It is due to greed of her father. His greed is as much his moral depravity exacerbated by aggressive masculinity as it is a symptom of times.

Suropati Chakraborty in Narendranath Mitra's *Sahridaya* represents the breed of enterprising bankers in Bengal. He is a very successful banker who has developed a small and under-staffed bank, Deshlaksmi Bank, in a rented flat in Calcutta's central business district, into the most prominent bank in Bengal with a chain of branch offices in other Indian cities; all by himself, his hard work and business sense. To him 'the mystery of money is more intriguing than abstruseness of a woman's mind, [it is] a tangled knot'. His relentless pursuit of wealth is almost erogenous. He is too willing to adopt any means which will further his business interest. His appearance bears it out:

> Curved by tortuous lines, the face is longish with a prominent jawbone and impaired cheeks. As if somebody has painted the lips with deep black colour, the sight of which reminds one of a leech, and one who sees it has an uncanny physical sensation . . . the sunken chin with the lips appear to be most merciless and ferocious.

Could this be an archetype of the greedy banker in those times?[19]

He is cautioned about his violation of business norms and the resultant risk of losing his bearing by his close friend. But Suropati eases him out of the board of directors of the bank in favour of an upcoming oil trader, who has invested a very large amount of money in Deshlaksmi Bank. In fact, Suropati is particularly interested in large investments from oil merchants and iron merchants.

His friend is not the only victim of Suropati's wayward business behaviour nursed by his insatiable ambition for riches. His wife, when alive, used to plead with him: 'Mind you, it is better that you remain poor but never think of doing wrong and injustice to others'. Suropati would retort:

> Listen, there is no correspondence between your [cherished] sacred stories and prayer poems in praise of deities with the worldly life. Its ways and customs are different. You live in the world of your religious values [represented by goddesses Lakshmi and Durga]; let me build my own world.

The well-meaning caution from his daughter, around whom widower Suropati's emotional life revolves, suffers the same fate. He is insistent on keeping morals and pursuit of wealth apart. Neither virtue ordained by religion nor reason based on experience, neither a woman's concern for her dear one nor a friend's anxiety for another's dignity, can restrain his greed for wealth and social standing. No wonder, the formation of a trade union of ill-paid bank employees in his organization is vehemently resented by him.

His relentless and devious search for capital is natural to his conception of masculine self. He believes that men set rules only to break them as and when the situation so requires. They have their own ways.

In order to reach the great highways, they have to traverse tortuous pathways. Once the men are successful, those pathways fade away on their own; even the men who have utilized them forget their use. Suropati has another justification for his endeavour.

> People trust [me] fully [and] hand over to me huge sums of their hard-earned money. Hence I have to keep an incessant vigil on their property notwithstanding risk and great hardship. The vigil is not for keeping the money under lock and key in safes but for circulation amongst people of the country for their welfare through banking services.

It is not without significance that he has named his bank as Deshlaksmi Bank, the bank for the wealth of the nation. A similar legitimatization is by the real-life bankers, like Narendra Laha. But deep down, Suropati is committed only to furthering his wealth as his closest confidant, a bank director and the intended son-in-law has found out.

> Suropati does not love his bank, he only loves himself. And his self-interest is only in money, conceived in digital measures alone. He has never given up an iota of self-interest when his own interest has conflicted with that of his bank.

Nor would he stay calculation of his gains even when his mainstay, the bank, starts floundering. Even when the bank's earnings have dropped by a half, he fakes profit in annual report on its status; just like Shipuchin in *The Anniversary*[20]and Samaresh in *Sedin Bangolakshmi Bankey* (In Bangolakshmi Bank on That Day).[21] This for him is a ploy to maintain the reputation of the bank and sustain employees' confidence in its viability. He does not believe in bad omens and takes calamities as a part of life experience of any enterprising man. Three other banks collapse in Calcutta; even his own bank has a 'run'. But he still exudes confidence in his public appearances. When the crisis eventually climaxes, Suropati secretively conspires with his trusted but apprehensive friend, to close down the bank. He even asserts his ability to bear the pain due to the sudden loss of his social esteem. He tells him at one point of time that there is some truth in his critics' assessment that he is heartless and hard like bricks. But he considers this to be the source of his strength and stamina.

He actually decides to run away secretively from the loss-making bank beyond the reach of the various stakeholders in their moment of reckoning. He does not believe in drowning in a sinking boat. For him, it is manly to swim to safety, and build anew. This is what he thinks of himself. But to those who have observed his ways from closest quarters, Suropati's strength is like that of a merciless hangman who can destroy anything, anybody to protect himself. And that he does by way of closing the bank, suddenly and surreptitiously. He pays hefty sums of money to his close employees to keep their mouth shut till he can execute his plan (of closing the bank). He enjoys immunity from public attention to unscrupulous bankers because of a public belief that Suropati would never damage his bank which is so dear to his heart, a belief he has carefully induced and nurtured over the years.

He reveals his unrestrained greed as he appropriates depositors' money even at the time of closing the bank. He ruins the poor employees, too, because he is unwilling to amalgamate his bank with viable banks because that would diminish his dominant position. Had he done this, the (deposited) money of the common people would have remained with them, and the poor employees and workers would not have missed their basic daily necessities. The public reaction to the sudden closure of the bank is collective expression of anger. Weak and hopeless, the ordinary depositors manage to fall back on everyday commonplace abuse. One can hear much shouting in front of the bank. Public anger disobeys the rules of decency. Slandering of Suropati becomes increasingly louder. Somebody enquires: 'Where is the big thief, get hold of him'; somebody thinks that he has escaped in the meantime. Suropati had already eluded the sense of shame, a cultural mechanism which mutes individual drives like greed. Shame is 'a kind of anxiety' due to 'fear of social degradation or, more generally, of other people's gesture of superiority'.[22]

At a personal level, the reaction on the part of the victims is of inconsolable anguish. A young widow, who is a teacher at corporation primary school, deposited about 2,000 rupees given to her by the Life Insurance Corporation after her husband's death. Stunned by her loss, she wonders what would befall her, her widowed mother-in-law and a minor son. That was her only saving. She represents numerous poor lower-middle-class depositors: sad, perplexed by an apprehension of losing everything and being compelled to struggle against poverty, misery and want.

Sujata's loss is entirely at the level of personal relationship because, unlike Nihar Bala, she has not lost her savings, and she has no fellow depositors to grieve with or fight for. Sujata loses her life at the hands of her doting father. She dies trying to save two precious relationships:

one with an employee in her father's bank and who commands her respect and adoration because of his morals; the other, with her father, Suropati, whom she admires for his diligence and dreams. Greed's destructive powers impinge the moral chord of intimate relationships. A run on a bank is more than a financial collapse.

In *Abataranika*, the protagonist is Arati, wife of a lowly paid over-worked employee of Joylaksmi Bank. She belongs to the lower mid-dle class, unlike Sujata; may be like Nihar Bala. The bank, like many 'which sprouted during the Second World War in every nook and cor-ner and started rounding up in 1946/47', collapses due to the machina-tions of some 'dishonest men'. Subrata and many employees like him always have trusted the soundness of the bank where they worked. On hindsight, Subrata realizes that he has been kept misinformed by the management of what is otherwise already a public apprehension of an impending collapse. He sufferes the ignominy of being publicly beaten by irate depositors in front of the closed bank gate. This is graphically depicted in Satyajit Ray's film, *Mahanagar*. What does Arati lose? She loses an income-earning husband, who loses much more: discomfiture because even the children at home have come to know about his loss of employment, and a sense of self-respect in the face of a reassuring wife on whose paltry earning the household must now depend.

Arati is exceptionally understanding and calm. But her normal-ity and her resilience hurt her husband. She has to suffer a husband suddenly gripped by the threat of a role reversal at home, and of emasculation. She has to sustain his ego through an intricate mix of admonition and affection. That is no easy task because Subrata has had an ambivalent position with regard to his wife working till late in the evening and being fond of her male boss. But he has to compro-mise his male ego because of her monthly contribution of her hard-earned income. He develops such a stake in her income after losing the job that he discourages any friction at her office or with its clients, afraid that might cost her the job.

His suffering is much more complex; so is Arati's negotiation of his misery. Even before losing his job in the bank, Subrata has not liked her long working hours and proximity to men in course of her work. Unable to contain her ego and forced to concede her an increasingly critical place in the household, he re-lives his early memories of his father beating up his mother and wishes to replicate his 'barbarity, heartlessness and cruelty'. He does not like that he must be decent; more so, because of his father's relentless suggestion that obstinate women must be dealt with physical retribution. Torn asunder between perverse patriarchal proclivity, his *bhadralok* civility and probably a sense of security in her income, he becomes morally emaciated, a carcass of a man. He becomes her problem, and she is clueless how she can restore him to male confident self.

The other man is her father-in-law, never happy with a working *bahu* (daughter-in-law). As his son loses his job and an income of Rs. 150 and he loses a certain comfort, he wants his erstwhile students to replenish it. He is pulled out of his civility by greed driven by want. Arati has the unenviable task of protecting him in the face of admonitions at home. She becomes a consoling woman. But she is under pressure to read the male expressions to deliver the necessary emotional succour to the two men in distress in her life. At the same time, she must do what the men in her life aggressively guard as their exclusive preserve: take charge of livelihood and the household. She copes with her androgynous tensions until she gives up her job in a rare gesture of fellow-feeling. A bank fails, the lower-middle-class home becomes its epicentre, and the female protagonist becomes a wreck.

The crisis completely destroys her dream of a reasonably comfortable life in a rented house in a respectable neighbourhood and son's good schooling. She is unfeminized by the unexpected turn of events, and she stops looking up for manly guidance because there is none. Focused on survival, she redefines the necessities of everyday life: dismisses her domestic help; she reduces the provision for milk, just enough for her child and his grandfather; she even becomes the washer woman at home. She moves from tolerable hardship in her early conjugal life to an insufferable pain of moral loneliness.

These are the narratives of collateral damage of banking crisis: man's greed, woman's disaster.[23] There are more popular stories read and talked about in literate Bengali homes, which have the male protagonist's fortuitous money trapping his wife in infectious greed. However, her eventual moral panic compels her to regain moral sensibility.[24] Women in these two realist fictions have to bear the emotional cost of coping with unbearable stresses in their intimate relations as crisis in the public sphere spoils their private spaces. In fact, in the period under study, men writers and playwrights use women's voice, otherwise silenced, to articulate moral critique – Sujata (*Sahridaya*) and Arati (*Mahanagar*). It is either a robust moral position (Bijoya in *Kalo Taka*), or moral panic (Giribala in *Parash Pathar*) or feminine foreboding (Sujata in *Sahridaya*) or a strong sense of justice (Arati in *Mahanagar*), which makes women intervene to mend moral ruptures.

For Nihar Bala, it was her sense of relative deprivation prompting her to demand authoritative intervention and implementation of the legal framework. Unlike the other women, she was focused on money saved but lost.

Notes

1 Indrajit Mallick and Sugata Marjit, *Financial Intermediation in a Less Developed Economy: The History of the United Bank of India* (New Delhi: SAGE, 2008): 49.
2 This is a wood-engraving by an unknown artist. The panic led to a great economic depression in Europe between 1873 and 1879. Source: Illustration in Frank Leslie's Illustrated Newspaper, 4 October 1873, p. 67, www.loc.gov/item/2002723398/, accessed on 1 August 2017.
3 Ibid.: see Chapter 1, C 183 IV, F 1336.
4 C 266, vol. 1, F 1744, RBI Archive, Pune, India
5 Ibid.
6 Letter to the Governor, RBI, Cal. form Pramatha Nath Mukherjee, President, Nath Bank Employees' Association, 13 March 1950; C 266, vol. 1, F 1744, RBI Archive.
7 Letter to the Governor, RBI, Bombay by Employees' associations. AMG/1/5/50, 7 June 1950. C 266, vol. 2, F 1745, RBI Archive.
8 Extract from Letter No. DBO 300/SB. 98–46, 7 December 1946 from the Deputy Chief Officer, Reserve Bank of India, Calcutta, F 592 NC 143. The banks were: Bengal Commercial and Agricultural Bank Ltd., Bhowal Industrial Bank Ltd., Bogra City Bank Ltd., Calcutta Exchange Bank Ltd., Calcutta Standard Bank Ltd., City Commercial Bank Ltd., Civil Bank of India Ltd., Eastern National Bank Ltd., India Exchange Bank Ltd., Federation Bank of India Ltd., Great Bengal Bank Ltd., Hazardi Bank Ltd., Indian Standard Bank Ltd., Jubilee Development Bank Ltd., Jubilee Overseas Bank of India and Burma Ltd., Kusthia United Bank Ltd., Nabadwip Bank Ltd., National Central Bank Ltd., National Mercantile Bank Ltd., Pioneer Industrial Bank Ltd., Puri Bank Ltd., Rajasthan Bank Ltd., Security Bank Ltd., Shree Bharat Industrial Bank Ltd., Union Industrial Bank Ltd., Union Mercantile Bank Ltd., East India Commercial Bank Ltd., Central Pioneer Bank Ltd., Continental Bank of Asia Ltd.
9 C 266, vol. 1, F 1744, RBI Archive, Pune, India.
10 Viviana A. Zelizer, 'The Social Meaning of Money: "Special Monies"', *American Journal of Sociology* 95, 2 (September 1989): 344, published by the University of Chicago Press, www.jstor.org/stable/2780903, accessed on 28 October 2013, 05:57.
    'Domestic money is a special money, not just a medium of economic exchange but a meaningful, socially constructed currency, shaped by the domestic sphere where it circulates and by the gender and social class of its domestic "money handlers"': 370.
11 Nancy Folbre, *Greed, Lust and Gender: A History of Economic Ideas* (Oxford: Oxford University Press, 2009): 324.

12 B. S. Guha, *Studies in Social Tensions Among the Refugees From East Pakistan*, B. S. Guha Memoir No. 1, 1954 (Delhi: Department of Anthropology, Government of India, Manager of Publications, Calcutta: Government of India Press, 1959).

13 Originally a story, *Abataranika* (Descent) was published in 1948. *Mahanagar* (The Big City) is a film based on the story renamed and by Satyajit Ray (1963). Satyajit Ray in fact drew on another short story by the author *Akinchon* (Desire) (1954). See *Chitrabhas*: Special Issue on Unpublished Writings of Satyajit Ray, nos. 48, 49 (2015): 57. For *Mahanagar* see *Uponnyas Samagro: Narendranath Mitra* (Collection of Novels: Narendranath Mitra), vol. 3, compiled and edited by Abhijit Mitra (Kolkata: Ananda Publishers, 2008): 665–716. For *Abataranika*, see Abhijit Mitra, ed., *Galpomala* (A String of Stories), vol. 1 (Kolkata: Ananda Publishers, 1986): 122–143. For *Akinchon*, see Abhijit Mitra, ed., *Galpomala* (A String of Stories), vol. 2 (Kolkata: Ananda Publishers, 1989): 208–217. For *Sahridaya, Uponnyas Samagro*, vol. 2, 2007: 457–589.

14 F 1339: Liquidation of Banking Cos. (01.05.51–16.7.52) [C 183B, vol. 1], Reserve Bank of India Archive, Pune. There is reference to her in G. Balachandran, *The Reserve Bank of India, Volume 2: 1951–1967* (New Delhi: Oxford University Press): 457. But here greater attention has been paid to the whole text of her letter.

15 Quoted in Abhijit Mitra, *Uponnyas Samagro*, vol. 3: 818.

16 *Capital*, 16 November 1950: 754–755.

17 It is difficult to trace the mythological reference of ALNESKER. It could be that Nihar Bala meant *Alkêsvara*, lord of Alaka, that is, Kubera.

18 There is no record in the relevant file in the archive that Nihar Bala received replies from the premier or his office, or from the persons to whom copies of the letter were forwarded.

19 Unfortunately, Bengal did not have a contemporary artist drawing/painting the Bengali financier which could be compared to Suropati's facial demeanor as portrayed in the novella. We cannot look for correspondence between sociological and literary and portraitures as Robert Nisbet has done in his *Sociology as an Art Form* (Oxford: Oxford University Press, 1976): Chapter 4 (Sociological Portraits).

20 Anton Chekhov, *The Anniversary*, https://ebooks.adelaide.edu.au/c/chekhov/anton/plays2/chapter14.html, accessed on 13 May 2017.

21 Ajit Gangopadhyay, *Nirbodhe O Sedin Bangolakshmi Bankey* (Calcutta: Shankar Pustakalaya, 1954).

22 Norbert Elias, *The Civilizing Process: Sociogenetic and Psychogenetic Investigations* (Oxford: Blackwell Publishing [1939], 2000): 415. Taking a cue from Elias one may argue that the bankers are prone to failures in self-restraint. Elias observes: 'The pattern of self-constraints, the template by which drives are moulded, certainly varies widely according to the function and position of the individual within this network, and there are even today in different sectors of the Western world variations of intensity and stability in the apparatus of self-constraint that seem at face value very large': 369. Following Norbert Elias, we can say that Suropati did not have the 'foresight . . . particularly marked in the classic bourgeois

syndrome'; Stephen Mennell, *Norbert Elias: Civilization and Human Self-Image* (Oxford: Basic Blackwell, 1989): 98–99.

23 Prasanta Ray, 'Conjugality in Times of Fortuitous Fortunes: *Alibaba* and *Parash Pathar*', Lecture delivered in Department of Modern History, Calcutta University, 2010.

24 Ibid.

5

GRASPING GREED

Elusive greed

The run on several banks in Bengal in the years of transition from colonial capitalism to post-colonial capitalism is obviously not a 'once-upon-a-time only in Bengal' episode. Universally, a mix of 'weak' regulatory capture and moral failure at individual–institutional levels trigger the collapse of banks and, with it, financial and moral ruin of individuals and households.[1] The storylines are fundamentally the same: stakeholders of unequal social power, the adiaphoric state, regulatory lapses and insensitive politicians; and, the situation of being on sufferance of the vulnerable due to lack of humanitarian governance.[2] The moral failure was due to avarice in Bengal of the 1940s – as elsewhere and in some other times, be it in Athenian society between 600 and 300 bc or in contemporary capitalism.[3] This has stimulated a perennial search for the reasons why individuals, institutions, people, state formations and economies become greedy. We have a great body of social knowledge, theological as well as secular, and philosophical as well as social-scientific. Grasping greed in the twin senses of understanding its roots and its institutional facilitators, and controlling its incidence, has indeed been a challenge. Broadly speaking, Sociology's endeavour in this regard stands out compared to that of Economics. Swedberg's comment is relevant here: He observes:

> While the superiority of capitalism as an economic system and growth machine has fascinated economists for centuries, this has not been the case with sociologists. For sociologists capitalism has mainly been of interest for its *social* effects – how it has led to class struggle, anomie, inequality and social problems in general.[4]

This temper informs sociology's analysis of greed, although largely in the form of sub-texts in the sociology of money, capitalism and modernity.

Classical sociologists did not engage in operationalizing greedy behaviour, something mainstream economists would demand. This is primarily because of greed's enmeshed existence in the midst of a welter of interests, values and emotions. They offered theories on economy, society and the state from which their understandings of greed follow. It is interesting that despite the universalistic projections, their analytical points of departure were their nineteenth-century European experiences of greed in which banks and bankers indulged. Such empirical foundation lent objectivity to what was avowedly a moral and political concern.

In secular understanding, which Sociology has fostered, greed is an inordinate desire to acquire or possess, usually material wealth, more than an individual needs. Evidently, there is no way to fix a universal human minimum, either by way of an item or an amount. Further, a moral undertone, which is not always monotonic, stands in the way of creating a general inventory of human conduct representing greed. This is because morals are diverse across social spaces and times. The secular interventions to regulate predisposition to greedy behaviour are through laws. Laws reduce *greed* to 'economic crimes' for obvious functional reasons. The laws usually take embezzlement as an act of financial greed. They thereby relate greed to the institution of property in a negative way because the greedy tries to gratify the urge by seizure or fraudulent dispossession of someone else's rightful possession. This notion of rightful possession rests on legal definition of legitimacy of possession and use; that is, on the notion of *legal* right and wrong. Obviously, the notion of 'an in ordinate desire' and the measure – 'more than an individual needs' – elude legal grasp. Compared to the moral breadth of theological discourses on greed with its myths and images, guilt and repentance, and sin and salvation, the legal discourse is understandably minimalist, although more systemized compared to morals.[5] Because of the ambiguity of moral definition and thinness of legal definition, we are cross-culturally impelled to set up metaphorical measures of 'more', for example, metaphors like 'a dwarf is trying to touch the moon'.[6] This is also a good example of everyday moral control. However, in sociological reflections on greed – which are recounted below, there is a consensus that the greedy eludes moral regulation and law.[7] But it is not denied that many abide by the moral principles which seek to ensure just behaviour because they have internalized the norms of conformity, or are afraid of social retribution.

Greed is usually an observer-labeler's category, usually directed to an individual. But greed is not always an individual's predisposition. Greed of the priestly class or corporate greed is a good example of collective greed. Institutions can be facilitators of individual or collective greed. They themselves can be greedy.[8] Further, nation-states and socio-economic systems like capitalism can engage in greedy extraction of resources within and beyond their frontiers. These can bestow certain normality to what in other's reckoning greedy behaviour: moralize it by espousing the goodness of greed and professionalize pursuit of greed by training talents to strategize drive for mean gains.

The observer-labeler's category implies a moral community or a legal regime to which a greedy person, class, or nation-state may or may not belong. Given the fact of moral diversity, it is common sense that what is greed and what is a morally permissible act can never be settled across meaning structures of the supposedly greedy persons, their victims – sometimes the greedy persons themselves and the 'bystanders' – 'the ordinary persons when he is in a position of observing other people's behaviour'.[9] Durkheim wrote:

> It can no longer be maintained nowadays that there is one, single morality which is valid for all men at all times and in all places . . . it is in the nature of things that morality should vary . . . [hence] there are . . . several and as many [moralities] as there are social types.[10]

Further, individuals in a complex society belong to a plurality of moral communities, each with its sense and code of what is right and what is wrong in human conduct.[11] It is not impossible that a person acknowledges his own greedy behaviour on hindsight, particularly if he is repentant and punished either by his significant others, by his inner conscience inflicting on him a sense of sin, guilt or shame, or by the state.[12]

What makes grasping greed further difficult is the fact of its germination in the intricate mix of interests, values, emotions and sentiments. Personal aspirations, ambitions and dreaming about the future are all positively encouraged by primary and secondary groups an ordinary individual passes through in his or her life cycle. But these socially celebrated desires are seed beds of greed. It is the ambivalence of acquisitive culture towards personal and collective ambition that allows them to swell into greed, particularly under institutional facilitation. That makes distinction between aspiration, typical of achievement orienta-tion, and greed difficult. It is like progressive deepening of a colour in which the terminal shades are starkly different from each other. The significant others of an aspiring/greedy person also have a stake in the gains of greed. The commonwealth too gains through these otherwise impermissible personal desires. Thus, extricating greed from a com-pound of desires, from their corresponding conduct, from interests and passions which greed gratifies, from a blend of senses of sin, guilt and shame a greedy person may suffer from, and from bi-moral nor-mative (religious–secular) matrix is very difficult.

What adds to the problem is the fact that greed is sometimes cele-brated as a worthy predisposition. It is not true that the idea of *wrong* pervades all attempts to conceive greed. At the level of social response to greed, the Scottish Enlightenment, as mentioned earlier, is ear-marked as a radical reversal of earlier denunciation of avarice.[13]*Greed* was re-defined as 'rational self-interest', which in turn became the ide-ological signature of capitalism. At the popular level, it found endorse-ments in such claims like Gordon Gekko's 'Greed captures the essence of the evolutionary spirit', and Deng Xiaoping's 'Poverty is not social-ism. To be rich is glorious'. Not to be outpaced, we had in Bollywood a popular song *Jannat Jahan/Jannat Takai* (money is heaven).[14] The issue of justice has steadily dissolved, making greed normal. We now have varieties of greed: elite greed, bourgeois greed and working-class greed – to connote shades of pleonexia, which is the desire to have more than others and more than one's share. As in ancient Athens, so in the late modern West and in neo-liberal India: moral subversion of the masses has been the effective instrument of domination.[15] An ad for ice cream, Big Ones (November, 2007) on billboards in Kolkata's highways signifies our neo-liberal consumerist turn when we happily overturn popular wisdom. It announces that greed is no longer sinful reversing the old Bengali proverb that greed is sinful. Displayed in Kolkata's Salt Lake, the billboard displayed women and men happily consuming with the motto, *greed is virtuous*. Could it be a visual sig-nal of India's arrival at the threshold of finance capital? How is this universal predisposition to be sociologically grasped?

The banking crisis and the Bengali sociologists

Returning to our focus on the banking crisis in Bengal in the 1940s and the 1950s, it is pertinent to inquire whether there was any effort in Bengal to grasp the happenings sociologically. It is well known that although sociology had its formal beginning in 1917 at Calcutta University, it could not make any headway in its birthplace at Calcutta. But outside the university, from the middle of the nineteenth century, there was interest in sociology and in sociological understanding of institutions in Bengal. This is indicated by serious discussions in vernacular journals on Comte and positivism.[16] Rev. James Long's initiated formation of The Bengal Social Science Association (1867–1878) was significant. It is interesting that collecting empirical data on 'banking operations' was in the agenda of the Department of Economy and Trade set up by the Association. In fact, the 'scheme of work' drawn up for this department gave 'Banking and Currency' priority. Among the 17 sub-areas on which enquiries might be instituted and information collected with advantage, was 'precautions against forgery'.[17] All these research fields were in pursuit of the basic objective of the Association 'to collect, arrange and classify series of facts bearing upon the social, moral and intellectual conditions of the people of Bengal, and by such means to assist in the promotion of measures for the good of the country'.[18] Along with such collective enterprise were outstanding minds like Bankim Chandra Chatterjee (1838–1894) who wrote essays on utilitarianism and positivism.[19] The interest in objectivity of understanding was evidently strong in late nineteenth-century Bengal.

The educated elite in Bengal was expected to be intellectually and culturally equipped to grasp sociologically the crisis in banking in Bengal in the 1940s and the 1950s. Benoy Kumar Sarkar (1887–1949) taught economics in Calcutta University (1926–1948). He, as already noted, was focused on the prospect of the economic development of Bengal and of banks owned and managed by the Bengalis. He was aware of bank failures in Bengal and also apprehensive of similar crisis in the future. But he did not take into serious account the moral failure of the men at the helm of the banking business in Bengal. In fact, institutional collapse had a small place in his otherwise extensive writings on the Bengal economy. This concern with moral failure could be present in the writings of Radhakamal Mukherjee (1889–1968), Benoy Kumar Sarkar's contemporary. This is because of his persistent engagement with values and the necessity of reconfiguring economic analysis. This makes a reference to his *Borderlands of Economics* (1925) urgent.[20] A professor of economics and sociology, he was the first Indian economic sociologist in the early twentieth century. Some commentators called him 'sociologist-economist', because of the primacy he accorded to sociology in his understanding of economic problems in India.[21] He wanted sociology 'to combat the tyranny of

Economics'.[22] He tried to develop 'a system of economics revivified at its foundations and renewed in its methods by a broad-minded cooperation of the sciences of life, mind, and society in keeping with the intellectual vogue of the day'. He observed:

> Economics still bases itself on an inadequate analysis of the primary springs of human action. It has thus reared up a system on a logical method, the insufficiency of which is now increasingly recognized and has taken only a fragment of real living man and a distorted though intensified shadow of his relations and activities.[23]

He appreciated that:

> Modern functional psychology, as we have seen, has resolved these classical economic motives into a number of impulses of different sorts and shorn them of their intellectual or rational basis. It has laid bare the falsity of the classical hypothesis of "enlightened self-interest" which, indeed, cannot explain the behaviour of man, rooted as it is in his unlearned original equipment of instincts and capacities.[24]

He wrote extensively on values and morals.[25] In his *The Dynamics of Morals: A Socio-Psychological Theory of Ethics* (1950), he regretted scholarly inattention to *values*. 'The endeavour during the last few decades to make sociology "value-free" has over-shot its mark. In the anxiety lest his personal valuation distort social reality, the sociologist leaves human values out of account, unexplored and unanalyzed'.[26] But, despite the possibility of at least a sub-text on avarice suggested by his observations on economics as 'a blend of hedonistic psychology and utilitarian ethics',[27] on the urgency of humanizing Economics,[28] and on pathologies of modern industrial capitalism, Radhakamal Mukherjee's focus on economic immorality did not go beyond a critique of 'dominant commercial interest' and the ruinous 'cash nexus' of capitalism.[29]

Curating Radhakamal Mukherjee's large corpus of writings to locate his thought on economic immoralities is never easy. Closest he came to implicitly acknowledging *greed*[30] – without using the notion – as social was when he proposed that instincts are to be reckoned with as springs of economic behaviour. Drawing on social psychology, he argued that 'the individual instinct acquires specific economic significance only when it coalesces and corresponds to the similar behaviour of the herd'.[31] On the acquisitive instinct, which one can argue – Mukherjee did not – has a strong probability of breeding greed, he was categorical that, in order to be a determinant of economic behaviour, it must be collectively endorsed. 'Nests and dwellings, feeding and hunting grounds, property and coins, are limited in supply, while their appropriation is encouraged by herd behaviour. Thus the acquisitive instinct partakes of an economic interest'.[32] The 'acerbities' of the 'collecting or acquisitive instinct', 'fed by the desire for mastery and exploitation', are distinctively human.[33] Mukherjee pointed out that 'values change for the worse instead of for the better, with the persistence of pathological groups, institutions and social policies'.[34] 'No doubt most of the personal maladjustments, tensions and neuroses arise today out of social-cultural disvalues destroying the sanity and corroding the morals of the individual'.[35] He did implicate the 'economic environment' in determining 'appropriation' and 'possession' as instincts in the economic realm.[36] These gleanings from his major works, which have 'a vertiginous quality', are parts of his macro concerns on values and morality,[37] and contain a critique of capitalism and an appreciation of socialism. He thought that reconstruction of value–framework and of economics should be simultaneous.

> The war has revealed that empirical description of forces is not the whole of economics. Economics can be no longer a mere handmaiden to business and industry, fitting its theories to the grooves of the present order. The different schools of socialism have shown economics to be the very quintessence of humanism and these now dominate modern social thought.[38]

Incidentally, this position is sharply contradictory with Benoy Sarkar's appreciation of what he called 'zamindari capitalism' and of his vital role as 'a helper and co-operator to the peasant by furnishing him with loans', as if he was the 'Ryot's banker'.[39]

Radhakamal Mukherjee himself did not address the problems of Indian banking the way this book does. He edited *Economic Problems of Modern India* in two volumes (1939/1941).[40] In the second volume, Sir S. N. Pochkhanwala (1881–1937) reviewed the Indian banking scenario in his article 'The Structure of Indian Banking'.[41] He was the founder of the first swadeshi bank, the Central Bank of India (1919). His observations were based on the experience of bank failures in India in 1913–1914. However, these would hold true about the banking crisis in the period examined here. He did point out lack of integrity on the part of the managers and the directors and their proneness to 'speedy accumulation of riches for themselves'.[42] This critique matches with Patrick Geddes' distrust of banks. It is well known that Geddes was a major influence on Mukherjee. Geddes, as a forerunner of Social Credit movement,

> believed that bankers were making use of public credit for private profit and demanded that this misfeasance be acknowledged and regulated. Maintaining that the ultimate source of credit was in the community . . . thought that credit should be used for socially beneficent investments.[43]

Despite this, sociology in Bengal and in India was inattentive to incidence of financial immoralities. Both Mukherjee and Sarkar were well-versed in West European sociology with a rich tradition of economic sociology. For grasping greed sociologically, we need to turn to it.

Socio-genesis of greed

The primary object of greed is money. Georg Simmel explained why it must be money.

> The nature and effectiveness of money is not to be found simply in the coin that I hold in my hand; its qualities are invested in the social organizations and supra-subjective norms that make this coin a tool of endlessly diverse and extensive uses despite its material limitations, it significance and rigidity.[44]

In everyday use of the notion of greed, it is sometimes greed for other socially significant resource also like sex, power and status which, however draw on money and create or enlarge access to money. But money has 'metaphysical quality' in its ability 'to extend beyond every particular use and since, it is the ultimate means, to realize the possibility of all values as the value of all possibilities'.[45] To Karl Marx, money is 'the fountainhead of greed'. Evidently, the strong association between money and greed is being continuously discovered;[46] also, intended and unintended relationships between financial institutions like banks and greed for money. Crisis in banking fuelled by greed has been very costly, particularly for the unsuspecting victims. But the standard practice among economists is to calculate the cost for the government or for the economy only.[47] What about costs of different orders, not all of which are quantifiable, inflicted on various categories of marginal people, for example, the workers, lower middle class, forced migrants – who have meagre chance of recovery? Their loss of precious savings disturbs their familial relationships and life chances. Cynicism about the state and political leadership develops as the state, and the politicians fail to offer them any succour.

Despite classical sociologists' concern with greed leading to institutional collapse, the lack of moral attention to this pathological disposition in economics is largely due to a positivism-induced disconnection between the mainstream economics and its humanist roots.[48] The prominence given to what Amartya Sen calls the engineering approach with its focus on logistics, has marginalized the critical importance of a vision of a moral order that places peoples at the centre of social life.[49] This accounts for neglect of victims of economic misadventures among economists. Banishing feelings for them is what the imperatives of objectivity stipulate. But this needs to be countered by what Zygmunt Bauman conceptualizes as 'morality of proximity': 'not a neutral, sociological "being-*with*-the-other" . . . but "a being-*for*-the other"'.[50] Friedrich Engels would be a rare early example of choosing to be face-to-face with human beings that makes possible morality of proximity. In the Preface to his *The Condition of the Working Class in England, 1944 (1845)*, he wrote:

> Twenty-one months I had the opportunity to become acquainted with the English proletariat, its strivings, its sorrows and its joys, to see them from near, from personal observation and personal intercourse, and at the same time to supplement my observations by recourse to the requisite authentic sources.

He was actually close to the victims of greed. He observed in the same tract: 'It [the English bourgeoisie] knows no bliss save that of rapid gain, no pain save that of losing gold. In the presence of this avarice and lust of gain, it is not possible for a single human sentiment or opinion to remain untainted'.[51] There is evidently a moral tone in Engel's observation. This was distinctive of early sociological examination of greed. This enterprise was an integral part of sociology of money, and fundamentally, of sociology of capitalism. It also adumbrated the notion of moral economy.

The moral tenor in classical sociology was in continuation of a deeply religious critique of greed in West European culture. Such was the power of the critique, that both Marx and Simmel highlighted the god-like attributes of money. Universally, the immorality of greed has provoked religious sanction because of its threat to human vitality and social cohesion. In the Christian life-view, greed, 'the Matriarch of the Deadly Clan', is one of seven deadly sins (wrath, greed, sloth, pride, lust, envy and gluttony). In fact, it is a part of a larger set of vices and virtues (humility, charity, kindness, patience, chastity, temperance and diligence).[52] According to *Śrīmadbhagavadgītā* (The Song of the God), there are three gates to self-destructive hell: lust, anger and greed.[53] This perception represents the individual-centric and astrological explanation of greed.

> When a greedy man sees a bag of gold and begins to think of its value, attachment for the thing grows in his heart; from attachment he feels intense longing to get possession of it and when anything or anybody interferes with the gratification of his desire it results in anger. From anger delusion rises, i.e., confusion of understanding; then his memory fails him, that is, he forgets his position and duty in life; and when he is in this state, without discrimination of right and wrong, he does things to cause his own ruin.[54]

The astrological dimension inheres in the belief that appropriation by malign planetary forces at birth will make the newborn prone to greedy indulgence in life.

The secular sociology of greed, despite its connect with the moral critique in religion, concedes that no moral and legal order is a sufficient deterrent to greedy indulgence. It is because of the universal social ambivalence to greed. So long as the threshold of viability of the economy and polity is not threatened by greed of the key members of the elite or crucial segments of the people, the ambivalence continues. When the threat is perceived to be disquieting, economic morals are refurbished to reset the thresholds of viability.

The trigger in the unsettling of the threshold was a crisis in banking, particularly for Karl Marx and Emile Durkheim. Marx wrote on cyclical crises related to the British banking reforms of 1844 and on the French Crédit Mobilier bank.[55] The crisis in the Paris Bourse in the winter of 1882 and the critical part played by the bank, Union Générale, drew Durkheim's attention. Weber referred to the Bank of

England and the South Sea Bubble (1720). There are distinct sub-texts on banking also in all of their writings including Simmel's – in their broader analysis of money and its institutions and in their theory of morals in which greed was an important issue.

The nodal point of Emile Durkheim's observation on greed is his theory of morals. His *Professional Ethics and Civic Morals* offers the best insight in this connection.[56] Durkheim's sociological mission was to espouse the role of professional ethics and civic morals to frame economic conduct in the face of a growing tendency of economy becoming detached from other social institutions. The state was to be the critical agency of moral restraint on individual economic conduct. The organ of moral discipline, the state should 'work out certain representations which hold good for the collectivity'.[57] He disapprovingly located the collective activity of business as 'outside the sphere of morals' and 'almost entirely removed from the moderating effect of obligations'.[58] For this, he castigated both classical economic theory and socialist theory because both held 'that economic life is equipped to organize itself and to function in an orderly way and in harmony, without any moral authority intervening'.[59] He wanted to bring back moral frames because he firmly believed that

> it is not possible for a social function to exist without moral discipline. Otherwise, nothing remains but individual appetites, and since they are by nature boundless and insatiable, if there is nothing to control them they will not be able to control themselves.[60]

Elsewhere, in *Suicide*, he elaborated on appetite for prosperity: 'From top to bottom of the ladder, greed is aroused without knowing where to find ultimate foothold. Nothing can calm it, since its goal is far beyond all it can attain'.[61] Durkheim was not at all optimistic about the prospect of morally taming greed.[62]

In his exposition on anomic suicide, he observed 'that economic crises have an aggravating effect on the suicidal tendency'.[63] Among a number of such crises he mentioned is the exceptional one involving the Paris Bourse in the winter of 1882. 'The relationship is found not only in some exceptional cases, but is the rule. The number of bankruptcies is a barometer of adequate sensitivity, reflecting the variations of economic life'.[64] The bank, Union Générale, played a central role in boom and subsequent collapse of the market. What happened by way of investors being lured by massive increase in the price of the share of the bank pointed to greed of the speculators who even printed counterfeit money. This vulnerability to temptation is due to 'man's activity ('s) lacking regulation ... leaving him without a check-rein'.[65] This economic anomie is 'a chronic state' in the sphere of trade and industry. This is because 'religion has lost most of its power. And government, instead of regulating economic life, has become its tool and servant'.[66]

> There upon the appetites [for prosperity] thus excited have become freed from any limiting authority. By sanctifying them, so to speak, this apotheosis of well-being has placed them above all human law. Their restraint seems like a sort of sacrilege. . . . Ultimately, this liberation of desire has been made worse by the very development of industry and the almost infinite extension of the market. . . . Now that he may assume to have the entire world as his customer, how could passions accept their former confinement in the face of such limitless prospects?
>
> Such is the source of the excitement predominating in this part of society, and which thence extended to other parts. There, the state of crisis and anomy is constant and, so to speak, normal. From top to bottom of the ladder, greed is aroused without knowing where to find ultimate foothold. Nothing can calm it, since its goal is far beyond all it can attain. Reality seems valueless by comparison with the dreams of fevered imaginations; reality is therefore abandoned, but so too is possibly abandoned when it in turn becomes reality.[67]

The same reading of the time is in Marx's third article on 'The French Crédit Mobilier'[68] He recounted the sense of alarm triggered by Saint-Simonian banking utopias.[69]

> Political life [in France] was replaced by the fever of speculation, by the thirst for lucre, by the infatuation of gambling. On all sides, even in our small towns, even in our villages, men are carried away by the mania of making those rapid fortunes of which there are so many examples – those fortunes achieved without trouble, without labour, and often without honour. . . . While the higher and middle classes – those ancient political classes – give themselves up to speculation, another labour presents itself among the lower classes of society, whence nearly all the revolutions emanated which France has

suffered. At the sight of this fearful mania of gambling which has made a vast gambling booth of nearly all France, a portion of the masses, invaded by Socialists, has been more corrupted than ever, by the avidity of gain. Hence an unquestionable progress of secret societies, a greater and deeper development of those savage passions.[70]

Durkheim was firm in his observation that 'the presence or absence of regulatory procedures by which it [money] is controlled' and 'the nature of these rules and regulations' was of critical importance in determining the effect of money on society.[71] On the limits of law in regulation of economic behaviour, Weber's conviction was similar to Durkheim's. His interest in law was a part of his focus on the role of the state in economy that indeed distinguished the early German tradition of economic sociology.[72] He categorically located reasons for inefficacy of legal restraint:

The second source of the limitation of successful legal coercion in the economic sphere lies in the relative proportion of strength of private economic interests on the one hand and interests promoting conformance to the rules of law on the other. The inclination to forgo economic opportunity simply in order to act legally is obviously slight, unless circumvention of the formal law is strongly disapproved by a powerful convention, and such a situation is not likely to arise where the interests affected by a legal innovation are widespread. Besides, it is often not difficult to disguise circumvention of a law in the economic sphere.[73]

It is . . . private interested parties who are in a position to distort the intended meaning of a legal norm to the point of turning into its very opposite, as has often happened in the past.[74]

Apart from the fact of subversion of legal restraints, there is also inefficacy of religion.

Everywhere, scepticism or indifference to religion are and have been the widely diffused attitudes of the large-scale traders and financiers.[75]

The morally corrosive character of greed and its cunning escape from moral and legal restraints is recognized also by Simmel. But he was not thoroughly negative in his attitude to money as such. David Frisby in his overview on Simmel observed: 'The ceaseless flux of the circulation of the money economy is elevated to a modern worldview. But despite illustrating the 'darker sides' of the money economy ('the complete heartlessness of money'), Simmel suggests that the same processes are also responsible for the "finest and highest elements of our culture"'.[76] Both 'the lighter and the darker sides of our culture' bring out Simmel's fundamental position that culture of things – in this case, money – become culture of human beings. Greed, which belongs to the darker side, is one of few psychological consequences Simmel analysed. To him, it was an example of 'the psychological growth of means into ends'.[77] The seeds of greed lay in the nature of money economy:

> Never has an object that owes its value exclusively to its quality as a means, to its convertibility into more definite values, so thoroughly and unreservedly developed into a psychological value absolute, into a completely engrossing final purpose governing our practical consciousness. This ultimate craving for money must increase to the extent money takes on the quality of pure means. For this implies that the range of objects made available to money grows continuously, that things submit more and more defencelessly to the power of money, that money becomes more and more lacking in quality yet thereby becomes powerful in relation to the quality of things.[78]

Today's reading of the power of greed offers much more cynical inventory of what succumb to money: 'Bread, cash, dosh, dough, loot, lucre, moolah, readies, the wherewithal: call it what you like, money matters'.[79] Simmel traced increase in 'intensity and expansion of this desire (greed)' to weakening of 'the modest satisfaction of individual life-interests, such as the elevation of the religious absolute as the ultimate purpose of existence'.[80] The inefficacy of the religious ethic to contain greed is re-stated by Simmel. Ironically, the metaphor of God turns out to be powerful in explaining a radical change in worldview of individuals. As Simmel analogizes, money assumes the status of 'the secular God of the World' by virtue of its elevation as 'the absolute means' into 'the psychological significance of an absolute purpose'. This conversion is distinctive of 'a developed and lively money economy', rather than of 'primitive economic levels'.[81] It is interesting that Marx also found the metaphor useful to convey money's critical status:

> wealth . . . exists, individualized as such, to the exclusion of all other commodities, as a singular, tangible object, in gold and silver. Money is therefore the god among commodities. . . . From its servile role, in which it appears as mere medium of circulation, it suddenly changes into the lord and god of the worldly commodities. It represents the divine existence of commodities, while they represent its earthly form.[82]

A corresponding development in such an economy, according to Simmel, would be increase in the scale of monetary systems: 'Progressive development strives in reality for the expansion, and consequently the centralization, of the institutions and powers that guarantee money values'.[83] Banks are both the outcome and the agency of such centralization. But this institution is subject to corruption.

> The guarantee, which is the vital nerve of money, naturally loses some of its force when the objective institution representing the community in fact represents only limited segments of the community and its interests. The private bank, for instance, is a relatively objective supra-personal entity interposed in the exchanges between individual interests. This sociological character enables it to issue money, but if its note issue is not soon transferred to a central institution under state supervision, the limitation of the area that it represents will become apparent in the imperfect 'money' character of its notes.[84]

Further, money is 'the breeding ground of economic individualism ("ruthless assertion of individuality") and egoism'.[85] 'Money's purely negative quality, that its use, unlike other forms of ownership, is in no way restricted by objective or ethical considerations, inevitably develops into inconsiderateness as a completely positive kind of attitude'.[86] Herein, he noted the possibility of catastrophic developments in money economy.

As to response to such crisis, Simmel made two observations on reactions of two social classes.[87] First:

> Owners of money usually profit from violent and ruinous economic upheavals, often to an extraordinary extent . . .

experience has shown that the big bankers usually make a steady profit out of these dangers (bankruptcies) that confront sellers and buyers, creditors and debtors.[88]

Second:

> People with small income, who are usually the owners of small notes, cannot as easily present them for redemption as the owners of large notes can. On the other hand, if a panic breaks out, the former press for redemption more violently and thoughtlessly or give the notes away at any price.[89]

In his *Philosophy of Money*, Simmel refrained from judging what was 'good and evil in the sense what is worth striving for and what not'.[90] He was in no way inclined to envisage reconfiguring of the normative framework to govern money and its institutions like banks.[91]

Marx was firm in his conviction that no normative innovation in regulation of money would be adequate to bring about a change of the fundamentals so long as such innovations remain within capitalist framework. Marx never subscribed to legal fetishism.[92] He observed:

> But none of them [forms of money], as long as they remain forms of money, and as long as money remains an essential relation of production, is capable of overcoming the contradictions inherent in the money relation, and can instead only hope to reproduce these contradictions in one form or another.[93]

Greed, for him, was both a logical and historical outcome of money in all its interconnected functions.

> Money is therefore not only *an* object, but is *the* object of greed. It is essentially *auri sacra fames* ('that accursed hunger for gold'). Greed as such, as a particular form of the drive, i.e., as distinct from the craving for a particular kind of wealth, e.g., for clothes, weapons, jewels, women, wine, etc., is possible only when general wealth, wealth as such, has become individualized in a particular thing, i.e. as soon as money is posited in its third quality (money as money – as an end in itself, which includes dimensions of money as hoard, as means of payment and as international money). . . . Money

is therefore not only the object but also the fountainhead of greed.[94]

Marx pointed to the possibility of greed becoming a common predisposition. 'Greed, as the urge of all, in so far as everyone wants to make money, is only created by general wealth'.[95]

According to the logic of this analysis, greed is not a case of individual perversion.

> Possession of it (money) is not the development of any particular essential aspect of his individuality; but rather possession of what lacks individuality, since this social [relation] exists at the same time as a sensuous, external object which can be mechanically seized, and lost in the same manner.

Marx conceded money's corrupting influence on an individual. 'A particular individual may even today come into money by chance, and the possession of this money can undermine him'.[96] But he discouraged 'the idea of seeking . . . final causes [of monetary crash] in the recklessness of single individuals'. As an example of collective greed, he would readily draw our attention to the wiles of bankers, the 'wolves of finance', and to one of their techniques, namely, 'evoking sudden, extraordinary fluctuations in the quotations of government securities'.[97] He was well aware that 'the irresponsible directors of banks' could fall 'a prey to their own caprices and interests'.[98] Even then he would point to eventual systemic imperatives: 'If speculation towards the close of a given commercial period appears as the immediate forerunner of the crash, it should not be forgotten that speculation itself is a result and an accident instead of the final cause and the substance'.[99] He took a similar position with regard to cheating:

> If one individual . . . cheated the other, this would *happen not because of the nature of social function in which they confront one another*, for this is *the same*, in this they are *equal*; but only because of natural cleverness, persuasiveness, etc., in short only the purely individual superiority of one individual over another.[100]

Given his primary interest in understanding regimes from the standpoint of monetary organization, he argued that the regime could be responsible for 'monetary panic'; in fact for more than that: it would lead to the 'eruption of general discontent' and sharpening of class contradiction: 'As against the shameless orgies of the finance aristocracy, the struggle of the people for prime necessities of life! At Buzançais, hunger rioters executed; in Paris, oversatiated *escrocs* [swindlers] snatched from the courts by the royal family!'[101]

The government evidently became an accomplice. Marx observed:

> In order to build up confidence in the republic's bourgeois morality and capacity to pay, the Provisional Government . . . paid out interests on . . . bonds to the state creditors (before 'the legal date of payment'). . . . [But this] robbed it [the Provisional Government] of its stock of ready cash. . . . It announced that no more money could be drawn on savings bank books for an amount of over one hundred francs. The sums deposited in the savings banks were confiscated and by decree transformed into an irredeemable state debt.[102]

'The petty bourgeois, domestic servants and workers had to pay for the pleasant surprise which had been prepared for the state creditors'.[103] But in Marx's understanding, money – '*the* object of greed' – would have more catastrophic consequences.

> Money . . . directly and simultaneously becomes the *real* community *[Gemeinwesen]*, since it is the general substance of survival for all, and at the same time the social product of all. But . . . in money the community *[Gemeinwesen]* is at the same time a mere abstraction, a mere external, accidental thing for the individual, and at the same time merely means for his satisfaction as an isolated individual. . . . The development of money in its third role . . . smashes this community. All production is an objectification *[Vergegenständlichung]* of the individual. In money (exchange value), however, the individual is not objectified in his natural quality, but in a social quality (relation) which is, at the same time, external to him.[104]

In his location of the connection between political regimes and management of finance, Marx adumbrated Weber's analysis of the role of the Bank of England in the context of 'politically oriented adventurers' capitalism' and its involvement in the South Sea Bubble.[105] And, also Pierre Bourdieu's conceptualization of the 'right hand of the state': 'the technocrats of the Ministry of Finance, the public and private banks and the ministerial *cabinets* [author's italics]'.[106]

Adam Smith also had admitted of the possibility of smashing up the community by the institutions of wealth.[107] 'The great mob of mankind are the admirers and worshippers, and what may seem more extraordinary, most frequently the disinterested admirers and worshipers, of wealth and greatness'.[108] It was 'the great and universal cause of the corruption of our moral sentiments'. The 'hypnotic admiration of wealth', E. G. West comments, 'was necessary among the poor, since it acted as a beneficial illusion which resulted in the maintenance of order in society'.[109] Smith pointed to the crucial role played by the men of 'rank and fashion' who have an 'easy empire over the affections of mankind' cultivate 'proud ambition and ostentatious avidity'. Those in 'middling and inferior stations of life' have different moral qualities.[110]

> In every civilized society, in every society, where the distinction of ranks has once been completely established, there have always been two different schemes or systems of morality current at the same time; of which the one may be called the strict or austere; the other the liberal, or, if you will, the loose system. The former is generally admired and revered by the common people: the latter is commonly more esteemed and adopted by what are called the people of fashion. The degree of disapprobation with which we ought to mark the hypnotic vices of levity, the vices which are apt to arise from great prosperity, and from the excess of gaiety and good humour, seems to constitute the principal distinction between those two opposite schemes or systems.[111]

Smith is more critical of the merchant class. On 'merchants and master manufacturers', he observed:[112]

> Their thoughts . . . are commonly exercised rather about the interest of their own particular branch of business, than about that of the society, [hence] their judgement, even when given with the greatest candour . . . is much more to be depended with regard to the former ('the interest of their own particular branch of business') of these two objects than with regard to the latter ('the interest of the society'). It is by their superior knowledge of their own interest that they have frequently

imposed upon his [the labourer's] generosity, and persuaded
him to give up both his own interest and that of the public. . . .
The proposal of any new law or regulation of commerce which
comes from this order ought always to be listened to with great
precaution, and ought never to be adopted till after having
been long and carefully examined, not only with the most scrupulous, but with the most suspicious attention. It comes from
an order of men whose interest is never exactly the same with
that of the public, who have generally an interest to deceive
and even to oppress the public, and who accordingly have
upon many occasions, both deceived and oppressed it.[113]

Smith recognized a clash between the profit earners and the general
social interest which was really the interest of those who live by rent and
those by wage – a clash in which the profit earners given their 'better
knowledge of their interests' due to their lifelong engagement with profit
making and their power and determination, and due to wage earners'
lack of power of comprehension and of voice, always dominate.[114]

Smith was outright in his rejection of Dr. Mandeville's argument
that 'private vices were public benefits, since without them no society
could prosper or flourish'.[115] But he could offer hardly any endur-
ing institutional solution of the problem of the power of private vices
over vulnerable individuals. 'That wealth . . . [is] often regarded with
respect and admiration . . .; and that the contempt . . . is often mostly
unjustly bestowed upon poverty and weakness, has been the complaint
of moralists in all ages'.[116] It was 'the great and universal cause of the
corruption of our moral sentiments'. Smith did envisage 'the silent
agency' of 'the Impartial Spectator' – 'the internal spectator or man
within the breast' – in assisting individuals in 'the quest for a general-
ized and comprehensive moral code in each separate society according
to its evolving circumstances'.[117] But Smith recognized the possibility
of corruption of the impartial spectator.

There are some situations which bear so hard upon human
nature that the greatest degree of self-government . . . is not able
to stifle, altogether, the voice of human weakness, or reduce the
violence of the passions to that pitch of moderation, in which
the impartial spectator can entirely enter into them.[118]

This is despite his position that 'There is no commonly honest man
who does not dread the inward disgrace of such an action';[119] and

despite 'a certain propensity in men to "sympathize with" each other's emotion and to do so with care and imagination which is both sincere and human'.[120] In case of failure of the impartial spectator, the only recourse left would be 'an appeal to a still higher tribunal, to that of all-seeing Judge of the world, whose eyes can never be deceived, and whose judgements can never be perverted'.[121]

For the profit earners employing 'the largest capitals', Smith did envisage institutional restraints rather than leaving it only to any theistic design. Smith wanted the legislator to avoid accommodating 'capitalist interests and power' and to counteract the tactics of the profit earners, which included narrowing of competition.[122] Indeed, the legislator representing a strong state should oversee market competitiveness and 'intervene to correct or counter (market's) socially and politically undesirable outcomes'.[123] Regulation of money and credit would be one such area of intervention by the state. Banks and bankers would come within the purview of this. Trust in banks would be of critical importance.

> When the people of a particular country have such confidence in the fortune, probity, and prudence of a particular banker, as to believe that he is always ready to pay upon demand such of his promissory notes as are likely to be at any time presented to him; those notes come to have the same currency as gold and silver money, from the confidence that such money can at any time be had for them.[124]

Smith advocated institutional correction of certain impermissible practices on the part of bankers. He observed:

> Where the issuing of bank notes for . . . very small sums is allowed and commonly practised, many people are both enabled and encouraged to become banker. . . . But the frequent bankruptcies to which such beggarly bankers must be liable, may occasion very considerable inconveniency, and sometimes even a very great calamity, to many poor people who had received their notes in payment.[125]

To prevent such a crisis, it is better that

> bankers are restrained from issuing any circulating bank notes or notes payable to the bearer, for less than a certain sum; and . . . are subjected to the obligation of an immediate

and unconditional payment of such bank notes as soon as presented, [then] their trade may, with safety to the public, be rendered in all other respects perfectly free. . . . It ["late multiplication of banking companies"] obliges all of them to be more circumspect in their conduct, and, by not extending their currency beyond its due proportion in cash, to guard themselves against those malicious runs, which the rivalship of so many competitors is always ready to bring upon them.[126]

Another practice requiring state overseeing would be that of banks circulating paper money in excess of gold and silver necessary for transacting the annual exchanges of paper money value.

Should the circulating paper at any time exceed that sum [of gold and silver], as the excess could neither be sent abroad nor be employed in the circulation of the country, it must immediately return upon the banks to be exchanged for gold and silver. . . . There would immediately, therefore, be a run upon the banks to the whole extent of this superfluous paper, and, if they shewed any difficulty or backwardness in payment, to a much greater extent; the alarm, which this would occasion, necessarily increasing the run.[127]

While Smith considered state institutional preventive measures for possible failures of banks, he did not consider ways to negotiate with injustice in the form of 'inconveniency, and sometimes even a very great calamity, to many poor people'. This is despite his observation: 'All men, even the most stupid and unthinking, abhor fraud, perfidy, and injustice, and delight to see them [the perpetrators] punished'.[128] As to response of others to injustice suffered by some individuals, Smith had this to observe at the general level: (1) 'We often struggle to keep down our sympathy with sorrows of others. Whenever we are not under the observation of the sufferer, we endeavour, for our own sake, to suppress as much as we can'[129]; (2) 'When there is no envy in the case, our propensity to sympathize with joy is much stronger than our propensity to sympathize with sorrow'[130]; (3) 'Though our sympathy with sorrow is generally a more lively sensation than our sympathy with joy, it commonly falls much more short of the violence of what is naturally felt by the person principally concerned'.[131] What about the distressed person?

The wretch whose misfortunes call upon our compassion feels with what reluctance we are likely to enter into his sorrow, and therefore proposes his grief to us with fear and hesitation: he even smothers the half of it, and is ashamed, upon account of this hard-headedness of mankind, to give full vent to his affliction.[132]

So the communitarian amelioration for the victims of private vice like greed would not be vigorous; nor would the appeal of the wretch be strong.[133] Smith had to settle down to punishment from within – something akin to the wisdom of the impartial spectator. He was definite that the perpetrator would be punished by his remembrance of his misdeed because they would be 'secretly pursued by the avenging furies of shame and remorse' and afraid that 'black and foul infamy' will 'overtake him from behind'.[134] But the penance of the perpetrator cannot restore to the loser whatever – savings, peace of mind, trust – he has lost because of a banker's greed.

What about punitive response from the state to wrong done to others by those drawn to 'proud ambition and ostentatious avidity' and ready to 'abandon the path of virtue'? What about wrong done by 'the candidates for the highest stations' in 'many governments' who exploit the opportunity of being 'above the law' and think that 'they have no fear of being called to account for the means by which they acquired it' (fortune)? After all,

> They often endeavour . . . not only by fraud and falsehood, the ordinary and vulgar arts of intrigue and cabal, but sometimes by the perpetration of the most enormous crimes, by murder and assassination, by rebellion and civil war, to supplant and destroy those who oppose and stand by way of their greatness.[135]

This is definitely violation of justice.

Apparently, Smith would not leave the issue of securing justice and meting out punishment only to 'sympathetic resentment of the spectator'. Smith pointed to an institutional provision when he observed: 'The . . . duty of the sovereign [is] of protecting, as far as possible, every member of society from the injustice or oppression of every other member of it, or the duty of establishing an exact administration of justice'. But for him such protection was more urgent for a particular kind of sufferer, namely, 'the owner of valuable property' who 'acquired (valuable property) by the labour of many years, or perhaps many successive generations'. For Smith, fundamentally, property was to be secured against passions: 'avarice and ambition in the rich, in the poor the hatred of labour and love of present ease and enjoyment, are the passions much more steady in their operation, and much more universal in their influence'. Between the two, Smith was more concerned about the threat from 'the indignation of the poor, who are often driven by want, and prompted by envy, to invade his [rich man's] possessions'. The poor were numerous too. 'For one every rich man, there must be at least five hundred poor, and the affluence of the few supposes the indigence of the many'. 'Civil government, so far it is instituted for the security of property, is in reality instituted for the defence of the rich against the poor, or of those who have some property against those who have none at all'.[136] The injured poor, in the Smithian scheme of justice, might receive some succour from the 'civil magistrate . . . entrusted with the power not only of preserving the public peace by restraining injustice, but of promoting the prosperity of the commonwealth, by establishing good discipline, and by discouraging all sort of vice and impropriety'.[137] The civil magistrate could sometimes resort to 'capital punishment of those who violate' laws of justice. But it might recoil on the invading poor and located as 'the disturber of public peace' might be 'removed of the world'.[138]

From Smith to Simmel – from *The Theory of Moral Sentiments* (1759) to *The Philosophy of Money* (1900) – the preoccupation with the problem of grasping greed in the two senses of comprehension and containment is evident. In Pierre Bourdieu's writings, approximately a hundred years from *The Philosophy of Money*, the ordinary people, 'denied [of] the means of acquiring a socially dignified existence' and 'poorly adjusted to the rapidly changing conditions of their lives', bear the 'weight of the world'.[139] Any questions against 'the discriminatory practices by the civil servants' by an individual or marginal group would make one vulnerable to be classified as irresponsible by the state. But the 'state nobility' gets away

> with all its violations of the obligation of disinterestedness, all the cases of "private use of public services" (from the diversion of public goods and functions to graft and corruption) . . . [and] the more perverse abuses of law and the administrative tolerances, exemptions, bartering of favours, that result from the faulty implementation or from the transgression of the law.[140]

The civil servants represent the state which monopolizes the legitimate use of the power of both physical and symbolic violence. In fact, the civil servants produce 'a "performative discourse" that both legitimates and constitutes the state as the wielder of symbolic domination in the struggle for power and domination'.[141] The power of deep penetration enjoyed by the state by virtue of statist capital is enormous. The field of power aligned to the state is the site 'which represents the upper reaches of the social class structure where individuals and groups bring considerable amounts of various kinds of capital into their struggles for power'.[142] The ordinary people, the victims of social suffering, remain out of this frame.

What about the judges and the judiciary: could they stand for the victims of capital-holders? Here is an observation by a French judge:

> There are cases that you must investigate and those you must not, all the fiscal fraud cases which are not followed systematically, and then the cases that are hushed up, not to mention political affairs; there too in a general way, and I'm not the only one to say so, people are starting to be sick of it, all the judges, or rather the great majority of judges, at seeing cases hushed up.[143]

This is an illustration how jurists and judges, the holders of juridical capital – a form of symbolic capital – ensure '*doxic* submission to the established order'.[144] As it has never been without struggle between the dominant and the dominated, the use of physical force as a form of capital to deal with 'resistance from below' from the dominated classes, has combined with production of cognitive structures which create the '*effect of universality*'. What about politicians as a source of succour? Bourdieu wrote: 'We had enough of the slipperiness and prevarication of all the politicians, elected by us, who declare us irresponsible when we remind them of the promises they made us'.[145] This 'us', for Bourdieu, includes the workers, but also many other categories in 'a complex classificatory prism'. This 'us' is subjected to state's symbolic violence.[146]

In the system of domination in the present times of 'transformation of the relationship between finance capital and industrial capital', bankers' position has been strengthened not only in the field of economic power but generally.[147] The bankers are 'the nobility of the bourgeois class'.[148] Their control over the economic field is expressed, among other interventions, in the structural violence inflicted by financial markets (layoffs, insecurity). Without 'everyday economic knowledge', workers are vulnerable to the bankers' misadventures;[149] and, not the workers or the poor only. In normal times, when there is no misadventure, the clients are routinely subjected to inattention by the staff and the authorities.[150] Thus, clients of financial institutions – depository (like banks), contractual (like insurance companies) and investment (investment banks) – remain vulnerable to force or fraud perpetrated by such institutions. This is contrary to a strong presumption in economic theory that 'one's economic interest is pursued only by comparatively gentlemanly means' or the 'discipline of competitive markets' can mitigate deceit, mistrust and malfeasance.[151] The clients are more helpless in today's virtual economy because of 'the extreme amplification of time- and space-lags and the lack of trust's traditional substrate identified in past relationships'.[152]

Further, the neo-liberal turn in the economy has also resulted in a 'return to individualism' and decomposition of the welfare state. This has made it easy for those who are secure in their share of various forms of capital to blame the financial illiterate; those are unaware of the ways of the 'right hand'.

> The return to the individual is also what makes it possible to 'blame the victim', who is entirely responsible for his or her misfortune, and to preach the gospel of self-help, all of this being justified by the endlessly repeated need to reduce costs of companies.[153]

and of the state. The financial market and the corporate media post-early twenty-first century are busy, as usual, in reframing the economic habitus and in the mould of 'blame the victim'. The blaming of the ordinary people, particularly the poor and the marginal, takes the form of stigmatizing them for their 'low effort' and 'innate mediocrity' in management of their own money. The successful and the powerful unabashedly show 'big and small acts of contempt, obliviousness, condescension, disrespect and coercion waged in everyday life as well as through the operation of institutions that deploy considerable resources and ingenuity to tell the "deserving" apart from the "undeserving"'.[154] This is noted in the contemporary 'social studies of finance':[155]

> The notion that such irresponsible dealings would have to be erased through the pain and suffering of ordinary citizens (who, as democratic voters, are now held responsible for their

governments' disastrous choices) is deeply troubling and a warning sign that Europe's economic designs may benefit no one but the most powerful.[156]

From the collapse of Union Générale leading to the 1882 crash of the French stock market to the very recent financial crisis in the United States, the bailouts have hurt common decency and standard notions of fairness in popular notions of justice, then and now. But that have hardly restrained financial tzars and the state nobility from their financial adventurism in pursuit of corporate greed. Regulatory institutions are not merely oblivious of their task. They are accomplices in financial adventures in the form of excessive risk-taking by private bankers.[157]

Left with no protection, the helpless, not always only the poor, turn to religious conception of justice.[158] But this is akin to Smithian optimism about recourse to the 'all-seeing Judge of the world'.[159] What has happened is that 'in three centuries of capitalist development in West Europe and North America, cultural constraints on the pursuit of individual self-interest have been loosened in different ways for different groups in different economic realms'.[160] The capitalist state has provided the juridical facilitation of unscrupulous pursuit of financial gains at the cost of the multitudes. It has also overseen the creation and nurturing of cultural legitimations normalizing corporate poaching of the economy.[161] It is this context that creates the contemporary urgency of attention to morality and ethics. In explaining resurgence of morals in economy, Fassin observes: 'The world of banking no longer finds its justification simply in expanding capitalism and speculators' wealth; savers and stockholders prefer to invest in ethical funds that claim to adhere to principles of solidarity and ecology'.[162] The Bengal story is quintessentially the same plot as its numerous versions elsewhere and later. Adam Quetelet wrote: 'Society prepares the crime and the guilty is only the instrument by which it is accomplished[163]. . . . There is a budget which we pay with frightful regularity; it is that of prisons, chains and scaffold'.[164] But Quetelet's budget did not include another round of cost incurred by the victims of both institutional and personal greed, which is at the centre of this tract.

Notes

1 '*Weak Capture* . . . occurs when special interest influence compromises the capacity of regulation to enhance the public interest, but the public is still being served by regulation, relative to the baseline of no regulation. In other words, weak capture prevails when the *net* social benefits

of regulation are diminished as a result of special interest influence, but remain positive overall'. See Daniel Carpenter and David Moss, eds., 'Introduction', in *Preventing Regulatory Capture: Special Interest Influence and How to Limit It*, The Tobin Project (Cambridge: Cambridge University Press, 2013).

2 The idea of humanitarian governance is derived from the concept of humanitarian government as in Didier Fassin, *Humanitarian Reason: A Moral History of the Present*, translated by Rachel Gomme (Berkeley: University of California Press, 2012). This is based on an orientation to human suffering, an orientation which articulates humanitarian morals with humanitarian politics and governance.

3 Ryan K. Balot, *Greed and Injustice in Classical Athens* (Princeton: Princeton University Press, 2001). For an excellent research on how the vulgar coexists with the sublime, see Alexander Lee, *The Ugly Renaissance: Sex, Greed, Violence and Depravity in an Age of Beauty* (New York, London, Toronto, Sydney, and Auckland: Doubleday, 2013). Lee thinks 'ugly' Renaissance is with us all in one way or another.

4 Richard Swedberg, 'The Economic Sociology of Capitalism: An Introduction and Agenda', in Victor Nee and Richard Swedberg, eds., *The Economic Sociology of Capitalism* (Princeton, NJ: Princeton University Press, 2005): 3.

5 Morris Ginsberg's pointer in his Huxley Memorial Lecture in 1953 that 'the systemization of morals compares very unfavourably with that achieved in the sphere of law' still holds true and always will. Morris Ginsberg, 'On the Diversity of Morals', in his *Essays in Sociology and Social Philosophy* (London: Penguin Books, 1968): 261.

6 The Bengali version of this popular saying is traced by some to *Sri Chaitanya-Charitamrta*, a biographical text on the life and teachings of Chaitanya Mahaprabhu (1486–1533), a Vaishnava saint and founder of the Gaudiya Vaishnava Sampradaya. It was written by Krishna Das Kaviraja (b. 1496), primarily in Bengali.

7 Neurologists, generally, and neuroeconomists, particularly, are wondering: 'Are the neural underpinnings of pleasure from money similar to the pleasure we get from food and sex?' They are 'optimistic that knowing how the brain works will tell us important facts about how we make decisions about money'. Chatterjee, *The Aesthetic Brain: How We Evolved to Desire Beauty and Enjoy Art* (Oxford: Oxford University Press, 2014): 93.

8 Lewis A. Coser, *Greedy Institutions: Patterns of Undivided Commitment* (London: The Free Press, 1974).

9 The term and the observation are from Adam Smith; see E. Royston Pike, ed., *Human Documents in Adam Smith's Time*, Routledge Library Editions, Adam Smith, vol. 5 (London: Routledge, 2010): 134–135.

10 Emile Durkheim, 'Effectiveness of Moral Doctrines' (1909), reproduced in Durkheim, *Essays on Morals and Education*, edited with an introduction by W.S.F. Pickering (London: Routledge and Kegan Paul, 1979): 130–131.

11 Steven Lukes, *Moral Relativism* (London: Profile, 2008).

12 Some contemporary researches on consumer behaviour locate later regret over moral abstinence by an individual. Although such findings

do not have a direct bearing on the assumption here that indulgence in greed can always lead to moral repentance, these create scepticism about moral hindsight of an economic actor. 'A series of studies showed that greater temporal separation between decisions and their (retrospective or prospective) evaluations enhances regret of righteousness and decreases regret of indulgence. The discovered temporal pattern of regret contributes to a fuller understanding of myopic and hyperopic self-control problem and is diametrically opposed to the traditional assumption that consumers are better off in the long run if they choose virtue over vice'. Ran Kivetz and Anat Keinan, 'Repenting Hyperopia: An Analysis of Self-Control Regrets', *Journal of Consumer Research Inc.* 33 (September 2006): 280. See also Keinan and Kivetz, 'Remedying Hyperopia: The Effects of Self-Control Regret on Consumer Behavior', *Journal of Marketing Research* 45 (December 2008): 676–689; Scott Rick and George Lowenstein, 'The Role of Emotions in Economic Behavior', in *Handbook of Emotions*, 3rd ed., edited by Michael Lewis, Jeannette M. Haviland-Jones and Lisa Feldman Barrett (New York: The Guilford Press, 2008).

13 Balot, *Greed and Injustice in Classical Athens*: 18.
14 *Wall Street* (1987 film), Deng Xiaoping, *Selected Works*, Hindi film *Jannat* (Heaven) directed by Kunal Deshmukh and produced by Mukesh Bhatt (2008). The song 'Jannat Jahan', sung by Rupam Islam, became a chartbuster. He created a Bengali version of that song, 'Jannat Takkai' (Money is heaven).
15 Prasanta Ray, 'Little Everyday Greed', *Autumn Annual*, Presidency University, Kolkata, 2015.
16 For a comprehensive analysis, see Bela Dutta Gupta, *Bange Dhrubabad* (A Treatise on Positivism in Bengal) (Kolkata: Paschim Bangla Academy, 2009); see also Bela Dutta Gupta, *Sociology in India: An Enquiry into Sociological Thinking and Empirical Social Research in the Nineteenth Century – With Special Reference to Bengal* (Kolkata: Centre for Sociological Research, 1972): Chapter 6.
17 Bela Dutta Gupta, *Sociology in India: An Enquiry into Sociological Thinking and Empirical Social Research in the Nineteenth Century – With Special Reference to Bengal*: 138.
18 Ibid.: 131, 132.
19 S. N. Mukerjee and Marian Maddern, *Sociological Essays: Utilitarianism and Positivism/Bankim Chandra Chatterjee* (Kolkata: Riddhi, 1986).
20 Radhakamal Mukherjee, *Borderlands of Economics* (London: Allen & Unwin, 1925). This is based on the lectures delivered between 1921 and 1925 in Lucknow University.
21 shodhganga.inflibnet.ac.in/bitstream/10603/17625/ . . . /08_chapter%20 1.p . . . accessed on 25 May 2017.
22 T. N. Madan, *Sociological Traditions: Methods and Perspectives in Sociology in India* (New Delhi: SAGE, 2011): 128.
23 Radhakamal Mukherjee: 32–33. 'Economics was grounded upon the rational side of human nature by the classical school who worked on the foundations of extreme hedonism and intellectualism in psychology': 31–32.

24 Ibid.: 39–40.
25 Radhakamal Mukherjee, *The Social Structures of Values* (London: Mac-millan, 1949). Also, *The Institutional Theory of Economics* (London: Macmillan, 1942); *The Dynamics of Morals: A Socio-Psychological Theory of Ethics* [1950] (London: Macmillan, London, n.d.).
26 Radhakamal Mukherjee quoted by Barbara Celarent, 'Review, "*The Dynamics of Morals: A Socio-Psychological Theory of Ethics*"', *American Journal of Sociology* 118, 6 (May 2013): 1742.
27 Radhakamal Mukherjee, *Borderlands of Economics*: 39–40.
28 Ibid.: Chapter 8, 'The Humanization of Economics'; See also, Barbara Harriss-White, 'India's Socially Regulated Economy', *Working Paper No 133*, Paper for the 7th International Conference on Institutional Economics, University of Hertfordshire, June 2005.
29 Radhakamal Mukherjee, *Borderlands of Economics*: 39–40:

In economic theory this tendency in reality has been the outcome of the old philosophy which believed that individuals are alone real, and has missed the fact that the individual is also a social product and ignored the dynamic and constructive role of the interplay between the individual and his institutional environment . . . Individualism, which was the keynote of the eighteenth and nineteenth centuries' thought till 1870, rested primarily on hedonism and utilitarianism, but was buttressed by the Smithian economics of laissez-faire and the dominant commercial spirit, the outcome of the Industrial Revolution. The gradual supersession of all human relations by the cash nexus and the loss of independence and status of the workingman, who is reduced to a mere automaton, were in keeping with the neglect and suppression of the social self. Indeed, the wage system, which is the development of modern industrial conditions, on the one hand has increased personal freedom, and on the other diminished, nay, destroyed, the strength of those personal and social ties which bind man to the family, the ethnic group or the neighbourhood.

30 The notion of greed has no place in his important texts.
31 Ibid.: 37.
32 Ibid.: 38.
33 Ibid.: 48–49.
34 Mukherjee, *The Social Structures of Values*: 13.
35 Ibid.
36 Ibid.: 90.
37 Barbara Celarent, 'Review, "*The Dynamics of Morals: A Socio-Psychological Theory of Ethics*"': 1739; the reviewer felt like many of his readers that 'Mukerjee's arguments do not flow with logical rigor from defined terms to grounded assertions. They swirl and overlap. Meaning emerges gradually and indirectly. Chapter subheadings float relatively free of the text they precede, being either starting points for meditations or – more likely – retrospective attempts to order a meditative oral text'.
38 Mukherjee, *Borderlands of Economics*: 31.

39 Pankaj Kumar Mukherjee, 'The Economic Services of Zamindars to the Peasants and the Public as Analysed by Benoy Sarkar', in *The Social and Economic Ideas of Benoy Sarkar*, edited by Banesvar Das (Calcutta: Chuckvertty Chatterjee & Co., 1939): 7, 51. Sarkar wrote in 1933 in *Liberty* and in *Arthik Unnati*: 'By allowing the rent to fall into arrears, the zamindars function automatically as *mahajan*s or bankers to the ryots who are thereby enabled to carry on their agricultural operations in a somewhat secure manner': 52.

40 Radhakamal Mukherjee, *Economic Problems of Modern India*, vol. 1 (London: Macmillan, 1939); vol. 2 (London: Macmillan, 1941).

41 Ibid., vol. 2: 325–352.

42 Ibid.: 341–342: He wrote: 'The Managers and the Directors of the Indian banks of the past did not display that amount of integrity and straightforwardness that is demanded of the bankers, and they were bent more upon the speedy accumulation of riches for themselves than on safeguarding the interests of depositors and shareholders. In order to achieve this selfish end, they indulged in dishonest transactions and wild speculation. In their anxiety to gratify their get-rich-quick desire they threw discretion to the winds and advanced large sums on securities not worth a name. They declared large dividends even in the initial stages without attempting to build up substantial resources for the rainy day. Their most serious crime lay in their transgressing the limits of legitimate banking business by giving preference to ordinary trading business. . . . It is no wonder therefore, that when the crash came it shattered most of the banks'

43 Tim Redman, *Ezra Pound and Italian Fascism* (Cambridge: Cambridge University Press, 1991): 53; Social Credit Movement was mainly a Canadian movement based on an ideal distributive system conceived and propagated by an Englishman C. H. Douglas (1879–1952). It was in favour of dispersing economic and political power to individuals. It proposed that 'absolute economic security' for individuals should be the basis of a new civilization.

44 Georg Simmel, *The Philosophy of Money*, edited by David Frisby, translated by Tom Bottomore and David Frisby, 2nd enlarged ed. (London: Routledge, 1990): 210.

45 Ibid.: 221.

46 Niall Ferguson, *The Ascent of Money: A Financial History of the World* (London: Penguin Books, 2009); Frank Partnoy, 'Infectious Greed: How Deceit and Risk Corrupted the Financial Markets', *Public Affairs*, 2009.

47 Gurbachan Singh, *Banking Crisis, Liquidity, and Credit Lines: A Macroeconomic Perspective* (New Delhi: Routledge, 2012).

48 All standpoint sociologies like feminism are informed by humanism. Currently, there is a significant humanist turn in sociology. See Ken Plummer, 'A Manifesto for a Critical Humanism in Sociology: On Questioning the Human Social World', in *Sociology: A Text and Reader*, edited by Daniel Nehring (London: Routledge, 2012); William Du Bois and R. Dean Wright, 'What Is Humanistic Sociology?', *The American Sociologist* 33, 4 (Winter 2002): 5–36; Ken Plummer, *Documents of Life: An Introduction to the Problems and Literature of a Humanist Method* (London:

Allen and Unwin, 1983); *Documents of Life 2: An Invitation to Critical Humanism* (London: SAGE, 2001); Alan Wolfe, *Whose Keeper? Social Science and Moral Obligation* (Berkeley: University of California Press, 1989); François Doss, *Empire of Meaning: The Humanization of the Social Sciences*, translated by Hassan Melehy (Minneapolis, MN: University of Minnesota Press 1999).

49 Amartya Sen, *On Ethics and Economics* (New Delhi: Oxford University Press, 1987).

50 Michael Hviid Jacobsen and Poul Poder, eds., *The Sociology of Zygmunt Bauman* (Farnham, Surrey: Ashgate, 2008): 64.

51 A contemporary engagement with morality of proximity is Pierre Bourdieu et al., *The Weight of the World: Social Suffering in Contemporary Society*, translated by Priscilla Parkhurst Ferguson et al. (Cambridge: Polity Press, 1999).

52 Phyllis Tickle, *Greed: The Seven Deadly Sins* (New York: New York Public Library, 2004). Some of the other scholarly works are the following: Nancy Folbre, *Greed, Lust and Gender: A History of Economic Ideas* (Oxford: Oxford University Press, 2009); Ferguson, *The Ascent of Money*; Roberto de Vogli, *Progress or Collapse: The Crises of Market Greed* (London: Routledge, 2012).

53 *Bhagavad Gita 16.21*: The Bhagavad Gita or *Śrīmadbhagavadgītā* (The Song of the God) is written in Sanskrit, authorship being credited to Ved Vyasa.

54 This is note derived from Chapter 2, verse 63 of Gita; see Lin Yutung, *The Wisdom of India and China* (New York: Random House 1942): 66; evidently, the individual is responsible for his greed and the adverse consequences are for him.

55 For Marx's analysis, see Lynn Shakinovsky, *The 1857 Financial Crisis and the Suspension of the 1844 Bank Act*, www.branchcollective. org/?ps_articles=lynn-shakinovsky-the-1857-financial-, accessed on 26 May 2017, Sergio Bologna, *Money and Crisis: Marx as Correspondent of the New York Daily Tribune, 1856–57*, www.wildcat-www.de/en/material/cs13bolo.htm, accessed on 26 May 2017.

56 Emile Durkheim, *Professional Ethics and Civic Morals*, translated by Cornelia Brookfield with a new Preface by Bryan S. Turner (London: Routledge, 2003).

57 Ibid.: 50.

58 Ibid.: 9–10. 'Now, this lack of organization in the business professions has one consequence of the greatest moment: that is, that in this whole sphere of social life, no professional ethics exist. Or at least, if they do they are so rudimentary that at the very most one can see in them may be a pattern and a foreshadowing for the future. Since by the force of circumstance there is some contact between the individuals, some ideas in common do indeed emerge and thus some precepts of conduct, but how vaguely and with how little authority. If we were to attempt to fix in definite language the ideas current on what the relations should be of the employee with his chief, of the workman with the manager, of the rival manufacturers with each other and with the public – what vague and equivocal formulas we should get! Some hazy generalizations on the loyalty and devotion owed by staff and workmen to those employing them'.

59 Ibid.: 10.
60 Ibid.: 12. Further: 'Let us see, then, how the unleashing of economic interests has been accompanied by a debasing of public morality. We find that the manufacturer, the merchant, the workman, the employee, in carrying on his occupation, is aware of no influence set above him to check his egotism; he is subject to no moral discipline whatever and so he scouts any discipline at all of this kind'.
61 Emile Durkheim, *Suicide: A Study in Sociology* [1897] (New York: Free Press, 1979): 255–256. Later reference to pathological consequences of prosperity in W. C. Mitchell's *Business Cycles and Their Causes* (Berkeley: University of California Press, 1941); found in Richard Swedberg, 'Major Traditions of Economic Sociology', *Annual Review of Sociology* 17 (1991). Swedberg quotes Mitchell: 'prosperity breeds crisis': 256.
62 In Indian wisdom, even locating the greedy was impossible. Kautilya observed in his *Arthaśāstra*: 'Just as it impossible not to taste the honey (or the poison) that finds itself at the tip of the tongue, so it is impossible for a government servant not to eat up, at least, a bit of the king's revenue. Just as fish moving under water cannot possibly be found out either as drinking or not drinking water, so government servants employed in the government work cannot be found out (while) taking money (for themselves)'. Quoted in Pranab Bardhan, *Scarcity, Conflicts, and Cooperation: Essays in the Political and Institutional Economics of Development* (New Delhi: Oxford University Press, 2005): 137.
63 Durkheim, *Suicide*: 241.
64 Ibid.: 242. See also Eugene N. White, 'The Crash of 1882, Counterparty Risk, and the Bailout of the Paris Bourse', *NBER Working Paper Series*, Paper 12933, 2007, www.nber.org/papers/w12933, accessed on 25 May 2017. A good part of Marx's theory of money was triggered by his polemics with Alfred Darimon (1819–1902), a prominent Proudhonist, on the issue of bank reform. Marx was reacting to Darimon's *De la réforme des banques*, 1856. See Karl Marx, *Grundrisse: Foundations of the Critique of Political Economy*, translated with a Foreword by Martin Nicolaus (London: Penguin Books, 1993): 115–127. It is interesting to note that the after-party of the recent Paris premiere of *The Wolf of Wall Street* (2013) was held at the former site of the Paris bourse. The film is 'based on the true story of Jordan Belfort, from his rise to a wealthy US stockbroker living the high life to his fall involving crime, corruption and the federal government'. The film belongs to a genre of film depicting moral collapse due to greed as in the film *Wall Street* (1987) and its sequel *Wall Street: Money Never Sleeps* (2010). Mia Shanley, 'Europe's Bankers, Investors Flock to "The Wolf of Wall Street"', Stockholm, 10 January 2014, *Reuters*. Gordon Gekko is a fictional character in *Wall Street*, but Jordan Belfort is a real character who wrote his memoir. But the difference between fiction and real melts as they both become 'a symbol in popular culture for unrestrained greed'.
   An early classic on greed is Erich Von Stroheim's *Greed* (1924). It is 'a dark study of the oppressive forces that decay and corrupt three people – a simple, uneducated former miner and dentist (McTeague) in turn of the century San Francisco, his miserly, vulgar and pathological wife (Trina),

and their mutual friend and McTeague's ultimate nemesis (Marcus) – all are caught up by their squalid, debased passion, compulsion and greed for gold. The wife's fixation on money causes the dentist to lose everything – he kills her, becomes maddened with the same lust for gold, then takes flight only to find himself handcuffed to his dead pursuer in the fateful conclusion. The film is a morality tale about how the characters are dehumanized by the influence of money upon their lives'. The film opens with a title card that reads: 'GOLD – GOLD – GOLD – GOLD Bright and Yellow, Hard and Cold, Molten, Graven, Hammered, Rolled, Hard to Get and Light to Hold; Stolen, Borrowed, Squandered – Doled'. The verse is taken from *Miss Kilmansegg: Her Moral* by the early nineteenth-century writer Thomas Hood.

There is nothing comparable in the history of Indian cinema. The closest comes is the Indian film *Stumble* (2003). The director, Prakash Belwadi writes about the middle class, and the film representing its greed. 'I see it as the great rip-off of the Indian middle class by the new economy. . .. For them, savings are the most crucial issue but with interest rates dropping, stock markets collapsing, there is no security of savings in the country. Coupled with this, the dotcom boom turned out to be one of the greatest mockeries of the new economy. This film is about how one nuclear family trips over money'.

65 Ibid.: 258.
66 Ibid.: 255.
67 Ibid.: 255–256.
68 Written in late June 1856. First published in the *New-York Daily Tribune*, no. 4751, 11 July 1856, marxengels.public-archive.net/en/ME0978en. html, accessed on 25 May 2017. The Crédit Mobilier was a French joint-stock bank founded in 1852 by the Péreire brothers. Under protection of the Napoleon III government, it engaged in speculation. It became bankrupt in 1867 and was liquidated in 1871. The third article was closely preceded by two articles available at marxengels.public-archive.net/en/ME0978en.html
69 This included Proudhon's proposal for a *Banque du Peuple* to emancipate the workers and to transform wage labour into associated labour within the framework of a single co-operative organization of society. A different order of banking was also introduced in France. The purpose was to change prevailing attitude of the French rentier-saver who were inclined to invest money in state bonds with fixed rates. This kind of investment bank wanted to mobilize agricultural savings to be eventually directed towards industry. 'The programmatic declarations of this new type of banking already explicitly indicate its role as a stimulus and as a means of transforming the French bourgeoisie'. Sergio Bologna, 'Money and Crisis: Marx as Correspondent of the New York Daily Tribune, 1856–57, Part 2', *Selected Writings of Sergio Bologna*, www.wildcat-www.de/en/material/cs13bolo.htm, accessed on 26 May 2017. We need to remember that the period (1848–1870) when the experiments were being proposed or made was the period of transition for French capitalism. About traditional as well as contemporary practices towards alternatives – those 'putatively animated by "social" instead of strictly

"economic" concerns' and those 'infused with or motivated by religious dogma and sentiment' – to mainstream financial institutions which subserve capitalist interests, particularly in 'illicit and illegal finance', see 'Poor People's Finance', in *The Oxford Handbook of the Sociology of Finance*, edited by Karin Knorr Centina and Alex Preda (New York: Oxford University Press, 2013): 416–421.

70 Ibid. Speech by Count Montalembert, in opposing a project of law to raise the postage on all printed papers, books and the like, on May 31, 1856, quoted by Marx in his third article on 'The French Crédit Mobilier'. See Note 68 above.

71 Durkheim in his review of Georg Simmel, *'Philosophie des Geldes'*, quoted in David Frisby, ed., *The Philosophy of Money*, translated by Tom Bottomore and David Frisby, 2nd enlarged ed. (London: Routledge, 1990): xviii.

72 Swedberg, 'Major Traditions of Economic Sociology': 258.

73 Max Weber, *Economy and Society: An Outline of Interpretative Sociology*, edited by Guenther Roth and Claus Wittich (Berkeley: University of California Press, vol. 1, Part 2, 1978): 335.

74 Ibid.: 336.

75 Ibid.: 479.

76 David Frisby, ed., 'Afterword: The Constitution of the Text', in *Philosophy of Money*: 517.

77 Ibid.: Chapter 3, section 2.

78 Ibid.: 232.

79 Ferguson, *The Ascent of Money*: 1. Also, Partnoy, *Infectious Greed*.

80 Simmel, *Philosophy of Money*: 236.

81 Ibid.: 238. 'Generally speaking, the threshold of the beginning of a real greed for money will be relatively high in a developed and lively money economy, but relatively low at primitive economic levels'.

82 Marx, *Grundrisse*: 221.

83 Ibid.: 183.

84 Ibid.

85 Ibid.: 437; Simmel thinks this to be a strong basis for being cynical to Comte's advocacy of placing 'bankers at the head of secular government in his utopian state'. Comte stipulated that 'the temporal rulers, in each state, would consist of the three most important bankers'.

86 Ibid.: 441.

87 Simmel characterizes a tripartite division between classes in terms of money: 'some possess no money at all (lowest), others save something (middle), a third class can live permanently from its interest (highest strata)', quoted in Nigel Dodd, 'Simmel's Perfect Money: Fiction, Socialism and Utopia in *The Philosophy of Money*', *Theory Culture Society* (published online 5 November 2012): 6. doi:10.1177/0263276411435570

88 Ibid.: 215.

89 Ibid.: 260.

90 Frisby, *Philosophy of Money*: xviii.

91 But there have been major debacles in contemporary capitalist economy, banking crisis being one of its manifestations. People are looking out for new forms of money: money not mediated through corporate

banks – may be, not through banks at all because the historical association between banks and ascendency of money is very strong. 'Although
varied in form, scale and design, most alternative money and credit systems have a discernible set of normative goals that could be described as
utopian in spirit: to foster a sense of community, to build local wealth
without allowing it to be siphoned off by large corporations and banks,
and to provide "free" banking. . . . Such schemes appear to work against
any idea of money as "soulless" . . . they are designed to enrich, not
erode, civic life. What Simmel calls money interests may operate in such
cases, but it is an interest that is grounded in local association – or more
specifically, sociation'. See Dodd, 'Simmel's Perfect Money: Fiction,
Socialism and Utopia': 2.

 92 Hugh Collins, *Marxism and Law* (Oxford: Oxford University Press,
    1987): 1–16.
 93 Marx, *Grundrisse*:123.
 94 Ibid.: 222.
 95 Ibid.: 224.
 96 Ibid.: 222, 223.
 97 Karl Marx, *The Class Struggles in France*, 1848–1850 (1850) (Moscow:
    Progress Publishers, 1975): 29. This text needs to be read with his *Grun-
    drisse* (1857–1858).
 98 Ibid.
 99 Marx quoted in Sergio Bologna, 'Money and Crisis: Marx as Correspon-
    dent of the New York Daily Tribune, 1856–57, Part 2', www.wildcat-
    www.de/en/material/cs13bolo.htm, accessed on 26 May 2017.
100 Marx, *Grundrisse*: 241. Marx followed up with penetrating analysis of
    the French Crédit Mobilier bank in his first article on this theme in the
    Chartist People's Paper, 7 June 1856, which was republished in the *New
    York Daily Tribune* on 21 June. He wrote two more on this issue on 24
    June and 11 July editions. In both, he examined the relationship between
    the bank and the regime. He showed 'the mobilisation of savings and the
    way they were sucked in through the Crédit subsidiaries . . . as one of the
    principal elements in mobilising otherwise unused resources and bring-
    ing them under the controlling hand of the regime'. In fact, Marx wrote
    on 'the problem of cyclical crises and questions related to the British
    banking reforms of 1844' in a series of articles in the *Neuer Oder Zei-
    tung*, 11, 12, 20 and 25 January, 1855. See Bologna, 'Money and Crisis:
    Marx as Correspondent of the *New York Daily Tribune*, 1856–57'.
101 Marx, *Class Struggles in France*: 32. 'Finance aristocracy' comprised
    'bankers, stock-exchange kings, railway kings, owners of coal and iron
    mines and forests, a part of the landed proprietors associated with them';
    ibid.: 28.
102 Ibid.: 41.
103 Ibid.
104 Marx, *Grundrisse*: 226.
105 Max Weber, *The Protestant Ethic and the Spirit of Capitalism*, translated
    by Talcott Parsons and Foreword by R. H. Tawney (New York: Charles
    Scribner's Sons, 1958): 186, note 6. For South Sea Bubble, see Peter Temin
    and Hans-Joachim Voth, *Riding the South Sea Bubble*, https://dspace.mit.

edu/.../ridingsouthseabu00temi.pdf%3Bjsessionid%3D47B79D27A66, accessed on 25 May 2017.

106 Pierre Bourdieu, *Acts of Resistance: Against the Tyranny of the Market* (New York: The New Press, 1998): 2.

107 It is evident that in this reconstruction of sub-texts on greed in Western classics does not follow the chronology of contributions. The reason for Adam Smith's late reference here is that he is usually taken as an economist who, according to Schumpeter in his *History of Economic Analysis, 1870–1914* (1954), was an economist adumbrating formation of economic sociology; see Swedberg, 'Major Traditions of Economic Sociology': 1991.

108 This was a 'most significant' addition by Smith in the seventh edition of the book in 1790, the year he died. E. G. West in his Introduction in Adam Smith, *The Theory of Moral Sentiments* (1759), with an Introduction by E. G. West (Indianapolis, IN: Liberty Classics, 1976): 20. This was well after *The Wealth of Nations* (1776).

109 Ibid.

110 T. D. Campbell, *Adam Smith's Science of Morals*, Routledge Library Editions: Adam Smith, vol. 3 (London: Routledge, 2010): 175.

111 Ibid.: 175: quoting Adam Smith, *The Wealth of Nations*, V.i.3 (II.315).

112 The bankers on whom this small tract focuses do not fall in the category of merchants, but in case of hearing of petitions and colonial government's consultations and in judicial litigations against the failing banks in Bengal, their pre-eminence is clear, making Adam Smith's observations relevant.

113 Adam Smith, *The Wealth of Nations*, Books 1–3 (1776), edited with Introduction and Notes by Andrew Skinner (London: Penguin Books, 1999): 358–359.

114 Giovanni Arrighi, *Adam Smith in Beijing: Lineages of the Twenty-First Century* (London: Verso, 2007): 47–48. Arrighi draws on *The Wealth of Nations* (vol. II, p. 255) to point to Smith's 'utter scepticism concerning the efficiency and usefulness of big business': 55.

115 Adam Smith, *Theory of Moral Sentiments*: 494; See E. G. West, Introduction, note 107.

116 Adam Smith, *Theory of Moral Sentiments*, edited by Sálvio Marcelo Soares (Sao Paulo: MetaLibri, 2005): 53.

117 Ibid.: 31. The impartial spectator can be 'an imagined or real person'.

118 Smith, *Theory of Moral Sentiments*: 73.

119 Ibid.: 236.

120 E. G. West in his 'Introduction', in Smith, *Theory of Moral Sentiments*: 31.

121 Smith, *The Theory of Moral Sentiments*: 228.

122 Arrighi, *Adam Smith in Beijing*: 42–48. Smith's fundamental dictum was: 'In general, if any branch of trade, or any division of labour, be advantageous to the public, the freer and more general the competition, it will always be the more so'; see Adam Smith, *The Wealth of Nations*, Introduction by Alan B. Krueger (New York: Bantam Books, 2003): 421.

123 Ibid.: 43.

124 Smith, *Wealth of Nations*, Introduction by Krueger: 372.

125 Ibid.: 412. Smith had a great concern for the poor. He wrote: 'No society can surely be flourishing and happy, of which the greater part of the members are poor and miserable. It is but equity, besides, that they who feed, cloath and lodge the whole body of people, should have such a share of produce of their labour as to be themselves tolerably well fed, cloathed and lodged'; see also 110–111.

126 Ibid.: 420.

127 Ibid.: 383.

128 Smith, *Theory of Moral Sentiments*: 171.

129 Ibid.:104. Smith observed: 'It is painful to go along with grief, and we always enter it with reluctance'; 106.

130 Ibid.: 105.

131 Ibid.: 106. He observed also in the same work: 'The compassion of the spectator must arise altogether from the consideration of what himself would feel if he was reduced to the same unhappy situation, and, what perhaps is impossible, was at the same time able to regard it with his present reason and judgment': 52. For Smith, the imperative on the part of others being told about somebody's misfortune was to give him or her attentive hearing. Because he thought: 'The cruelest insult which can be offered to the unfortunate, is to appear to make light of their calamities . . . not to wear a serious countenance when they tell us their afflictions, is real and gross inhumanity': 56.

132 Ibid.: 107.

133 Ibid.: 97. Particularly, because grief is a selfish passion: 'conceived upon account of our own private . . . bad fortune'.

134 Ibid.: 131–132.

135 Ibid.: 130–131.

136 Smith, *Wealth of Nations*, Introduction by Krueger: 901, 902, 907.

137 Smith, *The Theory of Moral Sentiments*: 159.

138 Ibid.: 169–170: 'The disturber of the public peace is hereby removed out of the world, and others are terrified by his fate from imitating his example'. In the same passage, Smith equates 'public peace' with the 'orderly and flourishing state of society'.

139 Bourdieu et al., *Weight of the World*. This work along with his *Acts of Resistance* was written when he was in active politics. 'Bourdieu's prominence increased exponentially during the 1990s, when he became a highly visible participant in political struggles against the neoliberal orthodoxy that was coming to dominate political discourse in Continental Europe'. Elliot B. Weininger, 'Foundations of Pierre Bourdieu's Class Analysis', in *Approaches to Class Analysis*, edited by Erik Olin Wright (Cambridge: Cambridge University Press, 2005): 82.

140 Pierre Bourdieu, Loïc J. D. Wacquant and Samar Farage, 'Rethinking the State: Genesis and Structure of the Bureaucratic Field', *Sociological Theory* 12, 1 (1994): 18.

141 David L. Swartz, 'The State as the Central Bank of Symbolic Credit', Lecture delivered at the 99th Annual Meeting of the American Sociological Association, San Francisco, 14–17 August 2004, people.bu.edu/dswartz/articles/10.html

142 Ibid.

143 Interview with a 'ground level' judge, Andre S., who served small provincial courts away from Paris by Remi Lenoir: The judge voiced his critical opinion on the working of the judiciary in 1991 from the midst of a stifling judicial hierarchy. 'The judiciary is in effect a highly hierarchical system in which the voicing of opinions is heavily monitored; unless they have a sufficiently elevated position in the hierarchy, those who speak out are disqualified in the eyes of their peers'. Bourdieu et al., *Weight of the World: Social Suffering in Contemporary Society*: 239–253.

144 Bourdieu et al., 'Rethinking the State': 15–16.

145 Bourdieu, *Acts of Resistance*: 78.

146 Weininger, 'Foundations of Pierre Bourdieu's Class Analysis'. The workers are not normally players in Bourdieu's field of power corresponding to economic capital. The 'us', the people who are subject to state's symbolic violence, include not only 'the subaltern, the mad, the sick, and the criminal. It bears upon us all, in a myriad minute and invisible ways'; Pierre Bourdieu, with collaboration of Monique de Saint Martin, *The State Nobility Elite Schools in the Field of Power*, translated by Lauretta C. Clough (Palo Alto: Stanford University Press, 1996): xviii.

147 'Large banking groups, which owing to the invention of new ways of concentrating capital and savings, manage to control entire branches of industry without being their exclusive owners. Bankers are thus in a position to impose their vision and expectations': 327; 'The top state chief executives . . . were "predestined", as it were, to occupy positions located at the *intersection* between the public and the private sectors or, better still, between banking, industry, and the state, the very locus of power today': 329; Bourdieu and de Saint Martin, *State Nobility Elite Schools*.

148 Ibid.: 308, and 441, note 18.

149 Bourdieu has drawn attention to the lack of 'everyday knowledge of economics' in his 1963 collaborative research with Luc Boltanski, and Jean-Claude Chamoredon on bank and its customers. This research represents his larger interest in relationship between 'economic and temporal dispositions' and attitudes towards spending, savings, credit and investing. The 'socialized subjectivity' or the habitus rather than the *homo economicus* governs perception and pursuit of economic interests which always have symbolic connotations. For reference to this unpublished report, Pierre Bourdieu, Luc Boltanski, and Jean-Claude Chamoredon, *Bank and Its Customers: Elements for Sociology of Credit* (1963), see Swedberg, 'The Economic Sociology of Pierre Bourdieu': 67–82. doi:10.1177/1749975510389712; Johan Heilborn, 'Economic Sociology in France', *European Societies* 3, 1 (2001): 41–67; Frédéric Lebaron, 'Pierre Bourdieu: Economic Models Against Economism', *Theory and Society* 32, 5–6 (2003): 551–565.

150 'As shown by the study we carried out in 1963 at the Campagnie Bancaire, even the semblance of an interest in the "person" of the client tends to disappear as the process of drawing up the contract progresses'. Pierre Bourdieu, *The Social Structure of the Economy* (Cambridge: Polity Press, 2005): 157.

151 Mark Granovetter, 'Economic Action and Social Structure: The Problem of Embeddedness', *American Journal of Sociology* 91, 3 (1985): 488.

152 Sandro Castaldo, *Trust in Market Relationships* (Cheltenhem: Edward Elgar, 2007): 61.

153 Bourdieu, *Acts of Resistance*: 7. In the late twentieth-century French social context, the 'right hand' comprises 'the technocrats of the Ministry of Finance, the public and private banks and the ministerial *cabinets*'; and the 'left hand', 'the social workers': family counselors, youth leaders, rank-and-file magistrates, and also, increasingly, secondary and primary teachers': 2.

154 Marion Fourcade, Philippe Steiner, Wolfgang Streeck, and Cornelia Woll, 'Moral Categories in the Financial Crisis', *Maxpo Discussion Paper 13/1*, Max Planck Sciences Po Center on Coping with Instability in Market Societies, Paris: 21.

155 The British Sociological Association listed sociologists in UK and US writing on the current financial crisis in response to a criticism by Aditya Chakrabortty in April 2012 of their insufficient attention. In fact, some sociologists have engaged in moral debates over market greed. www.guardian.co.uk/education/2012/apr/18/alternative-economics-people-mattered, www.guardian.co.uk/commentisfree/2012/jun/05/response-sociologists-financial-crisis?commentpage=1#start-of-comments. For a review of recent work of this genre, See, Ilkka Arminen, *Who's Afraid of Financial Markets?* ilkka.arminen@uta.fi, accessed on 23 May 2017.

156 Fourcade et al., 'Moral Categories in the Financial Crisis': 3. For impact of financial wrongs committed by powerful private players in the economic field, see John Bone and Karen O'Reilly, 'No Place Called Home: The Causes and Social Consequences of the UK Housing "Bubble"', *British Journal of Sociology* 61, 2 (2010): 231–255.

157 For review of such researches on private bankers control because of their routine supply of credit to entrepreneurs, see Lisa A. Keister, 'Financial Markets, Money, and Banking', *Annual Review of Sociology* 28 (2002): 39–61. doi:10.1146/annurev.soc.28.110601.140836, accessed on 25 May 2017. Researchers have established that it is not always that capitalists are caught unaware about financial fiasco. On contrary, they prefer to ride on the bubble. Temin, and Voth, 'Riding the South Sea Bubble'.

158 Fourcade et al., 'Moral Categories in the Financial Crisis': 2.

159 Smith, *Theory of Moral Sentiments*: 228.

160 Nancy Folbre, *Greed, Lust and Gender* (Oxford and New York: Oxford University Press, 2009): xxv. Capitalism's power of corrupting whatever it requires to corrupt includes knowledge systems. Hannah Devlin, 'Greed Imperils Good Name of Math: "Mathematics Has Lost Its Moral Purity as It Is Open to Misuse by Bankers [for Financial Gains] and Rogue Regimes [in Cyber Warfare]", According to One of Oxford's Most Celebrated Mathematicians, Andrew Wiles', *The Telegraph*, Kolkata, 5 October 2013.

161 This explains significant attention to greed and its consequences in recent times. It is interesting that the inaugural issue *Economic Anthropology* is focused on 'Social Economies of Greed and Excess'. Rahul Oka and Ian Kuijt, *Economic Anthropology* 1, 1 (2014).

162 Didier Fassin and Samuel Lézé, eds., *Moral Anthropology: A Critical Reader* (London: Routledge, 2014): 1.
163 Bourdieu, *Acts of Resistance*: 7. See note 152.
164 Adolphe Quetelet, *Recherches statistiques sur le royaume de Pays-Bas* (1829) (Research statistics on the Kingdom of the Netherlands), *Caprices of Man* (1835). It is difficult to find an English translation of the first treatise. His *A Treatise on Man and the Development of His Faculties* (Edinburgh: William and Robert Chambers, 1842) is available in English at https://archive.org/details/treatiseonmandev00quet

EPILOGUE

A search for the victims of greed for money does not bring forth a conclusion. Victims are being continuously bred – taking a cue from Manuel Castells's *Another Economy is Possible* – through 'the malevolent persistence of the bad old' capitalism.[1] To resume the Bengal story, revelations of a very large number of people being defrauded of their money in the form of savings point to continuing poaching of both public and personal money in Bengal. This is despite firmed up regulatory devices compared to what prevailed in the early decades of the last century. The bank is not the fraudulent institution any longer, although it is a site for criminal appropriation.[2] But planned misappropriation of other people's money continues. Some changes are evident, though. One: the status of the financial institution has changed from unscheduled and scheduled banks to Ponzi firms – more popularly, chit funds. The Ponzi phenomenon, it is well known, has become globally widespread. Two: the net to trap the gullible and risk-taking individuals has become expansive and dense. Three: the size of the losers has significantly increased. Four: the class character of the deceived has changed from the middle class to the middle class plus the poor. Five: so has the locus, from Calcutta to Kolkata plus its suburbs, and may be the rural interior also.[3] Six: efficient organization of the operatives networking with local politicians and police play a significant role in running the business. Seven: with increasingly key role being played by money in politics, politicians of different hues have become money-grabbers. Eight: The range of investments of money collected by the Ponzi firm owners has become varied. This includes film industry and education.

This much is evident that the Bengali pleonexia – the insatiable desire to have what rightfully belongs to others – is uncontainable, more so when the stakeholders improve their evasive skills. Those successful in arrogating other people's money to re-define their own lifestyles marked by conspicuous consumption attain social visibility. Since many of them had a modest beginning, their altered high-spending ways of living make them a new breed of nouveaux riches living off cunning extraction. It is just like in Bengali proverb which derides an individual spending another's money as one's own while people (observers) remain under a delusion that he enjoys the grace of Goddess Lakshmi – *parer dhone poddari, loke bale lakshmishree* (splurging on another's money as if it were one's own; onlookers see this as your good fortune).[4] Needless to insist, it is not an exclusively Bengali pathology. Incidentally, Bank of Commerce gave a series of advertisements in a serious Bengali journal *Prabasi* in 1944 with the partial proverb *parer dhone poddari*.[5] The bank authority was either not aware of the second part of the proverb (onlookers see this as your good fortune); or, left out the critique of such indulgence.

Such delusion, as referred above, dies faster these days because of new media's continuous and dramatic exposure of clever machinations of the rapacious few exploiting the trust of the gullible who are not all poor and financial illiterates. But this hardly deters another amoral individual re-enacting the same game, may be with a less insecure script; and another cohort of lazy money multipliers from handing over a small amount to a familiar agent, hoping that the promised high return will at least improve their physical quality of life. Because it does not involve hard work – even any work, it takes the character of unearned income. The moral failure of both the groups has apparently gained normality. Interestingly, each category of players in this economic field has its way of legitimising what it does. To the poor, it is not their greed because it is their survival tactics in the face of financial precariousness. Maybe, there is also the desire to move beyond the subsistence scale of living and access 'comfort' which one's current earnings do not permit. An acquaintance with middle-class lifestyle creates in them a sense of relative deprivation directing them to seek additional earnings. At the other end are the excessively greedy Ponzis and their props – the spoils-guzzling politicians, bureaucrats, policemen and bouncers – who want a radically re-defined lifestyle, more towards what Aristotle called a life of appetites. To them, their behaviour too is not pleonectic – morbidly greedy or covetous – but just entrepreneurial. It is just their enterprise and capacity to take risks. In some cases, it is beyond their power of comprehension that their greedy venture violates the principle of fairness. Many among them would not even care. Money painstakingly saved by the income of numerous insecure men and women is often wasted by a few owners and managers of fake firms in callous investments, or simply appropriated. For some biography-based explanation of why some individuals are generally prone to greed, we can turn to a repertoire of brilliant insights on human nature, from obsessive desire for happiness and pleasure (Epicurus), excessive love of self (Aristotle), to need for self-fulfilment and the narcissist turn in human character (Abraham Maslow).[6] To Erich Fromm, the greedy individuals have the non-productive exploitative orientation inclining them 'to take them [things] away from others by force or cunning'.[7] Universally, scholars have been reflecting on the practice of taking other people's money.

The expression 'other people's money' occurs in Adam Smith's *The Wealth of Nations* when he commented on the directors of joint-stock companies. He observed that

> being the managers rather of other people's money than of their own, it cannot well be expected, that they should watch over it with same anxious vigilance with which the partners in a private copartnery frequently watch over their own. . . . Negligence and profusion, therefore, must always prevail, more or less, in the management of the affairs of such a company.[8]

It broadly fits the experience in Bengal we have narrated here. The ordinary depositors were made inaudible and invisible in dominant reconstructions of bank runs and losses incurred by the ordinary depositors. Just about the same time when the Bengali lower middle class, including refugees, was going through the traumatic loss, Louis D. Brandeis was writing a series of articles in 1913 and 1914 on investment banks in the United States and elsewhere in the West, arguing that 'our savings banks are not banks *by* the people, nor, in the full sense, *for* the people' and that 'the depositors have no voice in the management'.[9] 'The money gathered in these reservoirs is not used to aid *productively* persons of the classes [wage earners, salaried people, or members of small tradesmen's families'] who make the deposits'.[10] The capitalists benefit from the savings of this class. We are reminded of the fundamental process of exploitation of the labouring class as explained by Marx. This exploitation takes the form of the ruling class in capitalism appropriating the *money form of the social surplus product* or, what amounts to the same, the money product of surplus labour.[11] The labouring class is the core of the other people. While the capitalist class is either callous about wasting other people's money in course of its financial misadventures, or scheming about its appropriation, they are exceptionally careful about their own money as indicated by enormous increase in their income and wealth, even in times of crisis in their own organizations. Their honesty and competence are questionable also.[12]

There are two kinds of victims of any financial fraud, be it in a bank, in an insurance company or in the so-called chit funds. One: the trusting depositors; the other, the fraudsters – masters of feigning trustworthiness – themselves found out by law-enforcing agencies they cannot buy off, or shaken off by their political masters. Both are victims of greed. Conjecturally observing, a combination of biography and present history makes some individuals fraudsters or some others their victims. However, one key factor is a cheat's ability to evoke in the potential subscribers/depositors some minimum trust in his promises on high return against a small deposit. On the other hand, a trusting predisposition, gullibility, intimate relationship with a neighbour who acts as go-between between a subscriber and the unknown men in charge of a cheat fund, lack of access to banks – make some form of informal saving the only option for many people who often have the misfortune of being dispossessed of their savings. Of course, there is the lure of 'big' money too. This takes us to the issue of trust between those who temporarily part with their money for saving often against a verbal promise of a higher return, and those who receive others' money as apparently trustworthy custodians. It is worthwhile to ponder why once betrayed in their trust, they or their likes, may be in the next generation, fall into the same 'trust' trap, and be victims again. This might mean that *(1)* because continuing distrust, both as a predisposition and as practice, is likely to interfere with the prospect of exploring new opportunities in gainful transaction, some kind of tentative trust becomes the only possible choice for those who want to explore further future transactions and take trust as only one of a number of factors which lead to economic decision-making;*(2)* estimation of trustworthiness is given up in the absence of reliable information on the predisposition and practices of the projected other party in transaction;*(3)* the choice among possible parties for an intended transaction is difficult in the absence of comparative data; or *(4)* the power of distrust wanes over time as the memory of betrayed trust weakens. So transactors in the present times – depositors in Ponzi firms – settle for 'thin' trust in available agencies that collect regular subscriptions from the multitude against almost no legally tenable record.[13]

179

We are evidently drawn to the question of character of the two players in the field, the fraudsters and their accomplices – individuals or institutions, and their victims. It was Aristotle who paid a critical attention to character, currently revisited by scholars who discuss the complex relationship between capital and character. Aristotle's notion of chrematistics, that is, money used to make more money, has resurged. Spencer J. Pack re-states the Aristotelian position thus: 'It [chrematistics] wrecks people's character, making them overtly greedy and desirous to accumulate more money. It causes people's passions to dominate their reason'.[14] In Aristotle, there is a 'particular sense of disdain for the slightly unsavoury skills of the commercial classes'.[15] Read with the Marxian position, it points out degradation of the moral character of the working class also through their subjection to 'low pay, overwork and tyrannical working conditions'.[16] As we try to grasp what happened in course of 'runs' and ruins in Bengal, and the cunning seizure of small cash of large numbers by Ponzi firms in recent years, we gain in insight by returning to Aristotle's 'conception [of] pleonexia [which] is not only greed for material goods, but also an excessive acquisitiveness of all divisible goods within a society, including honour and safety as well as material wealth'.[17] Aristotle conceptualizes this as 'tyrannical graspingness'.[18] This Aristotelian position directs us to a larger number of victims – the original and the collateral – at the many levels in which greed operates. In fact, he apprehended the possibility of civic strife – 'conflict between different groups in the state over the distribution of divisible goods' – because of 'the tendency of certain groups within a polis to take more than their share, and equally to believe that other groups are taking more than they deserve, both of which threaten the enjoyment of civic stability'.[19] It was Aristotle who raised so early the issue of pleonexia – a socially disruptive vice – as violation of the 'canons of distributive fairness within self-conscious communities'. Social movements, violent conflicts and the distrust of the state on the part of the multitude dispossessed of their rights to the natural and cultural commons as well as violent reprisal by the hegemonic classes and communities endorse the Aristotelian apprehensions.

That human character does not develop in a social vacuum is endorsed in a long tradition of social science analysis. The corruption of government and corruption of character have an interesting dialectic. A variety of theoretical positions endorse appropriation of the state by the rich and the powerful. The state continues to be the 'predator state': 'the systematic abuse of public institutions for private profit, or equivalently, the systematic undermining of public protections for the benefit of private clients'.[20] So does the production of victims of greed.

Understandably, any search for the victims of greed becomes a political project. In the long and complex history of financial fraud, the 'greedy wealth-getters', as Aristotle called them, have been of different kinds, of different political prowess.[21] Searching for the victims of greed in the past is no easy task; nor is it to develop a narrative on their total crisis. Jacques Rancière distinguishes between the 'words *of* history', 'the documentary evidence on which historians base their accounts of the past' and write 'words *about* history'. He regrets that only some of the words of history – words of the people, in our case victims of greed – find a place in official records. He wonders about our 'obligations to the words of the dead'.[22] Archival obliviousness forces us to look for any literal or visual trace of thinking and articulating in the past, particularly by the victims. To locate the victims, we need to engage in intertextual analysis and in data triangulation. The intention should be to develop a comprehensive understanding of the layers of victimhood. That might just about help us to develop a historical narrative. But it cannot stop with arrangements of facts. We need to analyse, to argue. We have to be careful that we are not dismissed as sentimental people, short on objectivity and credibility. Writing about contemporary victims of greed could be little easier data-wise. The victims are traceable, partly because media and inquiry commissions generate lots of information. But ideally, a researcher should be on its own, thereby avoiding bias institutional resources. One has to engage in painstaking, tracking and grasping their understanding of their experience of victimhood. In the ultimate analysis, the search for the victims of greed is essentially a political project, 'political' because it has to struggle against the official tendency to make real people anonymous by bracketing them into abstract categories like 'the multitude', 'the poor' or 'the lower middle class'.

Notes

1 Manuel Castells, *Another Economy is Possible: Culture and Economy in a Time of Crisis* (Cambridge, UK: Polity Press, 2017).
2 The expression *'run' on banks* re-appeared at least once when the economist ex-prime minister Manmohan Singh cautioned against the possibility of a bank run in times of recent demonetization. *Times of India*, 19 January 2017.

3 For a probing analysis of the modus operandi of Ponzi funds in con-temporary Bengal, see Subhanil Chowdhury, 'The Political Economy of Shadow Finance in West Bengal', *Economic and Political Weekly* 48, 18 (4 May 2013), www.epw.in/journal/2013/18/.../political-economy-shadow-finance-west-bengal.html, accessed on 28 May 2017.

4 Sushil Kumar De, *Bangla Probad* (Bengali Proverb) (Kolkata: Ranjan Pub-lishing House, 1945): 220.

5 It observed that banking then meant the very same behaviour because banks would gain profit by investing clients' deposits. It pointed out that an individual lacks the time and patience to make profit by investing money in gainful ventures on his own; nor could keep the money home secure from theft; it was not worthwhile either to spend money on one's relations. Bank of Commerce had established the reputation of being trustworthy. *Prabasi* (October–November, 1944): 19.

6 For a brief review, see Alexis Brassey, 'What Drives Man Toward Greed?', in *Greed*, edited by Alexis Brassey and Stephen Barber (New York: Pal-grave Macmillan, 2009): 94–111.

7 Erich Fromm, *Man for Himself: An Inquiry into the Psychology of Ethics* (London: Routledge, 2003): 46.

8 Adam Smith, *The Wealth of Nations*, Introduction by Alan B. Krueger (New York: Bantam Dell, 2003): 941.

9 Louise D. Brandeis, *Other People's Money: And How the Bankers Use It* (New York: Frederick A. Stokes Company, 1914): 217.

10 Ibid.: 218.

11 Ernest Mandel, *Marx's Theory of Surplus Value*, www.marxists.org/archive/mandel/19xx/marx/ch07.htm, accessed on 2 May 2017.

12 Spencer J. Pack, *Aristotle, Adam Smith, and Karl Marx: On Some Fun-damental Issues in 21st Century Political Economy* (Cheltenham: Edward Elgar, 2010): 200–202.

13 Geoffrey Hosking, *Trust: A History* (Oxford: Oxford University Press, 2014): 46–47.

14 Pack, *Aristotle, Adam Smith, and Karl Marx*: xii.

15 Ibid.: 16.

16 Pack, *Aristotle, Adam Smith, and Karl Marx*: Chapters 1, 2. For Aristotle, the proper and natural function of money is to help the circulation of goods. Hence, using money to make more money is a perversion of the natural function of money. For Marx's analysis of how capital degrades both capitalists and workers, see: 136–142.

17 Ryan Balot, 'Aristotle's Critique of Phaleas: Justice, Equality, and Pleo-nexia', *Hermes* 129, Bd., H. 1 (Stuttgart: Franz Steiner Verlag, 2001): 32–44, www.jstor.org/stable/4477400, accessed on 29 May 2017.

18 Ibid.: 37, 'Aristotle says that people can be pleonectic of money or honor or both. Even if these desires are conceptually distinguishable, they are both proper elements of Aristotelian pleonexia, whether money and honor are pursued separately, or united together as the targets of a very broad, almost tyrannical urge to acquire more of a variety of divisible goods, and sometimes even the polis as a whole. This is not simple greed for material possessions, but rather an expanded form of "graspingness" that aims at having it all'.

19 Ibid.: 38.
20 Pack, *Aristotle, Adam Smith, and Karl Marx*: 206.
21 Balot, 'Aristotle's Critique of Phaleas: Justice, Equality, and Pleonexia': 35. For a history of fraud, see David E. Y. Sarna, *History of Greed Financial Fraud From Tulip Mania to Bernie Madoff* (Hoboken, NJ: John Wiley, 2010).
22 Hayden White, 'Foreword: Rancière's Revisionism', in Jacques Rancière, *The Names of History: On the Poetics of Knowledge*, translated by Hassan Melehy, Foreword by Hayden White (Minneapolis: University of Minnesota Press, 1994): vii–viii.

APPENDIX 1
Banks in Calcutta, 1947

Bank Name	Status of Office
1. Abhoya Bank	Registered Office
2. Allied Bank	Branch
3. Associated Bank of Tripura 2	Registered Office; Branch
4. Bank of Bankura	Branch
5. Bank of East Asia	Registered Office
6. Beleghata Bank	Registered Office
7. Bengal and Assam Railway Employees' Co-operative Credit Society	Head Office
8. Bengal Bank	Registered Office
9. Bengal Credit Bank	Registered Office
10. Bengal Muslim Bank	Registered Office
11. Bengal Nagpur Railway Employees' Co-operative Urban Bank	Head Office
12. Bengal Secretariat Co-operative Society	Head Office
13. Bengal Union Bank 2	Central Office; Branch
14. Behrampore Bank	Branch
15. Bhowanipur Banking Corporation 2	Registered Office; Branch
16. Bishnupur Bank 2	Branches
17. Bogra Bank	Branch
18. Burmah-Shell Employees' Co-operative Credit Society	Head Office
19. Calcutta Central Telegraph Co-operative Credit Society	Head Office
20. Calcutta Corporation Co-operative Credit Society	Head Office
21. Calcutta Police Co-operative Credit Society	Head Office
22. Calcutta Tramways Employees' Co-operative Credit Society	Head Office

Bank Name	Status of Office
23. Calcutta University Co-operative Credit Society	Head Office
24. Central Calcutta Bank 4	Registered Office; Branches
25. Central Mercantile Bank	Branch
26. Chandpur Model Bank	Registered Office
27. Citadel Bank 2	Registered Office
28. City Bank 3	Registered Office; Branch
29. Comrade Bank 3	Branches
30. Co-operative Credit Society of the Port Commissioners of Calcutta	Head Office
31. Customs General Co-operative Credit Society	Head Office
32. Dhakuria Banking Corporation 2	Registered Offices; Branch
33. Dooars Union Bank	Branches
34. East Bengal Bank	Registered Office
34. East Bengal Commercial Bank	Registered Office
35. East Bengal Rural Bank	Branch
36. East Indian Railway Employees Co-operative Credit Society	Head Office
37. Eastern Bengal Railway Co-operative Credit Society	Head Office
38. Eastern Bengal Railway Junior Co-operative Credit Society	Head Office
39. Eastern Union Bank 2	Branches
40. Electro Urban Co-operative Credit Society	Head Office
41. Faridpur Banking Corporation	Branch
42. Gauhati Bank	Branch
43. Government of India Stationery and Printing Department Co-operative Society	Head Office
44. Great Indian Bank 2	Regional Office; Branch
45. Gun and Shell Factory Co-operative Society	Head Office
46. Hindusthan Bank	Regional Office
47. Howrah Banking Corporation	Branch
48. Imperial Bank Indian Staff Association Co-operative Society	Head Office
49. India Security Bank 2	Regional Office; Branch
50. Indian National Bank	Regional Office; Branches
51. Jubilee Bank 2	Regional Office; Branch
52. Kilburn Writers' Co-operative Society	Head Office

(Continued)

(Continued)

Bank Name	Status of Office
53. Kurigram Commercial Bank	Regional Office
54. Luxmi Industrial Bank	Regional Office
55. Manindra Banking Corporation 2	Central Office; Branch
56. Marine and Engineering Co-operative Thrift Society	Head Office
57. Martins Co-operative Credit Society	Head Office
58. Mercantile Co-operative Credit Society	Head Office
59. Mercantile Exchange Bank	Regional Office
60. Midland Trust (Bankers)	Regional Office
61. Midnapore Bank	Branch
62. National Economic Bank 7	Regional Office; Branches, Pay Office
63. National Exchange Bank 2	Regional Office; Branch
64. National Trust Bank	Regional Office
65. New Bengal Bank	Regional Office
66. Orient Bank of India	Branch
67. Patuakhali Bank	Regional Office
68. People's Credit Bank 3	Regional Office; Branches
69. People's Industrial Bank 3	Regional Office; Branches
70. Post and Telegraph Accounts Co-operative Credit Society	Head Office
71. Postal Co-operative Credit Society of Calcutta	Head Office
72. Prabartak Bank	Regional Office; Branches
73. Premier Co-operative Credit Society of Calcutta	Head Office
74. Rajsahi Banking Corporation	Branch
75. Shillong Banking Corporation	Branch
76. Survey of India Co-operative Society	Head Office
77. Treasury Buildings Co-operative Credit Society	Head Office
78. Union Bank of Bengal 3	Regional Office; Branch; Pay Office
79. Union Credit Bank 2	Regional Office; Branch
80. United Banking Corporation 3	Regional Office; Branches

Source: Appendix 1, Statistical Tables relating to banks in India and Pakistan, RBI, 1947, pp. 102–132.
Head office 27
Central office 2
Branch 36
Registered office 15

APPENDIX 2

Banks in liquidation

Calcutta area

Sl. No.	Name of Bank	Date of Liquidation	Dividends Paid to Depositors in Lakhs of Rupees	Dividends Paid to Shareholders in Lakhs of Rupees	Remarks
46	Aryan Bank Ltd.	20.3.1950	...	...	
47	Assam Central Bank	25.3.52	...	...	
48	Assam Corporated Bank Ltd.	4.8.48	...	...	
49	Associated Bank of Tripura Ltd.	19.12.49	0.04	...	
50	Bank of Calcutta Ltd.	1.4.49	...	...	
51	Bank of Commerce Ltd.	7.8.50	...	...	
52	Bank of Rajasthan Ltd.	7.9.53	0.13	...	
53	Beleghata Bank Ltd.	14.11.49	...	...	
54	Bengal Bank Ltd.	15.6.50	...	...	
55	Bengal Commercial & Agricultural Bank Ltd.	8.6.46	NA	NA	
56	Bengal Credit Bank	4.8.58	0.04	...	
57	Berhampore Bank Ltd.	14.11.49	1.61*	...	*Total outside liabilities
58	Bhagirathi Banking & Housing Co. Ltd.	4.6.47	NA	NA	

(*Continued*)

187

(Continued)

Sl. No.	Name of Bank	Date of Liquidation	Dividends Paid to Depositors in Lakhs of Rupees	Dividends Paid to Shareholders in Lakhs of Rupees	Remarks
59	Bharati Central Bank Ltd.	17.11.47	...	...	
60	Bishnupur Bank Ltd.	13.7.1954	0.01	...	
61	Bogra City Bank Ltd.	12.2.47	NA	NA	
62	Calcutta City Bank Ltd.	25.4.49	...	...	
63	Calcutta Commercial Bank Ltd.	12.9.49	2.52	...	
64	Calcutta Exchange Bank Ltd.	14.2.44	NA	NA	
65	Calcutta Industrial Bank Ltd.	27.1.48	0.03	...	
66	Calcutta Mercantile Bank Ltd.	20.6.49	NA	NA	
67	Calcutta National Bank Ltd.	30.4.53	39.28	...	
68	Calcutta Union Bank Ltd.	12.4.49	NA	NA	
69	Central Calcutta Bank Ltd.	9.5.50	0.54	...	
70	Central Hindusthan Bank Ltd.	27.2.52	NA	NA	
71	Chandpur Model Bank Ltd.	30.7.51	NA	NA	
72	Chittaranjan Banking Corporation Ltd.	8.1.40	NA	NA	
73	Chotanagpur Banking Association Ltd.	21.8.58	3.78	...	
74	Citadel Bank Ltd.	20.8.49	NA	NA	
75	City Bank Ltd.	4.7.49	0.34		
76	Comrade Bank Ltd.	20.2.51	NA	NA	
77	Continental Bank of Asia Ltd.	26.8.47	NA	NA	
78	Cooch Behar Bank Ltd.	25.8.52	1.76	...	
79	Dacca Central Bank Ltd.	14.11.49	NA	NA	

Sl. No.	Name of Bank	Date of Liquidation	Dividends Paid to Depositors in Lakhs of Rupees	Dividends Paid to Shareholders in Lakhs of Rupees	Remarks
80	Darjeeling Bank Ltd.	5.4.48	NA	NA	
81	Dhakuria Banking Corporation Ltd.	6.12.48	...	...	
82	Dinajpur Bank Ltd.	27.1.59	NA	NA	
83	East Bengal Commercial Bank Ltd.	30.11.48	NA	NA	
84	Eastern Bank of India Ltd.	2.8.43			
85	Eastern Continental Bank Ltd.	8.747	NA	NA	
86	Eastern Traders Bank Ltd.	12.4.49	0.01	...	
87	Economic Bank Ltd.	18.3.47	NA	NA	
88	Girish Bank Ltd.	8.12.49	0.60	...	
89	Great Eastern Bank Ltd.	21.6.48	NA	NA	
90	Hazradi Bank Ltd.	22.12.48	...	...	
91	Hindusthan Industrial Bank Ltd.	8.12.47	NA	NA	
92	India Public Bank Ltd.	21.4.41	NA	NA	
93	Indian United Bank Ltd.	18.2.52	...	...	
94	Kumerkhali Banking Corporation Ltd.	9.4.56	...	...	
95	Kurigram Commercial Bank Ltd.	4.12.50	NA	NA	
96	Kuver Bank Ltd.	6.8.48	NA	NA	
97	Laxmi Industrial Bank Ltd.	17.8.53	31.38	...	
98	Morris and Morris (Bankers) Ltd.	28.8.42	...	...	
99	Mercantile Exchange Bank Ltd.	8.8.49	NA	NA	
100	Nath Bank Ltd.	8.5.50	32.56		
101	National Economic Bank Ltd.	26.4.49	NA	NA	

(*Continued*)

(Continued)

Sl. No.	Name of Bank	Date of Liquidation	Dividends Paid to Depositors in Lakhs of Rupees	Dividends Paid to Shareholders in Lakhs of Rupees	Remarks
102	Northern Bank Ltd.	2.4.51	NA	NA	
103	Noakhali Union Bank Ltd.	4.4.49	. . .	. . .	
104	Orient Bank of India Ltd.	8.5.53	1.76	. . .	
105	Pacific Bank Ltd.	31.3.47	. . .	. . .	
106	Peoples Credit Bank Ltd.	30.1.51	. . .	. . .	
107	Peoples National Bank Ltd.	12.4.49	. . .	. . .	
108	Pioneer Bank Ltd.	12.7.49	2.04	. . .	
109	Pioneer Commercial Bank Ltd.	30.6.47	NA	NA	
110	Puri Bank Ltd.	5.4.48	1.23		
111	Purnal Deshbandhu Bank Ltd.	19.1.59	NA	NA	
112	Rajasthan Bank Ltd.	15.12.48	NA	NA	
113	Shillong Banking Corporation Ltd.	21.5.53	0.66	. . .	
114	Sonar Bangla Bank Ltd.	4.8.50	. . .	. . .	
115	Sree Bank Ltd.	3.8.48	NA	NA	
116	Sree Luxmi Bank Ltd.	21.6.48	NA	NA	
117	Sterling Bank Ltd.	16.1.51	. . .	. . .	
118	Suburban Bank Ltd.	20.7.48	0.08	. . .	
119	Tripura Modern Bank Ltd.	9.3.54	0.03	. . .	
120	Tripura Popular Bank Ltd.	9.3.54	NA	NA	
121	Tripura State Bank Ltd.	9.1.59			
122	Union Credit Bank Ltd.	20.9.49	NA	NA	
123	Alliance Bank of Simla Ltd.	9.5.1923	964.62	. . .	
124	Dacca Union Bank Ltd.	26.5.56	. . .	. . .	

Sl. No.	Name of Bank	Date of Liquidation	Dividends Paid to Depositors in Lakhs of Rupees	Dividends Paid to Shareholders in Lakhs of Rupees	Remarks
125	Great Bengal Bank Ltd.	19.4.49	NA	NA	
126	Liberal Bank Ltd.	23.10.49	...	...	
127	People's Bank Ltd.	8.3.59	...	...	

Source: Annexure No. 99 (vide Answer to Unstarred Question No. 588 Dated 28.2.61 Col. 2112).

Lok Sabha Debates (Second Series) Appendix 1, Thirteenth Session, 1961, Lok Sabha Secretariat, New Delhi, pp. 301–309. Archive, State Bank of India, Kolkata.

APPENDIX 3
Archival sources

RBI, Pune archive

1. Liquidation Proceedings of Banking Companies (F 1343).
2. Amalgamation of Banks in West Bengal (F 1744–1753).
3. Banking Crisis in West Bengal (F 1336–1339).
4. Liquidation of Banking Companies (F 1340–1344).
5. Policy Regarding Unclaimed Deposits with Banking Companies (F 13655–13661).
6. Schemes of Arrangement of Amalgamation, Liquidation (F 13758–13759).
7. Licensing of Banking Companies – Correspondence (F 13764–13765).
8. Bank Guarantee Schemes (F 1278–1279).
9. The Hindusthan Commercial Bank Limited – Inspection and Licenses (F 12834–12849).
10. Metropolitan Bank Limited (F 1284).
11. Bengal Bank Limited (F 1285).
12. Bank of Rural India (F 13281).
13. Bank of East Limited – in Liquidation (F 13282).
14. Bijairaj Bank Limited (F 13302).
15. Criticism of Proposals of Indian Bank Act (F 1356–1362).
16. Bank Act – Correspondence (F 1363).
17. Opinion on Banks (F 13763).
18. Das Bank Limited (F 13772–13774).

Secretariat library, writers' buildings, Kolkata

1. Report of the Bengal Provincial Banking Enquiry Committee, vols. I, II (Part I) and III (Part II), 1929–30.

2. Report of the Indian Central Banking Enquiry Committee, vols. I (Part I, II), II, III, 1931.
3. Statistical Tables relating to Banks in India with an introductory memorandum 1915 (2nd issue) to 1934 (11th issue), Department of Statistics, India.
4. *Bengal Economic Journal*, 1916, vols. 1, 2.

SBI archive in Kolkata

1. Annexure No. 99 (vide Answer to Unstarred Question No. 588 Dated 2 Feb 1961 Col. 2112), Lok Sabha Debates (Second Series), Appendix I, Thirteenth Session, 1961, Lok Sabha Secretariat, New Delhi: – 301–09.
2. *Capital*, Diamond Jubilee Number, 16 Dec 1948; all issues between 1949 and 1951.

Rare books and journals division, national library, Kolkata

All issues of *Ananda Bazar Patrika*, *Amrita Bazar Patrika* and the *Statesman*, Calcutta, between 1948 and 1951.

INDEX

Note: Page numbers in bold indicate a table on the corresponding page.

rational self-interest 138
Ray, Satyajit 7, 62, 84, 112, 119, 130
refugee-migrant families 95
refugees 3, 16, 90; income of 96
Reinhart, Carmen 8
repayments 41
resentment, emotion of 2
Reserve Bank of India 3, 65, 68–9, 71, 115, 116, 118, 126
The Reserve Bank of India 9
Reserve Bank of India Act 17
resurgent patriotism 40
revolutionary idealism 80
Rogoff, Kenneth S. 8
Roy, Acharya Prafulla Chandra 33
Roy, Bidhan Chandra 64, 125
Roy, Kiran Shankar 81
Royal Chronicle 24

Sahridaya 7, 85, 114, 119, 126
Samaddar, Jogindra Nath 28
Sampatti-Samarpan (Tagore) 6
Sanchoy 26
Sanyal, Amiya Nath 76
Sarkar, Benoy Kumar 29, 31–3, 43, 139, 141
Scheduled banks 78, 118
Scottish Enlightenment 138
Sedin Bangolakshmi Bankey 85, 128
Sen, Amartya 143
Sen, Patit Paban 34
Sen, S. K. 80
Sengupta, Amalendu 82
Sengupta, Sachindranath 83
Sett, Nihar Bala 19, 32
Shaw-pnachek Alamohan 31
Shishusiksha 46
Shonibarer Chithi 26
Sil, Hiralal 34
Simmel, Georg 142
Sinha, Harishchandra 27, 28
Sinha, Kaliprasanna 48
Sitar Bonobas 46
The Sleeping Kingdom 46
Smith, Adam 2, 39, 49, 153–7, 178

social bond 45
'Social History of Banking in Bengal in the Late Nineteenth and Early Twentieth Centuries' (Banerjee) 6
socialism 141
social reformers 43
social service 31
socio-genesis, of greed 142–61
Śrīmadbhagavadgītā 144
Srinivas, P. R. 62
Srirangam of Sisir Bhaduri 83
The Statesman 34
stock exchange crisis 36, 63
strike 113
'The Structure of Indian Banking' 141
Sudhin Datta, M. D. 38
Suicide 145
Sur, Atul 28
Sur, Sudhanshu Bhusan 20
systemic banking crises 8

Tagore, Dwarkanath 33, 48
Tagore, Gaganendranath 47
Tagore, Rabindranath 6, 35
Takaar Bazar (1948) 28
Tarkalankar, Madanmohan 46
Tebhaga movement 45
The Tennis Court Oath (David) 8
Thakurmar Jhuli 46
The Theory of Moral Sentiments (1759) 158
They Loved It So Much, The Revolution (Jaar) 8
trust, retrieving 60–88; announcement 66–74; civil society 83–5; colonial state 62–6; the press 75–80; protests 80–3
tyrannical graspingness 180

unemployment 91
universality, effect of 159

valuable property 157
victims 89–108; the loss 89–90; lower middle class 97–108; refugees 91–6

Vidyabinod, Kshirode Prasad 46
violation of justice 157

The Wealth of Nations 39, 49,
178
well-networked criminals 3
West, E. G. 153

West Bengal 16, 20, 44, 92, 124
West Bengal Provincial Congress
Committee 113
Woodhead, John Ackroyd 83
working-class struggles 45

zamindari capitalism 141